THE

GENESIS OF THE EARTH AND OF MAN:

OR THE
HISTORY OF CREATION,
AND THE
ANTIQUITY AND RACES OF MANKIND,

CONSIDERED ON BIBLICAL AND OTHER GROUNDS.

EDITED BY

REGINALD STUART POOLE,
M.R.S.L., ETC., OF THE BRITISH MUSEUM.

SECOND EDITION,
REVISED AND ENLARGED.

1860.

Copyright © 2013 Read Books Ltd.
This book is copyright and may not be
reproduced or copied in any way without
the express permission of the publisher in writing

British Library Cataloguing-in-Publication Data
A catalogue record for this book is available from the
British Library

Reginald Stuart Poole

Reginald Stuart Poole was an English archaeologist, numismatist and orientalist. He was born on 27th January 1832, in London, England – the son of the Reverend Edward Poole, a well-known bibliophile. His parents became estranged during his early childhood however, and his mother, Sophia Lane Poole, took her sons to Egypt to live with her brother, the Orientalist, Edward William Lane.

During their seven-year residence in Cairo from 1842 to 1849, Lane Poole wrote *The Englishwoman in Egypt*, while her son was imbibing an early taste for Egyptian antiquities. He began his Egyptian studies with relish, examining private collections in Cairo and Alexandria, and twice travelling up the Nile. Before he was seventeen, Reginald had contributed a series of articles to the *Literary Gazette which were* republished in 1851 as *'Horae Aegyptiacae', or, 'The Chronology of Ancient Egypt'*. In 1852, Reginald became an assistant with the British Museum, and was assigned to the department of coins and medals, of which in 1870, he became keeper. In that capacity he did work of the highest value, alike as a writer, teacher and administrator. In 1882 he was further responsible for founding the 'Egypt Exploration Fund', and in 1884 for starting the 'Society of English Medallists'. This latter society was founded with the hope of reviving the design and production of cast medals.

In his personal life, Reginald Stuart Poole married Eliza Christina Forlonge, daughter of William Forlone on 29th October, 1870. The couple had four children together.

Some of Poole's best work was done in his articles for the 9th edition of the *Encyclopædia Britannica*, on Egypt, Hieroglyphics and Numismatics; he also wrote for **Smith's** 'Dictionary of the Bible', and published volumes dealing with his special subjects. He was also the driving force in the production of British Museum catalogues of Greek coins, which still remain the standard reference set, and whose publication is the foundation-stone of modern Greek numismatics. In 1873 he published the first volume (on Italy), which was followed by three further volumes (Syria, 1878; Ptolemies, 1883; Roman Egypt, 1892).

Poole's principal contribution to Egyptology was his aforementioned founding of the 'Egypt Exploration Fund' (in 1882), in order to promote excavation and study of ancient Egypt. Poole devoted most of his spare time and energy to the fund, and was its honorary secretary (1882–5) and later its vice-president (1885–95). Many of his decisions are in retrospect considered misguided though, such as favouring Edouard Naville over the more meticulous archaeologist Flinders Petrie. His relations with the latter were for a time cool, after Petrie had blamed Poole for the fund's poor administration, which was largely owing to Poole's being seriously overworked.

In 1883, Poole was appointed by the Royal Academy as a lecturer on Greek, Egyptian and medallic art, a post which he held for the next two years. He was also awarded an honorary degree from Cambridge University in the same year. In 1889, he succeeded Sir Charles Newton as the Yates professor of archaeology at University College London. After this successful academic career, on **31st January 1893**, he retired from the British Museum and in 1894, resigned his professorship because of failing health.

Reginald Stuat Poole died of heart disease, at his home at 2 Gledstanes Road, West Kensington, London, on 8th February 1895 – at the age of sixty-three.

EDITOR'S PREFACE.

To the first edition of this work I prefixed a few prefatory remarks, in which I stated its character, but did not enter upon a consideration of the questions it discusses. Perhaps it was desirable that the first judgment formed of it should not be affected, favourably or unfavourably, by any arguments of the editor. This reason has now lost any weight it may have had, and I feel that I am bound to take this opportunity of giving a short review of the questions to which the work relates, and the manner in which the writer has treated them.

The subjects here discussed belong altogether to the ground between literature and natural science.* They have in every case a literary and a scientific side. When, in the days of Galileo, they began to attract attention, natural science was but in its

* In the following remarks I have sometimes used the term "science" for "natural science."

infancy, and literature was protected by powerful religious bodies. This neutral province at once fell under the dominion of literature, from which it was not wrested until the struggle caused by the new science of geology. The first discoveries of geology were discussed with the utmost arrogance by many of the clergy, who thought, or sometimes pretended to think, that they were crushing a heresy when they were denying without examination what might almost be called the lowest kind of revelation, since the truths of nature, as Scripture teaches, bear witness to the perfections of the Creator. In consequence of the false position into which the opponents of geology had thus put themselves, it became manifest, when their first clamour had subsided, that they were in the wrong, although the world did not care to inquire how. As might be expected, time has brought about the reverse of the old error. Subjects requiring high literary knowledge are discussed with the greatest dogmatism by men wholly devoid of this qualification, and any claim made by scholars to their right to be heard is met by derision. In the worst days of priestly bigotry nothing was done by the opponents of science surpassing the audacity of scientific men who, knowing little Greek, no Hebrew, and in complete ignorance of Semitism, set themselves to decide authoritatively the great question of the Biblical Cosmogony. Yet these are the first to protest against any similar imposture on the part of literary men.

I wish here to guard against a natural mistake. The reader may say, "You require such high qualifications that your neutral territory is forbidden ground to human intelligence." By no means. Natural science and literature are very different, at least in their present state. Natural science affords positive facts. We go to scientific men and ask them respecting the great antiquity of the world or any such matter, and are content to take their reply as either true or very near the truth. The scientific side of our question we have not to work out ourselves; but scientific men cannot come to us for such positive replies as they have given us. Science is allowed to have gained the facts we require, and the general agreement of scientific men is no slight guarantee of the correctness of those facts; for they no longer form an oppressed sect, which does not dare to preach its belief in the face of a hostile majority. Literature does not afford such data, and probably never will. The extreme disagreement of the best scholars shows that the discovery of positive results has not yet been made. Thus, while the scientific facts are at hand, the literary data require the largest preparatory study, and the most careful research. But the difficulty of the literary side of the question does not justify its neglect. It is one side, and the rightful property of literary men, who, if they abandon it to the other party, give the strongest evidence of their own incapacity.

Two questions are discussed in this work: the Biblical Cosmogony, and the unity or plurality of the origin of the human species.

I fully know what kind of reception the very mention of the Biblical Cosmogony meets from many who are content to take the judgment of scientific men. "The controversy," they say, "is settled. Why disturb so satisfactory a stumbling-block?" To these I would put this question, "You admit, as you must, that the Hebrews were an illiterate nation, with not even a rudimentary knowledge of science. You know that Egypt, Chaldæa, and Greece, were the homes of ancient science, and that their wise men held some great natural truths only recently recovered after having been lost in the darkness of the middle ages. Can you explain how it is that the cosmogonies of the Egyptians, Chaldæans, and Greeks, are utterly irreconcileable with natural truth, yet more, are hopelessly opposed to it, whereas that of the Hebrew Scriptures has not been proved to this day to contain an insurmountable difficulty? You seem to forget the theory of which you are always boasting, that the science of the Scriptures was derived from Egypt." I will unriddle this enigma. The Hebrew writer did not represent the knowledge of his people in the Cosmogony of Genesis. In no other way can the occurrence of a record not shown to be inconsistent with science, in the sacred writings of an utterly unscientific nation, be explained: but I can prove the truth of this assertion.

I wish very strongly to impress upon the reader this difference of the Hebrew and heathen cosmogonies. It seems, obvious as it is, to have been much overlooked. I may mention some facts which put it in a very clear light. In examining the literature of the ancient Egyptians, I have been struck by finding no traces of truth in their notions as to the origin of the material universe. Here, at least, the discovery of such traces might have been almost confidently expected. The religion of Egypt, notwithstanding its base superstitions, preserved some great doctrines that can only be ascribed to a primitive revelation. The belief in the existence of the soul after death, and in future rewards and punishments, cannot be supposed to have been discovered by man's reason. Some correct idea as to cosmogony might therefore surely be looked for; but the search would be in vain.

The Ritual indicates the ideas of the Egyptians on this subject, and we see that they resembled the fanciful speculations of the earliest Greek poetry. The case of the Chaldæans seems to be similar. In the fragments of Berosus, much that is based upon true tradition is preceded by a mythical cosmogony, almost as intangible as that of Egypt, though with some curious traces of truth; but it is not wise to speak confidently on this subject until the inscriptions have been brought in evidence. The case of the Greeks, and that of those Romans who mainly derived their knowledge from them, though of a somewhat complicated kind, points to the same conclusion. The earlier notions of the Greeks seem to be plainly borrowed, and to indicate the time when the national mind did not work for itself, but was content to learn from Chaldæa and Egypt. Afterwards, the philosophers reasoned out some great truths as to the nature of the universe which were discoverable by human reason. It is not until the time of those late writers who gathered from every available source that any account of the origin of the universe is found which bears traces of truth. But this was at a time when the notions of the Jews, and even the teachings of their Scriptures, were accessible to the Gentile world in the writings of the Alexandrian synagogue, and the disputes of the schools.

Thus tradition lost,—for civilized man must have once generally known,—and reason did not discover, the history of creation; and the Biblical Cosmogony stands alone, as of all ancient accounts of the origin of things the only one which is not on the very face irreconcileable with the truths of natural science.

I have said that the writer of Genesis did not represent the knowledge of his people in the narrative of creation. The correctness of this assertion is proved by the fact that the terms employed show the current opinion, while the truths they convey are wholly independent of it. Human language was used, and that language expressed the ideas of the people speaking it, so that from it we can discover the extent of their knowledge. But not alone must the mechanical language have been intelligible to those, for whose instruction the revelation was primarily made: the revelation itself must also have been not unintelligible to them, if but partially understood. The truths taught must, however, be true for all ages ; as true to us as to those who first received them. An opinion has lately sprung up, that, in reading the Bible, we are to inquire what each writer "meant." This is in direct contradiction to the express teaching of the Bible itself, and leads to error instead of to truth.

Many readers, accustomed to not uncommon notions on the subject, may here interrupt me by asking if I am not fighting a shadow; and whether I should not rather, with many scientific men, regard the early chapters of Genesis as not of the same authority as the doctrinal parts of Scripture. Without alleging the evidence of the truth of the Hebrew narrative of creation afforded by its marked difference from the cosmogonic speculations of heathen nations, I reply that its nature admits only of its being either revealed and true, or human and false. It relates events of which no man could have been a contemporary witness, and which no man could describe by his unassisted reason. Such theories as acknowledge in some sense its authority, and evade supposed difficulties by calling it poetical, are subterfuges that no honest man can dare to accept. There can here be no middle course: it must be either true or false.

It is not difficult to show that the language of the narrative of creation in Genesis expresses the notions of the ancient Hebrews, and is therefore independent of the truths which it conveys. The very second word, "bārā," has been held to signify "creation," as we commonly understand it; whereas it means, wherever its sense can be clearly defined, "making out of previously-existing materials." The Hebrew language is incapable of expressing in one word the metaphysical idea of creation; so that any attempt to find a closer meaning than that of "making" is only calculated to produce error. The word "hash-shāmaīm," rendered in the authorized version "the heaven," which almost immediately follows that just noticed, being a plural, should rather be translated "the heavens," and is consistent with the common belief of ancient nations, which was evidently shared by the Hebrews, that above the earth was a series of vaults one within another. The word "rākī'a," translated in the authorized version "firmament," in accordance with the renderings of both Septuagint ($\sigma\tau\epsilon\rho\acute{\epsilon}\omega\mu\alpha$) and Vulgate (*firmamentum*), is derived from the verb "rāka'," "he spread out by beating" (comp. Job xxxvii. 18, where this verb is used), and evidently described a solid concave vault which the Hebrews believed the lowest heaven to be. It is not necessary here to pursue this inquiry any further; but if the reader do so, he will find the whole phraseology of the Bible to be similar, making allowance for the difference of time and of language in the case of the New Testament, which was, at least mostly, written originally in Greek. This use of common terminology and phraseology is inevitable where common language is employed, addressed to common people, even when there is also scientific language. Thus we constantly speak of the sun as though we held the Ptolemaic system to be true; and a living poet who is famous for his accurate descriptions of nature speaks of the earth as though it were solid.

This last result will make some think that I have been wrong in saying that the investigation of these questions requires high literary qualifications. They will say: "If the terms used are not necessarily consistent with science, of what value is minute criticism?" I have, however, insisted on the accuracy of the truths conveyed, and in order to understand them rightly we must strive to discover the exact meaning of every word used. As in all other inquiries, inductive reasoning alone can lead us to the discovery of truth. Many men think it a little matter to acquire Hebrew enough to translate the Bible afresh. A certain amount of patience will make one master of accents and conjugations; but that is not all, nor is it even a right beginning. Semitic words rendered into the nearest corresponding Iranian words often do not express the same ideas. This is more strongly shown in the contrast of Turanian and Iranian speech. A Chinese poem translated word for word into English is unintelligible to an English mind. Where languages are essentially different, this must be the case. One who is thoroughly acquainted with the genius of the Semitic family of languages and with the Semitic mind can alone rightly understand a Semitic speech. It will not be until the difficulties of Hebrew scholarship are recognised, until it is acknowledged that as we have so small a fragment of the language its sisters should be patiently studied, and until Semitic learning is placed at our universities on the footing it merits, from its relation to revelation as well as its intrinsic excellence, that Biblical investigations will be rescued from the hands of well-intentioned smatterers.

The first chapter of the work contains an elaborate examination, on philological principles, of the Biblical narrative of creation. The reader will find that the writer has brought to his task the qualifications we have pointed out. The result is the conclusion that the revelation was made by means of a series of visions. This conclusion has been independently arrived at by the writer, although it had been felicitously guessed at by Coleridge, and reasoned out, but on rather doubtful principles of criticism, by Dr. Kurtz, from whom Hugh Miller adopted it.* I cannot here state the arguments by which the writer

---

* This theory was also advocated in an anonymous work, entitled "The Mosaic Record in Harmony with the Geological" (Edinburgh · Constable), which was not known to the author of this book when he wrote upon the subject. I have heard that the Rev. Richard Gwatkin also put it forth in a pamphlet, which I have not had the good fortune to see.

establishes his conclusion without repeating a great part of a long and elaborate chapter, and yet, by abridging it, weakening its force. I must add, however, that I think the unprejudiced reader who will take the pains to master this part of the work will agree with me that the conclusion is established in a triumphant manner. I am led to this opinion by the effect of the arguments on my own mind; but I am strengthened in it by observing how much annoyance these arguments and those of Hugh Miller have occasioned to the enemies of religion.

Before passing on to the second subject of the work, there is one matter I wish very clearly to lay before the reader,—the perfect independence of the two portions of which the book consists. The two questions to which they relate are distinct, and are separately treated. The results may be separately received or rejected. The author's principles and criticism are the same; but it does not follow that the subjects which he discusses are necessarily connected.

When such a question as the origin of the human race is mentioned, the cry of "Confugimus ad asylum ignorantiæ" is at once raised. But this course is no longer possible. The common opinion that man was first created six or seven thousand years ago is considered by all who have in any degree mastered the subject to be no longer tenable. Two new theories have been offered in its place. One clings to the one origin of our race, but assigns to it an enormous antiquity. The other suggests the existence of a Pre-Adamite race, and supposes the Biblical narrative to refer especially to a higher and later stock. No third theory seems possible.

The two theories have one thing in common: they both assert the great antiquity of man, the fact upon which the rejection of the current opinion depends. I advisedly call it a fact, since it is proved in a conclusive manner, by evidence of a very various character, the most important point of which is the discovery of flint-implements in tracts of drift, and in bone-caves; in both cases with the bones of animals now extinct. What we may consider certain is the immense antiquity of man, and his having been in the remoter age of his existence in a state of great barbarism.

Baron Bunsen, who may be considered the representative of a school, takes, apparently on grounds of sentiment, the unity of origin of the human race as the basis of his theory. He then examines the relation of languages on the supposition of their original unity, and roughly determines the length of man's dwelling on the earth by the time required for the origination and growth of the many varieties of human speech. He defines this period as about twenty thousand years B.C., divided midway by the Flood; and it is probable that those who belong to his school would not greatly shorten this vast space of time. Yet even this scheme is not sufficient without nullifying the Flood as destructive of the descendants of Adam; for ten thousand years is not enough, in his opinion, for the development of language. But it is a serious question whether any space of time would meet the difficulties of the case. Would mere time explain the growth, from Turanian (as Chinese), of the two other great families—Semitic (as Hebrew) and Iranian (as Greek)? I do not think that time is what is here needed: there is an essential difference that I do not see any lapse of ages would have produced. Iranian scholars, like Max Müller and others, are ready to admit that this theory is satisfactory; but no Semitic scholar has made the same concession, nor do I anticipate that any Semitic scholar ever will trace the Semitic family to the Turanian. Had it not been that Bunsen had started with a fixed persuasion that all languages had one origin, he would surely not have come to the conclusion he has reached. If he had examined the subject inductively, he would rather have held two sources; more especially if he had given due weight to the evidence of comparative ethnology and mythology. Those who consider that this theory is to be preferred on theological grounds, from its depending on the single origin of the human race, should remember that by putting Adam twenty thousand years, and the Flood ten thousand, before the Christian era, and by holding the Flood not to have destroyed all the Adamites, it so entirely sets at defiance the early part of the Bible as to make any appeal to the one agreement in its basis altogether nugatory.

The author of this work, taking up the subject with entire freedom from bias, first examines the Biblical data. In them he finds strong evidence of the existence of a Non-Adamite race both before and after the Flood. The reader must see in the book itself how he reconciles this inference with the statements in the Bible supposed to declare the unity of our race *in origin*, upon which one point the whole difficulty rests. Passing from the Bible to human knowledge, the author examines ethnology, chronology, history, and philology, each independently, in illustration of the controversy. From ethnology, he finds that the varieties of our species may be reduced to two stocks, but scarcely, except on the supposition of an unrecorded miracle, to one. In history, he sees that every civilized race tells us of a barbarous race expelled or subdued by its ancestors. In Pagan religions, when all traces of primeval revelation have been set aside, he perceives, in the case of nearly every one, two distinct elements; one intellectually very low, the other always much higher; the worship of stones and trees, combined with the adoration of the great luminaries or of intelligences. Philology, in like manner, leads him to the conclusion that many languages exhibit traces more or less clear of two sources of human speech widely distinct in character. In the case of the ancient Egyptian, which is of great importance from our having specimens of it four thousand years old, he discovers an example of the first contact of these two elements, which, mixed but not fused, like oil and water, compose this very ancient form of human speech.

This duality has never yet been explained in connexion with the theory of the unity of our race. Individual branches of the inquiry have been treated on the supposition that the latter is the correct theory with more or less success: but hitherto, in proportion to the degree of knowledge of the branch has been the violence of the reconciliation. In ethnology, the more moderate of the advocates of unity are beginning to treat the question of how the races of man came from one stock as a truth to be believed but not inquired into. Yet the author of this work has shown that it is not to be thus treated as a theological dogma while the evidence of the Scriptures is not conclusively in its favour. In history, no one has attempted to reconcile a mass of facts which, on the supposition of one origin, present no leading idea to guide the student in their arrangement. In philology, the agreement has been forced, and the consent of a large and independent body of students has not been obtained. The great difference between the author and the majority of inquirers is, that he collects facts to found a theory, whereas they start with a theory and then search for facts to confirm it. Right or wrong in his conclusion, he is undoubtedly right in his method, while they are as undoubtedly wrong. A right method is more likely to lead to truth than a wrong one.

I trust that the reader will give this book his full attention, and judge it with the candour with which it is written. Upon the manner in which the subjects of its inquiries are discussed, will, I believe, greatly depend the state of religious feeling among a large body of students. It is easy to treat such questions with dogmatism or flippancy, but it is impossible to calculate the mischief that may, and almost surely will, follow. Those who assert that the evidence of science is false, without examination, because it disagrees with their theological opinions, incur a fearful responsibility. It is to be hoped that a better temper pervades our Protestant clergy, and that they will enter upon this great controversy with a full acknowledgment of the sole authority of the Scriptures and the right of private judgment, those two great principles upon which hinged the Reformation.

REGINALD STUART POOLE.

JUNE, 1860.

POSTSCRIPT.—While this Preface is passing through the press, the discussions at the meeting of the British Association show that the antiquity and origin of man take the first place among the questions that interest scientific and literary men; and the manner in which theology has been introduced into the controversy proves that the old battle is to be fought again. I have, therefore, high authority to cite in confirmation of the conviction under which I have written these prefatory remarks.

AUTHOR'S PREFACE.

THE translators of the Bible whose versions have been authorized by the Churches have all been men to whom the science of geology had no existence, and to whom the difficulties involved in ethnology and ancient history were far less formidable, because far less known, than they are to the students of Scripture in the present day. If those learned men found a passage or a word, in the Sacred text, that might be literally interpreted as indicating that the earth and any of its occupants existed more than a few natural days before the creation of Adam, but that might possibly be rendered so as to convey the contrary meaning, they could not, for a moment, doubt that the latter meaning was the true one. Thus they read the Scriptures with a strong prejudice:—and so do *we*, in this more enlightened age:—but *their* prejudice was *against the truth*, whereas *ours* is *in its favour*. In the present day, however, men of science and learning, as apologists for the Bible, have laboured under *another* prejudice; for they have been impressed with the notion that the *versions* of which we have spoken are equally in what respects geology and ethnology and ancient history as in other matters free from grave inaccuracies; and hence they have generally been led, in some way or other, to strain those passages of Scripture which they would accommodate to acknowledged scientific or historical facts. But attempts to reconcile the Sacred Records with scientific and historical discoveries by strained interpretations of the former have never given general satisfaction.

Seeing this to be the case, and also that the Bible, though not designed to teach mankind geology or ethnology or any similar science, must, if rightly understood, agree with demonstrated geological facts, and greatly extend the knowledge derivable from other sources respecting the history of man, the writer of the following work was induced to try the contrary method,—that of adhering closely to the letter of the original in cases in which the authorized English version is loose or free, but combining with this method a constant comparison of Scripture with Scripture, as to words and also as to topics.

The principal results of this experiment were stated by the author in a pamphlet printed for private distribution, and afterwards (much extended) in a published volume, with a series of chapters, physical, chronological, historical, and philological, illustrating the main subject. He then did not expect that he might further advance, in any important degree, in the execution of the task which he had undertaken. But since the publication of the first edition of his essay, he has very carefully reconsidered the subjects of which it treats, and has made many and large additions to it (chiefly confirmations of arguments and opinions before advanced by him) constituting much more than one third of the present volume.

He has had no reason to be dissatisfied with the manner in which his first edition has been generally received. Nor has he seen any cause for discouragement in its treatment by opponents: for in every instance that has come to his knowledge, the only means employed to refute it have been garbled extracts and other misrepresentations, or mere *ex parte* arguments already examined, and weighed against *counter*-arguments, in the work itself.

The importance of the consideration of the principal subject has very greatly increased within the last few months, in consequence of a conviction expressed by many of our most eminent and cautious geologists, that flint-implements found in tracts of drift, and with other remains discovered in bone-caves, plainly show the antiquity of man to be immeasurably remote. It has, therefore, now become a matter of the utmost moment to decide whether such a conviction be compatible with belief in the truth of the records and doctrines of the Bible; and the writer of the following pages earnestly hopes that there may be no delay in the full and fair examination of this question by the ministers of religion, who have too often been responsible, in a great measure, for the infidelity that has resulted from new discoveries in science and history.

The author has to thank the editor of this essay for many important observations on passages in the first edition requiring elucidation or other improvement.

March, 1860.

CONTENTS.

CHAPTER I.

The Genesis of the Earth.

	PAGE
The First Narrative of the Process of Creation—In what Manner was it revealed?	1
The First and Second Narratives of Creation, considered as describing Revelations to Adam in Visions, reconcileable with Each Other, and also with Physical Facts, and with the Statement that, "in Six Days, the Lord made Heaven and Earth"	6
Various Opinions respecting the First Three Chapters of Genesis, and Remarks on the Third Chapter in particular...	12
The First Narrative of the Process of Creation contains Expressions apparently indicating its being a Description of a Series of Visions	17
Revelations in Visions entitled to be regarded as strictly true, and not confined to *Ideal* Things nor to *Future* Events	23
Consideration of the Statement that, "in Six Days, the Lord made Heaven and Earth"	25
The supposed Visions of the Events of the "Six Days" compared with Geological Opinions and Facts	28
Opinions of Hugh Miller and others, similar to those here put forth	37

CHAPTER II.

The Genesis of Man.

Caution required in the Examination of Ambiguous Passages in Scripture	45

Apparent Indications, in the Bible, of the Origination of All Mankind from a Single Pair:	PAGE
1. Adam being *alone*, a Wife was created for him ...	46
2. The Reason given for her being named "Eve" ...	47
3. "From the Beginning," God "made them Male and Female," or "a Male and a Female"	49
4. God "made of one Blood all Nations of Men" ...	50
5. "By one man (Adam) Sin entered into the World, and Death by Sin," etc.	53
Apparent Indications, in the Bible, of the Existence of Human Beings not descended from Adam:	
1. Cain's Fear, lest Others, finding Him, should slay Him—and the Mention of his Wife and Son, as well as of the Sons and Daughters of Seth, without any Intimation that either Cain or Seth had a Wife created for Him	65
2. The First Proclaiming of the Name of Jehovah ...	70
3. The Marriages of "the Sons of the Gods" with "the Daughters of the Adamites"—and "the Giants," or "Nephīlīm"	75
4. The Division of the "Isles of the Nations" by the Family of Japheth, etc.	84
5. Some of Mankind called "Sons of "Adam," as distinguished from "Sons of Īsh;" and the Former called "Ādăm," and the Latter called "Īsh"	88
The Deluge—its Extent with respect to the Earth and to Mankind, with Remarks on the Confusion of Tongues ...	91
Conclusion drawn from the Evidences examined in this Chapter	102

CHAPTER III.

Physical Observations.

Has Providence adapted the Different Varieties of Man to the Peculiar Physical Conditions of Different *Regions* of the Earth, or to Such Conditions of Different *Periods?*	106
Modifications of Form and Colour effected by Various Causes—the Former extremely slow—the Latter not found sufficient to account for the Hue of the Negro	108

CONTENTS. xxix

	PAGE
Instances of Races widely differing in Form and Colour, Conterminous in their Territories, and even Intermixed	109
Effects of the Mixtures of Races—Physical Characteristics of Jews in Eastern Countries—The so-called "Black Jews" of India and of Abyssinia—Grey-eyed Arabs: and "Black Arabs"	112
Adam and Eve supposed by some to have been Negroes, or Brown	116
Negroes, and Other Varieties of Man, represented upon Egyptian Monuments more than Three Thousand Years Old ...	117
Theory that the Descendants of Noah were miraculously adapted, in their Physical Organization, to Different Regions—shown to be an assumption of a needless miracle ...	118
The Different Varieties of Man shown to be adapted *rather* to Different *Periods* than to Different *Regions*, by Numerous Instances of Races supplanted by Other Races of Different Varieties	119
Propositions founded upon the Facts above mentioned, laid down to be tested and illustrated in Subsequent Chapters ...	122
A Succession of New Species, adapted to New Conditions of the Earth, proved by Geological Researches	130

CHAPTER IV.

CHRONOLOGICAL OBSERVATIONS.

Geological Evidences of the Period of the Origination of Man—Bone-caves and Tracts of Drift containing Human Remains and Implements	133
Biblical Chronology—The Chronologies of the Septuagint-Version and the Hebrew Text and the Samaritan Version, of the Period before the Birth of Abram, with a Table showing their Disagreeements	142
Longevity of Noah and other Patriarchs	150
Dates of the Deluge and the Dispersion	156

CHAPTER V.

HISTORICAL OBSERVATIONS.

Preliminary Remarks—Mankind supposed to have come into Existence *as soon as* the Earth was fit for their Habita-

tion—The First Race to have originated in the Equatorial Region of Africa—to have had a Natural Knowledge of God, but to have lapsed into Fetishism—and to have given Origin to the Pre-historic Population of Egypt 159
Ancient Opinions and Traditions respecting Egypt and the Egyptians in Pre-historic Times 162
The First Asiatic Settlers in Egypt 164
The Pharaohs and their Subjects—Their General Physical Characteristics such as are produced by the Mixture of Caucasian and Negro Races—Shown by Sculptures and Paintings to have differed greatly, in Features, Complexion, etc., from their Contemporaries in South-western Asia 167
Their Religion a Compound of Asiatic and Nigritian Elements; being a Mixture of Nigritian Fetishism with Higher Kinds of Nature-worship, and with some of the grandest Doctrines of Revelation 176
Their Language a Mixture of Asiatic and African Elements ... 187
Several Superstitions of the Ancient Egyptians under the Pharaohs, obtaining among the Modern Negroes of Africa, obtain also among the Indians ... ... *ibid.*
The Aboriginal and Later Races of India 188
The Races of Arabia, and their Fetishism in Ancient Times, and Belief in Pre-Adamite Genii ... ... *ibid.*
The Chinese and their Traditions... 190
The Traditions of the Ancient Greeks and Romans 192
Other European Nations 197

CHAPTER VI.

PHILOLOGICAL OBSERVATIONS.

Introductory Remarks on Comparative Philology considered as illustrative of Ethnology, with a Scheme showing the Author's View of the Mutual Relations of the Principal Families of Language 199
Opinions of Bunsen, Max Müller, and Renan, respecting those Relations... 207
Bunsen's Classification of the Semitic Languages 210
His Classification of the Iranian Languages 211

CONTENTS. xxxi

	PAGE
Max Müller's Classification of the Turanian Languages	215
Bunsen's Reasons for deriving these Families of Language from a Common Source—from the Ancient Chinese	220
As the Ancient Chinese Language is adapted to the Wants of a People considerably advanced in Civilization, may it not be inferred to have been preceded by Languages yet more simple and rude?—Reasons for answering this Question affirmatively	224
Bunsen's Theory of the Origin and Development of Language, and Our Own, considered in Relation to Sacred History ...	228
The Investigation retraced, from the Earliest Period, downwards	230
The Comparative Claims of the Ancient Chinese, and of a Ruder Kind of Language, to be regarded as the Earliest Form of Speech, again considered	ibid.
The African Languages	233
The Mongolian Languages	236
The Malaïc and Malayo-Polynesian Languages	ibid.
The American Languages	238
The Semitic Languages, and the Japhetic, or Iranian, or Arian; and Professor Müller's Opinion that they are possibly of Common Origin with the Turanian	240
Our Own Opinion respecting them	244
Of the Origin of the Semitic...	ibid.
The Geographical Distribution of the Descendants of Shem, Ham, and Japheth; and its Linguistic Consequences, more particularly as occasioning the Dialectical Varieties of the Semitic	246
The Egyptian Language particularly considered—Found to consist partly of Semitic Elements, and partly of Elements analogous to those of Languages now spoken by African Races	255
The Himyeritic and Ethiopic, the Assyro-Babylonian, and the Primitive Babylonian	268
The Japhetic Languages—Elements thereof found in the Ancient Egyptian, and also in the Primitive Babylonian, and traceable to Africa	271
Conclusion	275

CONTENTS.

NOTES.

		PAGE
1.	On a Passage in the Third Chapter of Genesis	277
2.	Hugh Miller's View of "the Three Geologic Days:" and Remarks thereon, and on his General View of the Revelation of the Process of Creation, extracted from the "Edinburgh Review"	278
3.	On the Appellation "Ādām," with Remarks on Arba and the 'Anākīm	282
4.	Further Observations on the Same Subjects	284
5.	On an Opinion recently proposed for Consideration, that the Deluge was a very destructive Overflow of the Nile	285
6.	Evidences presented by Natural History, showing that all Animals, in every part of the Globe, could not have been shut up in the Ark—Cuvier's Opinion, that the Deluge was not Universal; that the Mongolian Race probably escaped it, and that the Negroes did certainly	287
7.	On the Race formerly called "Beni-l-Kenz," and now called "the Kunūz"	289
8.	On Recent Explorations in Egypt, prosecuted by Direction of Mr. Leonard Horner, supposed by him to show that Pottery was manufactured in that Country 11,517 Years before the Christian Era	ibid.
9.	On the Question whether Man was originally in that Condition which is generally termed a State of Nature	292
10.	Extracts from a Lecture delivered by Sir Henry Rawlinson; with Observations thereon, showing that certain Results of his Researches remarkably confirm some Opinions expressed in the First Edition of the Present Work	ibid.

ERRATA.

Page 120, at the end of line 7, *add* almost
267, line 3, erase the comma.

THE GENESIS OF THE EARTH AND OF MAN, ETC.

CHAPTER I.

THE GENESIS OF THE EARTH.

THE narrative with which the Book of Genesis commences, ending with the third verse of the second chapter, altogether consists of a description of events which could not have been witnessed by any human being. Every one, therefore, who admits the truth of the Bible, whatever be his opinion of some other portions of it, must hold this narrative to be *a revelation*.

Now we find that revelations of this kind, of which the subjects are *events*, were generally conveyed in *representations to the sight*: and hence, by the safest and the most legitimate mode of judging, by comparing Scripture with Scripture, we are led to the conclusion that the narrative under our consideration is *most probably the relation of a revelation by means of a series of visions.* If we thus understand it as a description of a series of visions, we may naturally regard the words "and it was evening, and it was morning, day first"—"day second"—and so on (not well rendered in our authorized version), as denoting the limits of time between which the first vision and the second etc. occurred. The phrase here used, where it is said, "it was evening, and it was morning," is not like the expression "evening-morning" in Daniel viii. 14 (where "two thousand and three hundred evening-mornings" are mentioned as the period of the events represented in what is afterwards called "*the vision of the evening and the morning*," though no sound critic understands even these "evening-mornings" as natural days); nor is it like the term $\nu\nu\chi\theta\acute{\eta}\mu\epsilon\rho o\nu$ in 2 Cor. xi. 25. And the word rendered "day" in "day first," "day second," etc., is one which, in countless instances, it would be absurd to understand as meaning "day in opposition to night;" as, for example, in Exodus xii. 41, where it is said, "the self-same day it came to pass, that all the hosts of the Lord went out from the land of Egypt;" for it is said in the next verse that they went out by *night*.

We do not found the opinion here expressed, as to the manner in which the acts of creation were revealed, merely upon the general analogy of cases recorded in Scripture, without a consideration of the question, To whom was the revelation originally communicated? It is held by many (perhaps we might truly say by almost all) of the best Biblical critics, on grounds that appear to us to be such as hardly admit of any other inference, that the book of Genesis mainly consists of a number of distinct pieces or documents, not revealed to Moses, but collected and arranged by him under the guidance of inspiration. Several individuals, we know, received divine communications before the time of Moses. Among them were Adam, Enoch, Noah, Abraham, Isaac, Jacob, and Joseph; and we think that we have the strongest reason for believing that, to every one of these, God revealed his instructions, when not by means of an angel, as he did to prophets in general: that is, as He did to him of whom (spoken of as being one of a *class*, and designated by an appellation which signifies any man who makes known a revelation or any similar communication, whether relating to the past or the future,) He says, "in a vision I make myself known unto him; in a dream I speak with him:" not as He did to Moses, respecting whom He proceeds to say, by way of distinction and contrast, "mouth to mouth I speak with him; and apparently; and not in parables" (Num. xii. 6-8). These are the only modes of revelation that we find explained in the Old Testament; and as the last of them is restricted to the case of Moses, it follows that, if the events described in the first chapter of Genesis were (as so many of the best critics hold them to have been) revealed before his time, and not by means of an angel (a medium of communication not there mentioned nor indicated), *the Scripture warrants no other explication than that which we have proposed.* It is expressly stated at the close of the Pentateuch, and evinced by all that follows in the Bible, that "there arose not a prophet [or "spokesman of God" (see Exodus vii. 1 comparing it with iv. 16)] since in Israel like unto Moses, whom the Lord knew face to face," until the fulfilment of the prediction in Deut. xviii. 15 and 18 (of the coming of the Saviour); and clearly there was none such *before* Moses. Nor does it appear that any before or after him, until the Saviour's advent, received a revelation of any *event*, past or future, otherwise than by means of an angel (expressly mentioned or plainly indicated) or in a dream or vision; and hence the appellation *seer*. "Prophecy [or "the uttering of revelation"] came not at any time by the will of man; but being carried away [or "rapt" ($\phi\epsilon\rho\acute{o}\mu\epsilon\nu o\iota$)] by the Holy Spirit, the holy men of God spake" (2 Peter i. 21). See Ezekiel iii. 12 and 14, viii. 3, and xi. 1 and 24; where, when "the heavens were opened," and "he saw visions of God," the Prophet says, "the spirit took me up;" "the spirit lifted me up, and took me away;" "the spirit lifted me up between the earth and the heaven, and brought me in the visions of God to Jerusalem;" etc. As is the case of the ordinary dreamer, so was that of the seer in his dream or vision, receiving a revelation from God, inasmuch as his will had no agency to evoke or shape or modify what he saw or heard;

and though sometimes his mind was active, so that he reasoned upon these things with the Revealer, frequently it appears to have been wholly passive. Whatever may be thought of mere internal inspiration, as to its being verbal or not, the Scripture plainly teaches that in a revelation of the kind to which we refer that of the creation, the seer, in effect, "heard the words of God," and "saw the vision of the Almighty."

It was thus, by means of a vision, that the future desolation of Judæa was revealed to Jeremiah; and the scene is described by him (in chapter iv. verses 23-26 of the book of his prophecies) in a manner strikingly similar to that in which the state of the primeval earth is represented in the narrative of the creation; the general aspect in both cases being depicted by the very same words. He says, "I beheld the earth [or "land"], and, lo, [*it was*] *without form*, [so in the authorized version, but correctly "*desolate*,"] *and void*; and the heavens, *and they* [*had*] *no light*: I beheld the mountains, and, lo, they trembled, and all the hills moved lightly: I beheld, and, lo, [*there was*] *no man*, [or "*the Adam was not*,"] and all the birds of the heaven were fled: I beheld, and, lo, the fruitful place [was] a wilderness, and all the cities thereof were broken down at the presence of the Lord, by his fierce anger." And the late Professor Samuel Lee has observed (in the introduction to his translation of the Book of Job, page 16, remarking that Milton took the same view of the

CHAPTER I.

case), that the creation of Eve seems to have been thus revealed to Adam, who, in his "deep sleep," or ecstasy, appears to have seen God take one of his ribs, and make it a woman, and bring her unto him; as is related in Gen. ii. 21 and 22: with reference to the former of which two verses Professor Lee remarks (in the same introduction, page 74), ."It was in visions, seen in a sort of ecstasy (comp. Acts x. 10—'Ἐπέπεσεν ἐπ' αὐτὸν ἔκστασις, Griesb., the very Hebrew phraseology, *ib.* xi. 5, xxii. 17), that revelations were perhaps most frequently made under both Testaments." Elihu describes this mode of revelation, apparently as being common in his time : " God speaketh once, yea twice, [yet man] perceiveth it not : in a dream, in a vision of the night, when deep sleep falleth upon men, in slumberings upon the bed ; then He openeth the ears of men, and sealeth their instruction " (Job xxxiii. 14-16). The particular instances of revelations expressly shown to have been by means of dreams or night-visions are too numerous to need their being pointed out.

Professor Lee's opinion adduced above, relating to the account of the creation of Eve, we regard as highly important, not merely in itself, and as contributing to confirm our own view of the narrative with which the Bible commences, but also as leading us to discover the necessary consistency of the second narrative of the process of creation with the first in an instance in which there *seems* to be a plain disagreement. In the first chapter of Genesis, the birds are represented as created before the beasts, and the beasts before Adam; but in the second chapter, it is said that "the Lord God formed out of the ground every animal of the field, and every bird of the heavens, and brought [it] to the Adam, to see what he would call it." Thus it is distinctly implied that, if *creation* be here meant, the beasts and the birds were created *after* Adam. It has therefore been proposed that, instead of "formed," we should here read " *had* formed." So says Rosenmüller. But the verb is an *imperfect*: and to render an *im*perfect as a *plu*perfect in a case like this, when it is not grammatically connected with a preceding verb having a pluperfect sense, appears to us to be absolutely unjustifiable. The difficulty admits of a simple solution: for if it be meant by the woman's being "brought to the Adam" that she was brought to him in a dream or vision, in like manner we may most reasonably understand the beasts and the birds to have been brought to him. The passage at present under our consideration is intimately connected with what precedes and what follows it. The narrative relates to God's revealing to Adam the creation of the beasts and the birds and Eve, and Adam's giving names to them: the creation of Eve being represented in a peculiar manner, such as to show that the husband and his wife are to be regarded as one flesh. It commences with God's saying, "[It is] not good that the Adam should be alone: I will make for him a helper as a counterpart to him." And then the narrative proceeds thus, according to the most literal rendering that we can give:—"And Jehovah-Elōhīm was forming [or "shaping"] out of the ground every animal of the field, and every bird of the heavens, and was bringing [it] to the Adam, for to see what he would call it: and whatsoever the Adam was calling it, [namely] a living creature, it [was] its name. And the Adam was giving names to every beast, and to the bird of the heavens, and to every animal of the field: but for Adam, he found not a helper as a counterpart to him. And Jehovah-Elōhīm was causing to fall a deep sleep upon the Adam, and he was sleeping. [This last sentence, it should be observed, is parenthetic, and bears to what precedes it exactly the same relation that it bears to what follows it.] And He was taking one of his ribs, and was closing up flesh beneath it; and Jehovah-Elōhīm was building the rib which He had taken from the Adam for a woman, and was bringing her to the Adam. And the Adam was saying, This, now, [is] bone of my bone, and flesh of my flesh: this shall be called woman (ishshāh), for from man (īsh) has this been taken." He contrasts the creature whom, in his sleep, he saw formed from one of his ribs, and to whom he was to give a name, with the creatures formed out of the ground, to which he had given names before. Now we think that to any unprejudiced mind, the only reasonable inference to be drawn from the narrative here quoted must appear to be this:—that the whole is a relation of a revelation made to Adam in ecstatic sleep: and further, that it is a more circumstantial description of a portion of the revelation related in the preceding chapter, designed as an explanation of the earlier narrative, and as supplementary thereto.

Christian philosophers have been compelled to acknowledge that the first account of the process of creation is only reconcileable with demonstrated physical facts by its being regarded as a record of *appearances*. And if so, to vindicate the truth of God, we must consider it, so far as the *acts* are concerned, as the relation of a revelation to the *sight*, which was sufficient for all its purposes, rather than as one in words; though the words are perfectly true as describing the revelation itself, and the revelation was equally true as showing, by their proper images, or by images of analogous familiar things, the principal phenomena which a man stationed upon the earth would have seen had it been possible for him to be a witness of the events to which it relates; teaching in the most impressive and most intelligible manner the creation of those objects of which he to whom the revelation was made previously knew only the *existence*. It must be admitted that a representation of physical facts to the eye conveys a far more exact notion of them than can possibly be conveyed by words: and the former mode of representing the most important of the phenomena of the creation may have been the only one by means of which they could have been rendered sufficiently intelligible to the person to whom the revelation was made; as that person, we think (for a reason which we have already stated), was Adam, who himself, at least in part, apparently under the influence of inspiration, on this very occasion, framed his own language, when he gave names to the beasts and the birds and to Eve. It may be objected that such a person cannot be accounted to have been capable of sufficiently understanding the words that he heard, or seemed to hear, while contemplating the supposed visions; but we would rather infer that he may have been incapable of understanding those words unless they accompanied representations to the eye: and if we think that he did not fully comprehend them, we should take into consideration that the revelation was designed not only for his own instruction, but also, and much more, for the instruction of future generations. His case was like that of an inspired predictor, who imperfectly understood the words that he uttered. (See 1 Peter i. 11.) The passages in the Bible that bear upon science being necessarily adapted to very early stages of the progress of human knowledge, their meaning becomes more and more unfolded in successive ages, just as prophecies, in general, become more and more clear until they are fully explained by the events to which they point; and to seek for the true meaning of a passage of that kind by considering in what manner it was most probably understood by him through whom it was first given forth, we regard as worse than useless.

Further: if we view the narrative as the description of a series of visions, while we find it to be perfectly reconcileable (in a manner hereafter to be explained) with the statement in other parts of Scripture that "in six days the Lord made heaven and earth," we remove, with other difficulties, the only strong objection to the opinion of those who regard the "six days" as periods of undefinable duration; an opinion which has been urged as favoured by the statement that "one day is with the Lord as a thousand years, and a thousand years as one day," and by the fact that we are now in "the "seventh day," the day of rest, or of cessation from the work of creation. Certainly "the day of God," and "the day of the Lord," and the "thousand two hundred and threescore days" of the Revelation of St. John, and the "seventy weeks" in the prophecy of Daniel, are not to be understood in their primary and natural senses. It is therefore unnecessary to discuss the question, whether the eleventh verse of the twentieth chapter of Exodus be a gloss, or comment, as some suppose it to be on the ground that another passage is substituted for it in the repetition of the Decalogue (in Deut. v., where it is said, "*and he added no more*"), and whether the latter portion of the seventeenth verse of the thirty-first chapter of Exodus be also a gloss, and both be, in consequence, of doubtful authority. The only reason that we can see for regarding the last of these three passages as a gloss, and as being of uncertain authority, is the doubt which, in the opinion of some, is cast upon the first by the second; unless we regard as an additional reason the change from the first to the third person.

The question which we are considering is, in our judgment, one of very great importance: for it seems to us that there is no other alternative than that of accepting the explanation here proposed or conceding that the narrative to which it relates is a parable, and, moreover, a parable differing from every other in the Bible in being, as such, irreconcileable with truth. Some persons, it seems, can see nothing objectionable in the opinion that the first three chapters of Genesis, or at least the account of creation, may be considered as mythical, and yet inspired; but we would much rather hold the opinion that these portions of Scripture, ostensibly constituting the foundation of sacred history, are human inventions. With respect to the first chapter, especially, the former opinion, to say the least, seems to us to be utterly unreasonable; for an account of creation might be agreeable with truth in the order of the events, and at the same time adequate to convey the religious lesson that the Bible-narrative is obviously intended to teach, and adapted to the comprehension of the most uninstructed of mankind. The third chapter is, indeed, profoundly mysterious: in it we find several expressions hard to be understood; but some of these may perhaps be there used figuratively, since they are, by common consent, so used in other parts of Scripture; and thus its difficulties may in a measure be explainable. For instance, it is said in the last verse of that chapter, "And] He placed at the east of the garden of Eden the Cherubim, and the flame of the turning sword, to guard the way of the tree of life:" perhaps meaning "thunder-clouds, and lightning." (Compare Exodus xl. 35, where it is said that "Moses was not able to enter into the tent of the congregation because the *cloud* abode thereon and the glory of the Lord filled the tabernacle:" also, the mention of "*thunders and lightnings* and a thick *cloud*" in Exodus xix. 16.) The word rendered "turning," applied to the flaming sword, is used as applied to the *lightning-cloud* in Job xxxvii. 12: and in 2 Sam. xxii. 11, and Psalm xviii. 10, we read, "He rode upon a *Cherub*, and did fly:" in Psalm xcix. 1, "who sitteth upon the *Cherubim*:" in Psalm civ. 3, "who maketh *clouds* his chariot:" and in Isaiah xix. 1, "Jehovah [is] riding upon a swift *cloud*." It seems, then, that "cherub" may sometimes signify "a cloud:" and it may particularly mean "a thunder-cloud;" for Ezekiel speaks of *lightning* going forth from the *Cherubim* which he describes by the appellation of "living creatures," going "whithersoever the *wind* (hā-rūăh) was to go," in the first chapter of his prophecies. Ezekiel also (in ch. xxviii. vv. 13 and 14) likens the King of Tyre, adorned with brilliant gems (afterwards called "stones of fire"), to a "covering, *expanded* Cherub," apparently meaning a lightning-cloud; and his residence, to "Eden, the garden of the Lord," and to "the holy mountain of God." We do not venture to assert positively that the Cherubim of the garden of Eden were thunder-clouds; but the opinion that they were really living creatures has occasioned a very grave error—that of regarding them in the same light as the "griffins" described in a Persian fable as the guardians of the gold-producing mountains; a fable to which that opinion apparently led, as well as to that of the dragon represented as guarding the orchards of the Hesperides, and to the placing of human-headed bulls and lions at the entrances of Assyrian palaces. That they were *perhaps* thunder-clouds may be argued not only from the passages cited above, but also from the facts that *lightnings* are called "*arrows*" in Zech. x. 1; and *lightning* is called the "*arrow* of voices" in Job xxviii. 26 and xxxviii. 25: while, on the other hand, *arrows* are called "*lightnings* of the bow" in Psalm lxxvi. 4 (in our version 3); and a glistening *sword* is called "*lightning*" in Job xx. 25: so that a weapon and lightning are convertible terms.—There are also several other expressions in the same chapter that may perhaps be figurative. (See Note 1.) But no ingenuity of interpretation can much diminish the mysteriousness of its contents; and this very quality, since the New Testament plainly shows that the *events* related in it are to be understood as matters of *fact*, should rather *confirm*

THE GENESIS OF THE EARTH. 15

than *shake* our belief in the narrative (comparatively simple and natural) of the process of creation.

No interpretation of the latter narrative that does not treat it as a true statement, or that assigns to any word in it a meaning which that word is not generally acknowledged to have elsewhere, or a meaning not fairly deducible from an acknowledged radical signification, is, in our opinion, deserving of consideration. If this narrative, however, be a revelation in *words* only, we think that it must clearly be understood as relating that the heavens and the earth, with all the animals and plants of the latter, including man, were created in six *natural* days, or rather nights; which no sound geologist will admit. It has been urged that the sun and moon and stars are not represented as *created* on the *fourth* day, but *appointed* on that occasion "to rule over the day and over the night, and to divide the light from the darkness;" because we are told that on the first appearance of light, "God divided the light from the darkness; and God called the light day, and the darkness He called night:" but this is only a way of lessening, without removing, *one* of *many* difficulties attending the narrative considered as a *verbal* revelation. We think that this case, if the revelation be merely verbal, presents a much greater difficulty than that of the sun's standing still at the command of Joshua: for if we adopt a rendering proposed by Dr. Adam Clarke, "the sun stood still in the [upper] hemisphere of heaven, and hasted not to go down, when the day was complete," we may infer that the phenomenon was occasioned by an extraordinary refraction; the sun being near the horizon; and still the event, taking place at the word of Joshua, and in order to prolong the daylight for the accomplishment of a great moral object, was clearly miraculous.—The hypothesis of the intervention of a vast period between the first creation and the "six days' work," combined with the opinion that those were *natural* days, is now pronounced unsatisfactory by a large majority of the most eminent of the geologists; and by a far larger majority, the supposition that the "six days' work" relates only to a portion of the globe. Some writers have even asserted that six distinguishable periods of undefinable extent cannot be shown to be consistent with geological facts. But as long as the geologists themselves agree in distinguishing several successive periods as "azoic" and "palæozoic" etc., or as long as they distinguish any relative ages of organic remains, *which they must always do*, they cannot, we think, show any good reason for denying that there have been six distinct enormous periods in the universally-acknowledged progressive conditions of the earth.

A writer in a periodical publication ('the Journal of Sacred Literature,' July, 1855), remarking upon an abstract of a small pamphlet to which we originally intended to confine our observations on the subjects here treated, and which had been printed for private distribution, objects to our view of the record of the acts of creation, and says that "the seer does not give the remotest intimation that it is not the most rigidly historical narrative." We think that he *does* give an intimation, and one not remote, of its being the relation of a series of visions, in the words "and it was evening, and it was morning, day first"—"day second"—and so on. For these words appear to us very plainly to denote that the events after the mention of which they occur are represented as though taking place in the *night*, between evening and morning; not between evening and evening, in four-and-twenty hours; nor between morning and evening; and we can hardly suppose that *the events themselves* took place in periods which can either properly or metaphorically be termed "nights." We think that in one *night* the darkness was seen to withdraw itself, and the *light* to appear: that in another, the *sun* was seen, as well as the moon and the stars: and that in the night of the seventh day no vision of creation was beheld, God having then "rested" "from all his work which He had made." But what we have before advanced as the grounds of our opinion must, we think, be admitted by every impartial judge to be at least sufficient to show that it is *most probably* correct; and this is, perhaps, all that we should expect to establish, and all that can be reasonably desired by the geologist who wishes to believe the sacred record. We should ourselves be fully satisfied, without other evidence, by the consideration that the narrative of the creation is manifestly true if it be a relation of events revealed to the eye, accompanied by explanatory words, and that it is not so otherwise: for some undoubted visions are related in the Bible without any statement of their being revelations of this kind; as the vision of Jeremiah which we have already mentioned, that of Jacob at Mahanaim, and that of Micaiah. It is therefore not a case without parallels if the person to whom the revelation in question was made received it in a series of visions, and related it to his children or others in ambiguous terms, withholding (as Cornelius did in relating his vision to St. Peter) the explanation that he received it in this manner; an explanation which might have excited doubts of its truth in the minds of his hearers, who probably knew no other instance of revelation with which to compare the mode of its manifestation.

By this observation we do not mean to retract an opinion which we have already expressed, and so to concede that the narrative in the first chapter of Genesis is devoid of any indication of its being the relation of a revelation by visions. We have mentioned what we hold to be one such indication; and we believe that we have discovered another. The words rendered in the authorized version "and God *saw*," occurring seven times, may signify, without the change of a letter or even of a vowel-point, "and God *showed*." Thus we may read, "*And God showed the light, that* [*it was*] *good:*" then, "*And God showed* that [*it was*] *good:*" and at the close of the narrative, "*And God showed everything that He had made, and, behold,* [*it was*] *very good:*" or, to be more exact, instead of "*showed,*" we may read, "*was showing.*" Now, as the expression of which we propose this rendering is unquestionably equivocal, we cannot dare to assert that the meaning which we prefer to assign to it here is certainly that which is intended: but for the very same reason, none should presume to assert that the rendering in the authorized version is certainly the right one. In favour of this latter, it may be urged that, beside some other instances of the same kind more obviously figurative, we find a similar expression in Gen. xi. 5, where it is said, that "the Lord came down to see the city and the tower:" but afterwards He seems to speak of his going down with attendant angels; apparently that *these* might see, and might act as his ministers to smite and to scatter, as the angel of the Lord did among the host of Sennacherib (see 2 Kings xix. 35, comparing that passage with 2 Sam. xxiv. 15 and 16; and see also 2 Kings vii. 6 and 7). In favour of the other rendering, we contend that we should rather avoid interpreting an expression in the Bible in such a manner as to exhibit so extraordinary a kind of anthropomorphism as that which is here presented by the authorized version when it admits of a meaning which is literal and proper: and that the rendering which we prefer is perfectly appropriate and unstrained cannot be questioned. The Hebrew word to which we propose to assign in this case the meaning of "he showed," or "was showing," is the imperfect (or future with "vāv conversive") of a verb signifying "to see," and (as in 2 Kings xi. 4) of a derivative therefrom signifying "to cause to see," and hence "to show," *often occurring in descriptions of dreams and visions;* as in Gen. xli. 28, and Jer. xxiv. 1, and Ezek. xi. 25, and xl. 4, and Amos vii. 1, 4, and 7, and viii. 1, and Zech. i. 9, etc.; in several of which instances it is followed, as in the last verse of Gen. i. (which we would render, "And God showed everything that He had made," etc.), by the demonstrative particle rendered "behold;" the very frequent occurrence of which in similar cases (as Gen. xxxi. 10, and xxxviii. 7, and xl. 9, and xli. 1, 2, 3, 5, and 6, etc.) we regard as a corroboration of the rendering which we have proposed in the case in question. Thus it is at least evident that the narrative of the acts of creation admits of its being *literally* rendered as *expressly describing* a succession of *revelations to the eye*, accompanied by explanatory *words*.

If we be right in our opinion respecting the passages in the Bible that bear upon science, that, as they are necessarily adapted to very early stages of the progress of human knowledge, their meaning becomes more and more unfolded in successive ages, just as is the case with the generality of prophecies, —and we see not how this can reasonably be doubted by him who believes them to be revelations,—we should expect to find in such passages ambiguous expressions, susceptible, without being strained, of different interpretations. And such is the case in more than one instance in the principal narrative of the creation. It has been thought necessary, in rendering the second verse of the second chapter of Genesis, to read "And God ended on the *sixth* [instead of "the seventh"] day his work which He had made," on the authority of the Septuagint and Samaritan and Syriac versions; though this is apparently only a conjectural emendation: or to read "And God *had* ended on the seventh day," etc.; but this is a license exactly the same as one upon which we have before remarked, as being, in our opinion, absolutely unjustifiable. Both of these expedients are made needless by rendering the first verb in the verse "*caused to disappear*," "*to vanish*," or "*to be no longer seen;*" and we *therefore* regard this rendering as decidedly preferable. The same rendering of the same verb is perfectly appropriate in several other instances, in which it is rendered in our authorized version "consumed," or the like. This verb is the active causative form of one which, among its significations, has that of "it disappeared," "vanished," or "became no longer seen;" said of a *cloud* (so in Job vii. 9), and of *smoke* (so in Psalm xxxvii. 20); and the verb in the clause next before that in which we have proposed the new rendering is the passive causative of the same. We may therefore, commencing with the last verse of chapter one, with which these two clauses are closely connected, read thus:—" And God showed everything that He had made, and, behold, [it was] very good. And it was evening, and it was morning, day the sixth. *And the heavens and the earth and all their host were caused to disappear* [or "*be no longer seen*"] *: and* [or "*for*"] *God caused to disappear* [or "*be no longer seen*"]*, on day the seventh, his work which He had made:* and [or "for"] He rested, on day the seventh, from all his work which He had made." Thus, on the seventh day, no work was represented as done: and thus understood, the words in this passage prefigure with striking exactness (an exactness which we can hardly regard as merely accidental) the last and greatest of *sabbaths*, the "sabbatism" spoken of by St. Paul (in Heb. iv. 9), and *likened by him to the rest here described;* that sabbath which St. Peter (in his second Epistle iii. 10) calls "the day of the Lord," "in which *the heavens shall pass away* with a great noise, *and the elements,* burning with fervent heat, *shall be dissolved, and the earth and the works thereon shall be burned up;*" or, as in the words of Isaiah (li. 6), when "*the heavens shall vanish away like smoke, and the earth shall waste away* [or "*come to nought*"] like a garment, *and they that dwell therein shall die* [or "*perish*"] *in like manner;*" the period at the commencement of which St. John foresaw, in one of the grandest of his *visions* (Rev. xx. 11), that "*the earth and the heaven fled away.*" The close agreement of our proposed rendering of the first two verses of the second chapter of Genesis with these parallel passages, that is, of the words describing the *type* with those describing the *antitype*,—consistency of this kind being generally the most satisfactory criterion by which to judge of the correctness of an interpretation,—*in addition to its explaining what has been considered a great difficulty*, or rather an apparent contradiction, *in the Hebrew text*, entitles it, we think, to be regarded as decidedly preferable to the rendering in the authorized English version, and as confirmatory of our opinion of the whole narrative of the process of creation.

The writer to whom we have referred, as objecting to our view of that narrative (exhibited only by an abstract of the small pamphlet before mentioned), says further, "To assume that the record is one of *appearances* and not of *facts*,"—although we have expressly contended for the perfect truth of the revelation,—"is to strip it of its historical character." And again, he says of our explanation of that record, "Does it not reduce it to a dream, a waking dream if you will—but still a dream?" Would he venture to say thus of *unquestioned* visions related in the Bible? And if he must allow that revelations made in dreams, and apparently in such a manner as to be, in effect, only *heard*, are entitled to be regarded as strictly true when found related in the Bible (as in several instances which we are about to mention), will he, after a moment's reflection, say that we impair the credibility of the record of the creation by explaining it as a series of dreams in which some of the revelations were, in effect, both *heard* and *seen?* Admitting that "the revelation of *future* events may have been by vision" (as though even this were doubtful), he asks, "but where can we find a revelation of *past* events, of which this can be said and proved?" We have given what we regard as a sufficient answer to this question by a quotation from Professor Lee respecting the creation of Eve: and we might content ourselves with asking, in our turn, a question of our objector: Where can we find in the Scriptures a narration of any past event beside the two instances mentioned above (both of which we believe to relate to the same revelation), and those which are represented as relating to spiritual matters, but such as might be given on the authority of human witness, without being revealed either in the more usual manner (that of a vision) or otherwise? But several past events, including some which might have been made known without any divine revelation, can be "said and *proved*" to have been sometimes revealed in dreams, in which the revelations thus imparted were, in effect, *heard*; as in the instance of the dream of Abimelech, related in Gen. xx. 3, informing him of a fact which Abraham and others could have made known to him; and in the instances of two dreams of Joseph, the husband of the mother of the Saviour, related by St. Matthew in ch. i. v. 20, and in ch. ii. vv. 19 and 20, of his Gospel. The last of the chapters to which we have here referred is remarkable as relating three dreams which were revelations of future events, as well as one revealing a past event. And in the second chapter of the book of Daniel we find two dreams mentioned:—one a revelation of future events, namely, Nebuchadnezzar's dream; and the other, of a past event, namely, the same dream apparently repeated to Daniel, being "revealed" to him "in a night-*vision*," and therefore so as to be *seen* by him, and accompanied by the revelation of the future events which it signified, so as to be, in effect, *heard* by him. Again, in the ninth chapter of the Acts we read of a vision relating to past and future events. Thus we have given five instances of the revelation of past events in dreams or visions; and one of these dreams was to give assurance of the greatest miracle recorded in the Bible!

The same writer questions whether this view be consistent with the statement that "in six days the Lord made heaven and earth." But if the record be a relation of six visions, in which were seen the aspects of events of six distinct periods of equal (though undefinable) length, we assert, incontrovertibly, that these periods may be termed "days" in later passages of the Bible with as much propriety as the periods which are so termed in the Revelation of St. John, or as other periods in the book of Daniel are termed "weeks." In saying this, with respect to the term "days," we believe that we are even understating the case; for we have the strongest reasons for regarding each of the "days" of creation, after the first, as a new period of *life*, following a period of *death*, such as, though not universal, was on a very extraordinary scale (numerous entire species becoming extinct,—if by slow degrees, the more agreeably with the analogy which we are pointing out,—to be superseded by others better suited to new conditions of the earth): and the period of human *life* is called in Scripture " *day ;*" like as that of *death* is termed " *night ;*" as in St. John's Gospel, ix. 4. For this reason, therefore, with others, like as the Hebrew civil day consists of a *natural night* and a *natural day*, so each of the six " days " of creation may be regarded as consisting of a *figurative night* and a *figurative day*, as we shall hereafter more fully explain; and hence the passage in Exodus xx. 9—11 may mean, "Six of thy days (natural days) shalt thou labour, ... but the seventh of those days is the Sabbath, ... for in six of his days (figurative days) the Lord made heaven and earth, ... and rested the seventh of those days." And for the same reason, also, we think that the latter periods may with propriety be termed " days " if of *unequal* (as well as undefinable) lengths; even if as unequal as the lives of any six human beings.

It is, perhaps, not unworthy of notice, that the Indian cosmogony, which agrees in several remarkable particulars with that of the Bible, so nearly as to convince us that it is partly borrowed from this latter, describes many successive creations and destructions, as the events of so many *days ;* and represents each of these *days of the Creator* as lasting *many thousand ages*. And the opinion that the "days" of the Biblical cosmogony are to be understood figuratively may be traced, in writings of ancient authors, Christian and Jewish, more or less distinctly, up to the time of Philo; so that even the objection of novelty cannot be urged against it.

Some persons have argued, that to represent the "six days" of creation as other than *natural* days is to annul the propriety and force of the reason for the institution of the *sabbath*. But in arguing thus, they appear to have disregarded the fact that the day of the Creator's rest was *not* a *natural* day; for it evidently extends from the last act of creation to the general resurrection: therefore, if the six preceding days were natural days, and the law respecting labour and rest must literally correspond with the reason assigned for it in Exodus xx. 8—11, and xxxi. 15—17, a man would be required to labour six natural days, and then to rest for the remainder of his life! They seem, moreover, not to have considered that the institution of the sabbatical *year* obviously rests upon the same foundation as that of the sabbath-*day* (see Exodus xxiii. 10—12, and Lev. xxv. 1—7). Nor are these three—the *day*, the *year*, and the *period between the last act of creation and the resurrection,*—the only sabbaths: there is yet to come the *eternal sabbath*, the σαββατισμός spoken of by St. Paul (in Heb. iv. 9), and, as we have before observed, *likened by him* (in the next verse) *to God's rest from his works of creation.* Thus it is evident that one objection to the regarding of the "six days" of creation as periods of unknown duration falls to the ground: and we are not acquainted with any other objection ostensibly derived from the Bible, except one founded upon a misinterpretation of the words (in Gen. i.) which signify "and it was evening, and it was morning, day first," etc., combined with the opinion that the revelation in which they occur was *merely verbal;* an opinion involving difficulties that can never, we feel assured, be reasonably solved.

The explanation which we have proposed is obviously consistent with the theory of the continuity, as well as with that of the discontinuity, of the series of changes which the earth and its appertenances have undergone. For it regards each of the supposed visions as relating to some one, or more, of the principal phenomena characterizing that series of changes, without *necessarily* denoting any absolute interruption, from first to last. Nay, rather, by the correspondence of each night-vision to a period afterwards termed a "day," it implies a succession of *gradual* changes, each like the change from day to night; which latter, be it observed, is not a period of *total* privation of light. It is therefore perfectly consistent with the fact that certain species of animals and plants have become wholly (though gradually) destroyed while others have survived and new ones have been brought into being: a case somewhat similar to that resulting from a pestilence in a country inhabited by different races, some of them more obnoxious to its fatal influences than others. It admits that the periods to which it relates *may* have been as intimately connected, one with another, as those of a history represented only by a few scenes of a drama; and that many of the changes which geology makes known to us, as having taken place in the condition of the earth and of its animals and plants, may have occurred during only *one* of those periods. In short, it concedes to the philosopher all the license that he can desire to enjoy in his speculations. For while unmistakeable evidences of some of the facts which it indicates, and of the verisimilitude of all the rest of them, as far as appearances are concerned, are conspicuous in the discoveries of geologists, and in the inferences which are drawn from those discoveries, it leaves an inexhaustible source of study open to scientific research by its regarding the revelation as confined to the exhibition of a few scenes represented by images of objects familiar to the sight of all mankind.

First, it seems that a region of the earth "desolate and void," overspread by *water*, and enveloped in the "darkness" of "*night*," was disclosed to view by the appearance of the "light" of "*day*," at the bidding of the Creator. Such appears to have been the scene beheld between the first "evening" and "morning;" and such seems to have been the condition of the whole earth during the first (so-called) "night" and "day," or the first of the "six days." Accordingly, the earliest organisms with which we are acquainted, both plants and animals, are wholly *marine;* and all consist of species that became extinct unnumbered ages before the creation of man; whence we may reasonably account for their not being represented in the revelation made to him. But their *origination* may be signified by the statement that "the Spirit of God"—according to several ancient and modern translators "the *wind* of God," or "*a potent wind,*" by which the vivifying Spirit was perhaps represented in the vision, for the same expression bears these meanings as well as the first meaning,—[was] "hovering," or "brooding," "upon the face of the waters." It is generally conceded by the geologists that the absence of terrestrial organic remains in the most ancient deposits affords almost a proof that the waters of the sea covered the whole, or nearly the whole, of the primeval earth. Doubtless there existed elevations from which those deposits derived their origin: but these elevations may have been beneath the surface of the waters, which we can hardly suppose to have been everywhere of equal depth. From such elevations, by the constant action of the ocean, chiefly by the tides, may have been washed down the primary deposits, in which, as a necessary consequence, we find none but marine organisms. Or *some* elevations may have been *above* the surface of the waters consistently with our explanation; as the word rendered "earth" is very frequently applied to a *portion* of the earth; and we do not suppose that the semblance of the earth appeared rotating before the eyes of the person to whom the revelation was made, so as to display to him every part, and thus to convey a knowledge of its globular form, which, probably, was not even suspected until a comparatively late age.

Secondly, that the waters in the atmosphere were seen to become separated by an "expanse" (which—whatever be the literal meaning of the term thus rendered—was supposed to be a solid concave hemisphere) from the waters beneath; agreeably with the generally-admitted fact of a gradual cooling of the earth: for in proportion as the sea is warmer than the atmosphere, so much greater is the quantity of vapour, or fog, resting upon the surface of the former. —A great change must be inferred to have then taken place in the organisms existing in the sea; that is, a general, or very extensive, though gradual, extinction; or, in other words, a figurative *night*, preceding the second *day*: and similar extinctions of species may also be inferred to have taken place on the occasion of each of the succeeding acts of creation.

Thirdly, that there was seen a "gathering together of the waters" "under the heaven" "into one place," with an emerging of land, forming "earth" and "seas," in accordance with undoubted facts of geology; and that the dry land was seen to produce "sprouting herbage," and "seed-bearing herbs," and "fruit-bearing trees," represented by images of *existing* species, but of such kinds that the description of them is suitable to the earliest land-flora, of any considerable extent and variety, with which we are acquainted. Many geologists have inferred from the general character of that ancient flora, and especially from the great abundance of ferns displayed by it, judging from the remains that are found in the coal-measures, that the climate in which it grew was warm, damp, and cloudy; and the record of the creation appears to demand this inference. Another inference drawn from the same flora, and amply confirmed by the circumstances of place, is also one which seems to be required by the scriptural record; namely, the insular character of the land that produced it. (See some interesting remarks on this subject in "Cosmos," vol. i. p. 282, of Otté's Translation.) And this inference (which is agreeable with the characters and paucity of the species of terrestrial animals of the same period) obviously corroborates the former one, by its implying a temperature more equable over the globe than that of the present age, and an atmosphere more charged with moisture. Enormous must have been the destruction of life when tracts of land thus, for the first time, rose above the sea, to be covered with vegetable produce. This, then, may be termed a figurative *night*, preceding the creations of the third *day*. It was probably of vast duration, like the "days" between which it intervened; for the upheaval of the land, here indicated in the narrative, is generally believed, on geological evidences, to have been extremely slow and gradual.

Fourthly, that the sun, hitherto concealed by an unbroken canopy of clouds, and now required to exert its unobstructed influence upon more advanced species of creations, was first beheld; evaporation having decreased with the decrease of the surface of the waters; and that with it were seen the moon and the stars.—The great atmospheric change thus indicated must have been attended by a very extensive gradual extinction of vegetable and animal species; and thus, again, we find evidence of another figurative *night*, that which preceded the fourth *day*.

Fifthly, that there appeared a multitude of aquatic animals (small and large reptiles), and of birds, represented, like the creations of the third period, by images of *existing* species, but designated by terms equally applicable to these and to earlier species of aquatic creatures and of birds, of an age immensely later than the land-floras of the carboniferous rocks, and yet very long anterior to the great period of land-animals. With respect to the term rendered "whales" in the authorized version, it should be observed that it applies to various large aquatic and amphibious creatures; particularly to crocodiles; and to serpents; but certainly not to any species exclusively of all others.—As each of the first four "days" appears to have been preceded by a figurative night, we may reasonably infer that so was this (the fifth) day, and the next also; and the many and great successive changes in the physical conditions of the earth, made known by geology, attended by the extinctions of numerous entire species, rather demand than forbid the conclusion that such was the case.

Sixthly,—agreeably with what took place when the features of the land and sea, and the characters of their animal and vegetable occupants, were about to become, for the most part, nearly what they now are,—that cattle, and other animals of the land, came into view, as though brought forth by the earth; the representation of these, also, being similar to that of the aquatic animals and the birds, and that of the plants: and then, man, represented by him to whom the revelation was most probably made, together with his wife. The words by which the last act of creation is introduced we would literally render, "We will make Adam, in our image, after our likeness; and they shall have dominion" etc.: understanding these words (not as the expression of a desire, seemingly addressed to ministering angels, as the pseudo-Jonathan supposes, but) as an announcement, made to the seer, of the event next to be represented.

The Creator is then shown to be *resting* "from all his work which he had made;" probably by the disappearance of the earth and the heaven, as in St. John's vision of the *eternal sabbath*, of which this last portion of the revelation is affirmed by St. Paul to be a *type*, as we have already observed. But this term "*resting*" is not to be understood in its fullest sense: it is obviously *relative* as well as *figurative;* by no means implying that those very laws by which *continual* changes were effected in former periods, from the earliest existence of the earth, are not in operation *now;* but only that since the last recorded act of creation God has originated in our earth *no new species*. —The sixth "day" may be said to have gradually changed into *night,* a night of *extinction,* with respect to multitudes of its species, remains of which are found with those of species still existing. And especially with respect to *man,* it may be said, agreeably with the language of Scripture, that the "day" of his creation has been followed by a *night,* that night of *moral darkness* in the deepest gloom of which came the Flood. Then *light* dawned again upon a portion of the earth, and (although often obscured) shone more and more until the *sunrise* of the *seventh day,* when "*the Sun of Righteousness*" rose "to give *light* to them that sat in *darkness* and in the shadow of *death*." But the full light of truth then shone upon *Judæa only,* thence to extend to other countries; wherefore St. Paul said, addressing the *Romans,* "The *night* is far spent; the *day* is at hand:" and still *the night of heathenism* overspreads the greater part of the globe. We have already shown that we hold the vision of the seventh "day" to have been *prophetical* as well as *typical*.

The main design of this most sublime revelation seems to have been, first, to teach the seer, and, through him, others, that all the natural objects of which the existence was known to him were created by One Supreme Being; later generations being left to understand the same respecting similar objects discoverable by scientific explorations: secondly, and consequently, to show the impiety of the worship of such objects (a worship prevailing even in our own days, in various forms and disguises, throughout many regions of the earth): and thirdly, to make known the institution of the sabbath, or at least to supply a reason for its after-observance, and to foretoken the day of Christian light and also the eternal "sabbatism." All this was effected, not in a manner suited to convey scientific instruction, but in a manner perfectly consistent with scientific truth, if the narrative be understood in the only way in which the Bible authorizes our understanding a revelation belonging to a class in which this record is included; that is, as a revelation of events not shown to have been originally communicated to Moses nor by means of an angel. If our explanation, therefore, be right, it is not from a want of evidence in the Bible that it has not been elicited before; but chiefly because men have failed to apply to this case a clear Scriptural rule, of which numerous examples are found throughout the books of the Old Testament.

We have here made large additions to our observations on the same subject in the first edition of this work; and we had done so without knowing, or even suspecting, that any other writer had previously expressed an opinion similar to that here presented, as to the manner in which was revealed the process of creation described in the first chapter of Genesis. The publication of the late Hugh Miller's "Testimony of the Rocks" has, however, shown us that such was the opinion of Coleridge, in whose "Aids to Reflection" (page 111) we find the following passage:—"Let us carry ourselves back, in spirit, to the mysterious Week, the teeming Work-days of the Creator; as they rose in vision before the eye of the inspired Historian of 'the generations of the Heaven and the Earth, in the day that the Lord God made the Earth and the Heavens.'" And it has also made known to us that two other writers had expressed a similar opinion; having seen in the narrative of the process of creation what they held to be satisfactory evidences of its being a description of a series of visions, though differing from us in supposing those visions to have been beheld by Moses, and in their reasonings on the subject. In the fourth lecture in his work above mentioned, entitled "The Mosaic Vision of Creation," Mr. Miller manifests a decided preference of this opinion above every other. He there states it to have been put forth, and discussed, by Dr. J. H. Kurtz, in his *Bibel und Astronomie* (second edition, 1849); this writer arguing " that the pre-Adamic history of the past being *theologically* in the same category as the yet undeveloped history of the future, that record of its leading events which occurs in the Mosaic narrative is simply *prophecy* described backwards; and that, coming under the prophetic law, it ought of consequence to be subjected to the prophetic rule of exposition." Mr. Miller then continues, "There are some very ingenious reasonings employed in fortifying this point; and, after quoting from Eichhorn a passage to the effect that the opening chapter in Genesis is much rather a creative picture than a creative history, and from Ammon to the effect that the author of it evidently takes the position of a beholder of creation, the learned German concludes his statement by remarking, that the scenes of the chapter are prophetic tableaux, each containing a leading phase of the drama of creation. 'Before the eye of the seer,' he says, 'scene after scene is unfolded, until at length, in the seven of them, the course of creation, in its main *momenta*, has been fully represented.' The revelation has every characteristic of prophecy by vision,—prophecy by eye-witnessing; and may be perhaps best understood by regarding it simply as an exhibition of the actual phenomena of creation presented to the mental eye of the prophet under the ordinary laws of perspective, and truthfully described by him in the simple language of his time. In our own country," he adds, "a similar view has been taken by the author of a singularly ingenious little work which issued about two years ago from the press of Mr. Constable of Edinburgh, 'The Mosaic Record in Harmony with the Geological.'" And he also mentions the present work, quoting a portion of its first chapter.

In perusing Mr. Miller's work cited above, we have seen nothing to add to the arguments upon which we had previously founded the opinions advanced in the foregoing pages, beyond a few observations which we shall here quote, generally, but not entirely, agreeing with our own inferences. We think most decidedly that the revelation of the creation was not made to Moses, but to Adam: yet, if to Moses, it may have been by vision; for it seems probable that the "burning bush" was exhibited to him in this manner, as well as "the pattern of the tabernacle, and the pattern of all the instruments thereof." This, therefore, is not the chief point; but we have shown that it is one of considerable importance; and we think that the evident vision of Adam described in the second chapter of Genesis, compared with the preceding chapter, is alone sufficient to determine it.

Upon the main point, the *manner*, or *mode*, of the revelation, Mr. Miller appears to us to argue with much sagacity and force. After remarking that "the *reason* why the drama of creation has been *optically* described *seems* to be, that it was in reality *visionally* revealed," he proceeds thus:—" A further question still remains: *If* the revelation was by vision, that circumstance affords of itself a satisfactory reason why the description should be *optical;* and, on the other hand, since the description is decidedly *optical*, the presumption is of course strong that the revelation was by vision. But why, it may be asked, by vision? Can the presumption be yet further strengthened by showing that this visual mode or form was preferable to any other? Can there be a reason, in fine, assigned *for* the *reason*,—for that revelation by vision which accounts for the optical character of the description? The question is a difficult one; but I think there can. There seems to be a peculiar fitness in a revelation made by vision, for conveying an account of creation to various tribes, and peoples of various degrees of acquirement, and throughout a long course of ages in which the knowledge of the heavenly bodies or of the earth's history, *i.e.* the sciences of astronomy and geology, did not at first exist, but in which ultimately they came to be studied and known. We must recognise such a mode as equally fitted for the earlier and the more modern times,—for the ages anterior to the rise of science, and the ages posterior to its rise. The prophet, by describing what he had actually seen in language fitted to the ideas of his time, would shock no previously existing prejudice that had been founded on the apparent evidence of the senses: he could as safely describe the moon as the second great light of creation as he could the sun as its first great light, and both, too, as equally subordinate to the planet which we inhabit. On the other hand, an enlightened age, when it had come to discover this key to the description, would find it *optically* true in all its details. But how differently would not a revelation have fared, in at least the earlier time, that was strictly scientific in its details, —a revelation, for instance, of the great truth demonstrated by Galileo, that the sun rests in the centre of the heavens, while the apparently-immoveable earth sweeps with giddy velocity around it; or of the great truth demonstrated by Newton, that our ponderous planet is kept from falling off into empty space by the operation of the same law that impels a descending pebble towards the ground! A great miracle wrought in proof of the truth of the revelation might serve to enforce the belief of it on the generation to whom it had been given; but the generations that followed, to whom the miracle would exist as a piece of mere testimony, would credit, in preference, the apparently-surer evidence of their senses, and become unbelievers. They would act, all unwittingly, on the principle of Hume's famous argument, and prefer to rest rather on their own *experience* of the great phenomena of nature, than on the doubtful testimony of their ancestors, reduced, in the lapse of ages, to a dim, attenuated tradition. Nor would a geological revelation have fared better, in at least those periods intermediate between the darker and more scientific ages, in which ingenious men, somewhat sceptical in their leanings, cultivate literature, and look down rather superciliously on the ignorance and barbarism of the past. What would sceptics such as Hobbes and Hume have said of an opening chapter in Genesis that would describe successive periods,—first of molluscs, star-lilies, and crustaceans, next of fishes, next of reptiles and birds, then of mammals, and finally of man; and that would minutely portray a period in which there were lizards bulkier than elephants, reptilian whales furnished with necks slim and long as the bodies of great snakes, and flying dragons, whose spread of wing greatly more than doubled that of the largest bird? The world would assuredly not receive such a revelation. Nor, further, have scientific facts or principles been revealed to man which he has been furnished with the ability of observing or discovering for himself. It is according to the economy of revelation, that the truths which it exhibits should be of a kind which, lying beyond the reach of his ken, he himself could never have elicited. From every view of the case, then, a prophetic exhibition of the pre-Adamic scenes and events by vision seems to be the one best suited for the opening chapters of a revelation vouchsafed for the accomplishment of moral, not scientific purposes, and at once destined to be contemporary with every stage of civilization, and to address itself to minds of every various calibre, and every different degree of enlightenment."

After some further remarks, which we reluctantly refrain from quoting, he thus continues:—" What may be termed the three *geologic* days,—the third, fifth, and sixth,—may be held to have extended over those carboniferous periods during which the great plants were created,—over those Oolitic and Cretaceous periods during which the great sea-monsters and birds were created,—and over those Tertiary periods during which the great terrestrial mammals were created. For the intervening or fourth day we have that wide space represented by the Permian and Triassic periods, which, less conspicuous in their floras than the period that went immediately before, and less conspicuous in their faunas than the periods that came immediately after, were marked by the decline, and ultimate extinction, of the Palæozoic forms, and the first partially-developed beginnings of the Secondary ones. And for the first and second days there remain the great Azoic period, during which the immensely-developed gneisses, mica schists, and primary clay slates, were deposited, and the two extended periods represented by the Silurian and Old Red Sandstone systems. These, taken together, exhaust the geologic scale, and may be named in their order as, *first*, the Azoic day or period; *second*, the Silurian and Old Red Sandstone day or period; *third*, the Carboniferous day or period; *fourth*, the Permian and Triassic day or period; *fifth*, the Oolitic and Cretaceous day or period; and, *sixth*, the Tertiary day or period." (See Note 2.) He then makes an attempt to conceive "how they might have appeared pictorially, if revealed in a series of visions to Moses, as the successive scenes of a great air-drawn panorama;" and the result is a description much more ample and circumstantial than that which we have ourselves offered; perfectly agreeing with the *descriptions* of the supposed visions, but not, we think, with the *visions themselves*. For the *visions*, considered abstractedly, were only for the instruction of the *seer;* and therefore we regard them as exhibiting only images of *existing* physical objects: but the *descriptions* are designed for the instruction of *mankind in general*, throughout all their generations; and therefore we regard them, in their relation to vegetable and animal creations, as equally applicable to existing species and to the most remarkable species peculiar to successive *past* periods. Except in making this distinction, which we hold to be absolutely indispensable, and in believing that the revelation was to *Adam*, there is no important point on which we differ in opinion from Mr. Miller.

If the general correctness of the explanation which we have here offered be admitted, we are not to infer that the narrative of the process of creation does not leave some important facts to be supplied by other portions of Scripture; and with this observation, we may proceed to the second part of our inquiry.

CHAPTER II.

THE GENESIS OF MAN.

WHEN a passage, or a collection of passages, in Holy Scripture, is known to be susceptible of two different interpretations, without any forced construction, it is our right and duty to refrain from forming an opinion in favour of one of those interpretations, and against the other, until we have carefully weighed all the circumstances of the case, not suffering the evidence on either side to be swayed by any educational bias, or by any tradition that might be brought to bear upon it, and have found a decided preponderance of probability in one scale of the balance. It is one of our most precious privileges, as Protestant Christians, to hold this axiom; and astronomy and geology have sufficiently rebuked us for neglecting it.

The passages in the Bible that are commonly regarded as deciding the question respecting the origin of the human species demand a reverential caution of this kind in him who examines them: for while these apparently indicate the origination of all mankind from Adam, there are others which apparently imply the existence of human beings not his offspring. Almost all Biblical critics who have compared and discussed them have endeavoured to reconcile the latter with the commonly-understood import of the former: but it is only by reversing the method which they have pursued that we can vindicate the truth of the first quarter of the book of Genesis, consistently with the opinion now held, respecting the antiquity of man, by many—we believe we may say, the majority, if not all,—of our most eminent geologists, and also by many ethnologists, and other men of science and learning. To persons who have adopted this opinion (that the antiquity of man is immeasurably remote), it can hardly be satisfactory to regard the portion of Scripture above mentioned as mythical or allegorical, though retaining belief in the rest.

Of the passages that apparently indicate the origination of all mankind from Adam, the following are those that are generally esteemed the most weighty in their evidence.

1. *"And the Lord God said, [It is] not good that the man ["the ādām"] should be alone: I will make him an help meet for him."* (Gen. ii. 18.)

This passage certainly seems, at first sight, to imply that Adam was the only human being then existing. But if we regard him as the first individual of a new variety of a species which had universally sinned but not become extinct, we may not only understand why God *created* a female for him, but also why we find no mention of the creation of wives for his sons. The sinless Adam needed a sinless wife:

but in the cases of Cain and Seth, the same necessity did not obtain; they having been *born* fallen creatures.

It may be objected that Adam and Eve may have originated *naturally*, if any earlier human race existed: but to reason thus would be to argue only on *physical* grounds respecting a matter of *revelation.* That they originated *supernaturally* is, to our mind, an absolutely-unavoidable inference from the circumstances of the case; and therefore, in all that we have to advance in relation to them, we must be considered as holding this tenet. We readily admit the *unity* of our *species;* and that, as far as our experience goes, we always find that *varieties* originate *naturally:* but there may be *exceptions* to a physical law, though there cannot be *contradictions.* From the *general natural* originations of varieties, we have no more reason to presume that there have been no *particular supernatural* originations (which is the meaning that we assign to "creations") than, from the *general uniform course of nature* in other respects, we have reason to presume that there have been no such events as *miracles.* When Bacon denounced the attempt "to find natural philosophy in the first chapter of Genesis, the book of Job, and elsewhere in Scripture," as leading "not only to a fantastical philosophy but also to a heretical religion," he neglected not to add that we should "*give unto Faith the things that are Faith's.*"

2. "*And Adam* [or "*the ādām*"] *called his wife's*

name Eve, because she was the mother of all living." (Gen. iii. 20.)

To understand what is here said, we must first observe, that it has an obvious reference to the announcement previously made to Eve (*who, it is clear, was not yet a mother*), that she should "bring forth children;" so that the verb here rendered "was" must be one of the numerous instances in which the preterite in Hebrew is used as an emphatic future; as in Gen. i. 29, and xv. 18, and xvii. 20, and xxiii. 11 and 13, etc. : and secondly, that the Hebrew noun which is here rendered "all," when the noun to which it is prefixed is without the article, as it is in this instance, often signifies "*many*," or "*a variety*," or "*all kinds*," or "*all sorts;*" as in Gen. xli. 57, and Lev. xix. 23, and 1 Chron. xxix. 2, and Neh. xiii. 16, etc. We therefore believe that Adam called his wife's name Eve because she *should be* the mother of many children, like as God gave to Abram the name of "Abraham" because he was *to be* "a father of many nations." If the meaning be "all living," we have no right to infer from it more than that Adam was as yet in ignorance of the existence of any human beings beside himself and his wife; and it is not unreasonable to suppose that he may have been originally placed apart in the garden of Eden because that ignorance was necessary to the preservation of his innocence. Before his fall, he had known good only: not evil. Hence, also, if we suppose (as many persons do) that the revelation of the process of creation was made to Adam, in Paradise, and further assume that a race of men existed before him, *we may readily account for the fact that the earlier creation of man was not made known to the seer:* and that Adam was the person to whom that revelation was made, we have shown to be, in our opinion, more than probable.

3. "*And He answered and said unto them, Have ye not read, that He which made from the beginning* (ἀπ' ἀρχῆς [as in the fourth verse following]) *made them male and female* [or "*a male and a female*"]? *And He said, For this cause shall a man leave father and mother, and shall cleave to his wife; and they twain shall be one flesh.*" (Matt. xix. 4 and 5.) Or, "*From the beginning of the creation* (ἀπὸ δὲ ἀρχῆς κτίσεως) *God made them male and female. For this cause*" etc. (Mark x. 6.)

As the words thus rendered were said in explanation of the divine law of marriage, we think they may reasonably be understood to mean that God's making male and female, or a male and a female, signified that the female is the necessary complement of the male, and that the two should be inseparable; and that our Lord said, to show this more plainly, quoting the words of Adam, "For this cause" etc. We do not see that they necessarily imply the non-existence of Pre-Adamites; but rather believe them to mean that God has ever proportioned the females to the males so as to show that for every male there was designed a female for his counterpart.

4. "*And hath made of one blood all nations of men for to dwell on all the face of the earth.*" (Acts xvii. 26.)

In the passage thus rendered, the manuscripts of the original, and the versions made from it, present several variations. The most important of these variations is the omission of the word signifying "blood," namely αἵματος, in the Vatican and Alexandrian manuscripts (which seem to be justly regarded by the best critics as generally the most accurate of all), and in several others, as well as in the Vulgate, and some other old versions. The rest do not materially affect the subject of our inquiry; but all of them, considered together, show that it would be presumptuous to found upon this passage a decided opinion that the human species originated entirely from one pair. We agree with those who hold that αἵματος is not a likely word to have been interpolated, as implied in ἑνὸς: but in our opinion it matters little whether it be so or not. If it be an interpolation, we think that we are only justified in inferring that the word implied is either ἀνθρώπου or ἔθνους; and that the passage therefore means, "And hath made of one *man*," or "of one *nation*," "all nations of men" etc. Thus the most obvious import would still be the assertion of our universal consanguinity. We cannot, however, be sure that "*all nations of men*" means more than "*every nation under heaven*" in Acts ii. 5, applied only to all the nations among which were Jews. Moreover, sup-

THE GENESIS OF MAN. 51

posing that αἵματος is not an interpolation, the learned Dean Alford holds that the meaning is not "hath made of one blood", etc., but "*caused every nation (sprung) of one blood to dwell*" etc.; and refers to Matt. v. 32, and Mark vii. 37. (See his N.T. vol. ii. pp. 180 and 181.) If so, the passage imports no more than Gen. ix. 19 ("These [are] the three sons of Noah, and from these," or "by these," "the whole earth was scattered," or "dispersed"), considered in a later portion of this chapter. But we are content to argue the case on the supposition that the authorized English version represents the true text correctly.

As the expression "one flesh," where it is said (in 1 Cor. xv. 39), "there is one flesh of men, another flesh of beasts, another of fishes, another of birds," denotes *only a similarity* in the flesh of a whole species, and even of a class consisting of various orders and genera and species, so the expression "one blood" may denote only *a specific, not an absolute*, unity of blood. Or the latter expression may denote *consanguinity*, but *without implying unity of origin:* for we say of the children of the same parents that they are "of one blood," but not of the parents unless we can actually trace them both to one ancestor; and if we knew the father and mother to be descended from different pairs of protoplasts, we should still say the same of their children. But if "blood" denotes consanguinity in a few instances in the Bible, so does "flesh" in about the same number of cases (as in Gen. xxix. 14, and xxxvii. 27, and Judges ix. 2, and 2 Sam. v. 1, and xix. 12 and 13); and yet we see in how lax a manner the latter term is used by St. Paul in an instance mentioned above. Dr. Pye Smith candidly admits that " we cannot indeed affirm it to be an *impossibility* that the Almighty Creator should have seen fit to bring originally into being duplicates, triplicates, or other multiples of pairs, formed so alike that there should be no specific difference between them." And he afterwards observes, "With regard to Acts xvii. 26, it cannot be proved that 'one blood' necessarily signifies descent from a common ancestry: for, admitting a specific identity, though having proceeded from distinct foci of creation, both the physical and the mental characteristics would be the same in all essential qualities." ("The Relation between the Holy Scriptures and some parts of Geological Science:" ed. of 1852: Supplementary Note E.)

We think that these words are mainly designed to convey a *figurative* meaning. The context seems plainly to indicate this, declaring the doctrine of a unity of mankind far above that of physical consanguinity, by teaching that God " giveth to all life, and breath, and all things," and that "*we are his offspring;*" in order to show the folly of idolatry and polytheism, and of the Athenians' imagining themselves to differ in origin from others by being the offspring of their own soil. In like manner, also, the Saviour says (Matt. xxiii. 8 and 9), " Be not ye called Rabbi: for one is your Master, [even] Christ; and *all ye are brethren*. And call no [man] your father upon the earth: for *one is your Father, which is in heaven.*" Here the figurative meaning is still more plain; though these words appear chiefly to point to a yet higher unity, to which we shall have to advert in considering the two passages of Scripture next following. But we strongly incline to the opinion that the words in Acts xvii. 26, if αἵματος be not an interpolation, have *also* a *literal* meaning; though by no means conceding that they disprove the existence of Pre-Adamites; for if there have been two creations of man, each consisting of one pair, and the children of the second pair intermarried with descendants of the first, then, literally speaking, *one blood pervades the whole human species*, although in a very large portion thereof intermixed with *another* blood, that of the man created "in the image of God." It is obvious that there may have been *several* creations of man (though we think it improbable that there have been more than two) and yet all mankind may be connected by consanguinity.

5. "*By one man sin entered into the world, and death by sin, and so* [the sentence of] *death passed throughout* (διῆλθεν) *to all men* [of his descendants], *for that* (ἐφ' ᾧ, in the margin of the authorized version "in whom,") *all have sinned.*" (Rom. v. 12). And "*Since by a man* (δι' ἀνθρώπου) [*is*] *death, by a man* [*is*] *also the resurrection of the dead: for as by* (ἐν) *Adam all* [who partake of the nature which he

transmitted] *die, even so by Christ shall all* [who partake of the nature which he assumed] *be made alive.*" (1 Cor. xv. 21 and 22.)

Considered abstractedly, these two passages seem to assert that sin *first* entered into the world by one man, namely, Adam; and that the sin of that man brought death upon himself and *all our species*. But neither of these assertions can be admitted. The first is inadmissible because Eve sinned before Adam: the second, because Adam's sin did not bring death upon Eve, for she died for her *own* sin; nor upon Enoch; nor upon Elijah. Hence it appears to be meant by the former passage, that the *sentence* of death (which was pronounced conditionally before the commission of the sin, and which was afterwards made ineffectual in the cases of Enoch and Elijah,) passed throughout (*not to all absolutely*, in consequence of Adam's sin, since it was brought upon his wife by herself, but) to all men *of his descendants*. If so, supposing the existence of Non-Adamites, these are excluded; and the reasons for their exclusion are sufficiently obvious. That it was the *sentence* of death that passed throughout is expressly shown in one of the verses following the former passage, in the same chapter; where it is said, "the *sentence* (κρίμα) [was] for one [offence] to condemnation."

Before geological discoveries had brought to light abundant and overwhelming evidence of the fact that irrational animals lived and died upon this earth countless ages before the time of Adam, these passages of Scripture were commonly regarded as teaching that death was unknown in the world before Adam's transgression. It requires but little consideration to see that this was an unjust, or at least an unnecessary, inference; that the death here spoken of is only that which Adam brought upon himself, and, by the transmission of his sinful nature, upon his descendants: and as these passages do not declare, contrary to demonstrated facts, that death in an absolute sense was unknown before Adam, neither do they prove that rational beings did not exist before him, dying for a cause different from that which brought death upon him and his seed. Both assert that one man brought death upon his posterity; and this fact is by no means inconsistent with the existence of multitudes of other men of whom every one died for his own transgression against the law written in his heart. They teach that death as a punishment for transgression of a divine commandment is by one man, namely, Adam; and the latter of them, with its context, teaches that the resurrection of the dead as a gratuitous compensation for that punishment is also by one, namely, Christ; in like manner as the former, with what follows it, is designed to show that, "as by one man's disobedience the many were made sinners, so by the obedience of one shall the many be made righteous." Therefore, all that we may reasonably infer from them, with respect to the question of the existence of human beings before Adam, seems to be this:

that if such beings existed, they did not sin against an express divine revelation: and the existence of Pre-Adamites without such a revelation is surely less wonderful than the fact that there have been, and still are, Post-Adamites without it: but there exists no people whose genealogy can be traced up in the Scriptures to Adam without some *relic* thereof, small though it be; and this is an argument for the existence of Non-Adamites; for we think that the revelation made to Adam can never have become extinguished among his posterity.

"Sin is the transgression of law" (1 John, iii. 4); for "through law (διὰ νόμου) [is] the knowledge of sin" (Rom. iii. 20): "where there is no law [there is] no transgression" (Rom. iv. 15): "sin is not imputed where there is no law" (Rom. v. 13). But law, in this definition of sin, has a twofold acceptation: there is a revealed law and a natural law. St. Paul speaks of the former where he mentions those who "have sinned without law" (Rom. ii. 12); and he draws a distinction between the former and the latter where he says, "when, therefore, the Gentiles, who have not a law, do by nature the things contained in the law, these, not having a law, are a law unto themselves, which show the work of the law written in their hearts" (Rom. ii. 14). Therefore sin, also, has a twofold acceptation. And hence the same Apostle says afterwards (perhaps more particularly referring to the latter half of the first chapter of his Epistle to the Romans, in which he has recounted the enormous sins committed against the law of nature by Gentiles "professing themselves to be wise"), "we have before proved both Jews and Gentiles (Hellenes) to be all under sin" (Rom. iii. 9): the sin of the former being against a revealed law; that of the latter, against the law of nature. Now the sin spoken of in the former of the two passages to which these observations are appended, and alluded to in the latter of them, was only of the former kind; therefore these passages do not prove that sin of the latter kind did not before exist: and the death of which they speak being likewise only that which was occasioned by the former kind of sin, they do not prove that there was no death of human beings for a different cause before the sin of Adam, any more than they declare the refuted doctrine that death in an absolute sense was unknown before his time.

It may be observed also, that the expression rendered "the world" (τὸν κόσμον), in the former of the passages to which these remarks apply, may mean "the world of Adam's race;" for it is often used so as to exclude many of the human species; as, for instance, in 1 John, v. 19, where "*the whole world*" (ὁ κόσμος ὅλος) denotes *all who are not of God*.

And here, too, we may observe, that Adam is called, according to most of the manuscripts, and our authorized version, "*the first man Adam*," and simply "*the first man;*" but only where Christ is called "*the last Adam,*" and "*the second man*" (1 Cor. xv. 45 and 47); and we should not insist that an appellation must be literally understood when it has a correlative which *cannot* be so understood. The propriety of these appellations may be sufficiently seen from the consideration that Adam was our first federal head, and that Christ is our second and last: or from the fact that Adam was *the first man who bore "the image of God,"* in respect of qualities possessed by none other before the incarnation of the Saviour; and that *the second and last who received that image unimpaired by sin* was Christ, "who is the image of the invisible God" (Col. i. 15), "the express image of his person" (Heb. i. 3), in the highest sense; which image believers are to bear at the resurrection, *as the Apostle goes on to show after using the appellations which we have thus explained* (1 Cor. xv. 49). But in at least four manuscripts, including that of the Vatican (which is generally esteemed the most accurate of all), in verse 45, the word "man" is not found. Therefore we may be correct in reading thus:—"The first Adam was made a living soul: the last Adam, a quickening spirit.... The former man [is] from the earth, earthy: the latter man, from heaven. (We omit "the Lord," in the last clause, because Tertullian says that it was added by Marcion.)

The religious bearings of this question seem to have caused most Christians who have thought upon it to *lay too* much stress upon the apparent Scriptural evidences of the non-existence of Pre-Adamites, and to overlook or evade the apparently contrary evidences which we have yet to examine, and which are of the same paramount authority. But many persons have taken too gloomy a view of the condition, with respect to a future state, in which human beings not descended from Adam, if there be, or ever have been, such, must be considered as placed. "For there is no respect of persons with God: for as many as have sinned without law shall also perish without [being judged by] law; and as many as have sinned under law shall be judged by law: for not the hearers of the law [are] just before God, but the doers of the law shall be justified: when, therefore, the Gentiles, who have not a law, do by nature the things contained in the law, these, not having a law, are a law unto themselves, which show the work of the law written in their hearts." (Rom. ii. 11-15.) Moreover, the Scripture teaches that *persons in this condition,* having the gospel made known to them, *may obtain salvation by faith in the atonement,* like others. " For the Scripture, foreseeing that God would *justify the heathen* through faith, preached the gospel before unto Abraham, [saying,] *In thee* shall *all the nations* be blessed. *Wherefore they who are of faith are blessed with faithful Abraham.*" Thus says St. Paul, addressing *Gentiles* (Gal. iii. 8 and 9). And again, addressing the same people, he says, " *Ye are all the sons of God by faith in Christ Jesus; for as many of you as have been baptized into Christ have* put on Christ: there is neither Jew nor Greek, there is neither bond nor free, there is neither male nor female; for ye are all one in Christ Jesus: and if ye [be] Christ's, then are ye Abraham's seed, and heirs according to the promise" (Gal. iii. 26 to the end of the chapter).

There was a time when even an Apostle required a special revelation to convince him "that God is no respecter of persons; but in every nation he that feareth Him, and worketh righteousness, is accepted with Him." And in the present day, most of our theologians, falsely supposing that general consanguinity necessarily involves unity of origin, and taking it for granted that the sacrifice of Christ can only be effectual to the salvation of persons allied to Him by blood, argue that there can be no race of men not descended from Adam; while many, on the other hand, have expressed their belief that the benefits of the atonement may even extend to the inhabitants, if there be any, of other worlds beside our own!

A late devout and philosophic author, whom we have before cited, while, at least, very strongly inclining to the popular belief in the origination of the entire human species from one pair of ancestors (originally asserted by him to be "a fact which lies at the foundation of revealed religion," and in his latest observations upon it reaffirmed), nevertheless plainly showed his conviction that it cannot be proved from Scripture; and was led by this conviction to make the following important observations on the question in its relation to ourselves as Christians, supposing the limitation of the posterity of Adam to the narrowest compass which the Bible, by any fair construction, can be held to allow.—" If the two first inhabitants of Eden were the progenitors, not of all human beings, but only of the race whence sprung the Hebrew family, still it would remain the fact, that *all* were formed by the immediate power of God, and all their circumstances, stated or implied in the Scriptures, would remain the same as to moral and practical purposes. Adam would be a 'figure of Him that was to come,' the Saviour of mankind; just as Melchizedek, or Moses, or Aaron, or David: the spiritual lesson would be the same. The sinful character of all the tribes of men, and the individuals composing them, would remain determined by the most abundant and painfully demonstrated proofs, in the history of all times and nations. The way and manner in which moral corruption has thus infected all men, under their several heads of primeval ancestry, would be an inscrutable mystery (—which *it is now;*—) but the need of divine mercy, and the duty to seek it, would be the same; the same necessity would exist of a Saviour, a redemption, and a renovation of the internal character by efficacious grace. That the Saviour was, in his human nature, a descendant of Adam, would not militate against his being a proper Redeemer for all the races of mankind, any more than his being a descendant of

Abraham, Judah, and David, at all diminishes his perfection to save us, 'sinners of the Gentiles.'" ("The Relation between the Holy Scriptures and some parts of Geological Science;" by Dr. Pye Smith: ed. of 1852: Supplementary Note E.) That this is Scriptural doctrine is plainly shown by the tenth chapter of the Acts, and by our citations from the third chapter of the Epistle to the Galatians; as it is, also, by the remarkable words of John the Baptist, "Think not to say within yourselves, We have Abraham to [our] father: for I say unto you that God is able of these *stones* to raise up *children unto Abraham.*"

But here it is important to observe that, according to the view which we have taken, of the mutual relation of all mankind, the Saviour, as man, is connected by consanguinity with the whole human species.

Supposing the existence of a race of Pre-Adamites, all of them sinners against the law of nature, our argument, in brief, is this:—that Adam, by creation, received a *physical* nature specifically the same as that of the Pre-Adamites; that by his fall, he assumed a corrupt *moral* nature, rendered more guilty than that of these latter by his superior knowledge; that he transmitted this *physical* and *moral* nature to his sons and daughters; and that these, by their intermarriages with persons of Pre-Adamite origin, while they transmitted the same physical and moral nature to their descendants, effected also *a union of*

THE GENESIS OF MAN. 65

which appear to indicate the existence of human beings not descended from Adam.

1. Cain's saying, "*I shall be a fugitive and a vagabond in the earth; and it shall come to pass [that] every one that findeth me shall slay me.*" And the consequence of that saying: "*And the Lord said unto him, Therefore whosoever slayeth Cain, vengeance shall be taken on him sevenfold. And the Lord set a mark upon Cain,* [or "*gave a token unto Cain*"] *lest any finding him should kill him.*" And the subsequent events related of him: "*And Cain went out from the presence of the Lord, and dwelt in the land of Nod,* [or "*land of exile,*"] *on the east of Eden. And Cain knew his wife; and she conceived, and bare Enoch: and he builded a city, and called the name of the city, after the name of his son, Enoch.*" (Gen. iv. 14-17.)

Cain may be supposed to have expected the great increase of Adam's posterity which happened during his life-time, and thence to have feared the vengeance of a kinsman: but this is certainly not the obvious meaning of his words: and moreover, he was, on the day of his saying thus, "driven out from the face of the earth" [or "land"], evidently meaning the land of his parents, and became "a fugitive and a vagabond." How, then, should he fear the vengeance of his own kindred?

His wife is commonly supposed to have been his sister: and at least one of Adam's sons must have married his sister if no other human race but that of Adam existed: but this is contrary to an express law of God (Lev. xviii. 9): and the marriage of a brother with a sister in circumstances forbidding the supposition that they may have been unacquainted with their mutual relationship, and in a case altogether such as that of Adam's immediate offspring, we think improbable in the highest degree. It has been argued that a marriage of this kind was unobjectionable until it was expressly forbidden; and some have gone so far as to urge in its favour David's *presumed* willingness to give his daughter Tamar, *contrary to law*, to her *half*-brother Amnon: but an infidel might argue thus with respect to adultery, and even murder. Dr. Johnson, in his Dictionary, though not referring to this particular case, terms such a union "unnatural and criminal." On this point, however, we may appeal to the Scripture itself: in Lev. xviii. a union of this very kind, *before the promulgation of the Law*, is mentioned among those *abominations that defiled the land in which they were committed*. It was one of the customs of the Canaanites (as well as of their brethren the Egyptians) mentioned again in Lev. xx.; where it is also said, "*they committed all these things, and therefore I abhorred them.*" And no exception to the condemnation of it is made elsewhere in Scripture. It is not like the marriage with a brother's wife; the prohibition of which is shown to relate only to the brother's life-time, by the *command* (in Deut. xxv. 5) to marry a childless brother's *widow*. From our finding it to be thus included in a catalogue of crimes for the commission of which God "abhorred" even the idolatrous nations that committed them, as well as from our finding it to be generally viewed with abhorrence by such nations themselves (though some have been led by evil example and false religion to approve it), surely we may infer that *nature* teaches it to be unlawful. Some persons have *assumed* that the marriage of brothers with sisters was *necessary* in the case of Adam's children; as though there were "anything too hard for the Lord," so that He who created one man and one woman could not, if there existed no other family than that of Adam, create others. The Scripture teaches us that, to prevent the necessity of breaking his law, God wrought a special miracle in giving to the Israelites, in the wilderness of Sin, "on the sixth day, the bread of two days." Is it, then, lawful to suppose that God necessitated the commission, knowingly, of one of those acts of which He has expressly declared his abhorrence? We think it is not. The case of Abraham (who, as some suppose, married a sister, not a niece as others contend, but a sister *by the father's side only*, and was under no necessity to do so,) cannot be adduced as a parallel case to the marriage of a son of Adam with his sister; much less, as showing that a positive law of God, affecting the very foundations of society, was not always binding: still less, as we have indicated above, will it avail to adduce examples of the marriages of brothers with sisters which were held lawful, and practised, in the fullest extent, among the ancient Egyptians, and, with the limitation to the sister by the father's side only, among the Athenians, according to an old tradition an Egyptian colony.

We must therefore conclude, unless we presume to impute inconsistency to the *moral* law and government of God, in one of the cases in relation to which that law seems to be known instinctively, and in a case in which we cannot suppose the conscience to have been blinded by evil example, that, beside the family of Adam, there existed a race of other origin, with whom his sons and daughters intermarried. And if so, we must further infer, that, in the times of the third and subsequent generations after Adam, while one portion of mankind was wholly Non-Adamite, another portion was in a greater degree Non-Adamite than Adamite, and a third portion was that to which the apellation of Adamite may be most properly applied. The race of Cain (who was "cursed from the earth" [or "land"], "a fugitive and a vagabond," "driven out from the face of the earth" [or "land"], expatriated, and in a manner excommunicated, who "went out from the presence of the Lord, and dwelt [apart from his kindred] in the land of Nod" [or "land of exile"], and there had a wife,) cannot, we think, be included among the Adamites: for if (as we suppose him to have done) Cain married a woman of another race, his children, we may most reasonably assume, living apart from all their collateral relations, generally did the same; thus producing a progeny in which the Adamite blood must have been much less than that with which it became intermixed. On the other hand, the brothers and sisters of Cain, though, like him, intermarrying with another race, produced · families of cousins, who most probably intermarried among themselves (setting an example which we find to have been followed by many of their posterity), and thus preserved less deteriorated the Adamite blood. Of such a race as we suppose that of Cain to have been, it might be said that they were not Adamites, though of an Adamite, in a stronger sense than it is said of others (in Rom. ix. 6 and 7), "they [are] not all Israel, which are of Israel; neither, because they are the seed of Abraham, [are they] all children: but [God said,] In Isaac shall thy seed be called." In explanation of these words, it is added, "That is, they which are the children of the flesh, these [are] not the children of God: but the children of the promise are counted for the seed." Now Seth was of the children of the promise, for of his seed, according to the flesh, was to be the Saviour; and he had a title to be called "a son of God" as well as "a son of Adam," seeing that he was, as St. Luke says (iii. 38), "[the son] of Adam, which was [the son] of God:" but not so Cain: the latter lost his title to be called "a son of God," as is shown by St. John's contrasting (in his first Epistle, iii. 9 and 12,) him who is "begotten of God" with him who is, "as

Cain was, [begotten] of the wicked one;" and hence, also, we may infer that he lost his title to be called "a son of Adam." Eve, moreover, seems to have alluded to his having ceased to be reckoned as her offspring when "she bare a son, and called his name Seth: for God [said she] hath appointed me another seed instead of Abel, whom Cain slew." The appellation of "the Adamites" may also be supposed to be used so as to exclude the race of Cain for *another* reason, because this probably constituted a comparatively small portion of the collective races which were in part descended from Adam, like as the appellations of "Israel" and "all Israel" are used so as to exclude the tribes of Judah and Benjamin.

2. "*Then a beginning was made for proclaiming the name of Jehovah.*" (Gen. iv. 26.)

The passage which we have thus translated has been regarded as one of which the meaning is extremely obscure. In the authorized version it is rendered, "then began men to call upon the name of the Lord," or, as in the margin, "to call [themselves] by the name of the Lord;" and according to the former of these interpretations, the meaning is generally supposed to be, that men then began to celebrate the public worship of the Lord: according to the second, that righteous men then began to call themselves "sons of God;" and thus the passage has been regarded as connected with the beginning of Gen. vi., which is separated from it only by a parenthetic chapter. The difficulties which attend the admission of either of these interpretations, if we hold the common opinion, that at the time to which this statement relates, soon after the birth of Enos, there existed no human beings beside the family of Adam, are sufficiently obvious to need no comment: and with respect to the latter of them, a further difficulty arises from a critical examination of the meaning of the appellation rendered "sons of God" in the authorized version in Gen. vi. 2 and 4 (as we shall have to show in considering the passages in which it occurs), standing, as it does, in the same sentence with "the daughters of the Adamites." But if we admit that there then existed other human beings beside the family of Adam, both these interpretations appear to be suitable; for we may regard the latter as meaning that certain men then began to call themselves the servants of Jehovah.

In this case, however, the rendering which we have given seems to be far more suitable. It is agreeable with the rendering in the authorized version in Ex. xxxiii. 19, "I will make all my goodness pass before thee, and *I will proclaim the name of the Lord before thee:*" and in the next chapter, verse 5, "And the Lord descended in the cloud, and stood with him there, and *proclaimed the name of the Lord.*" The like rendering is also, evidently, the most appropriate in 1 Chron. xvi. 8, and Ps. cv. 1, "Give thanks unto the Lord; *proclaim his name; make known his deeds among the people;*" and in Is. xii. 4, "Praise the Lord; *proclaim his name; declare his doings among the people; make mention that his name is exalted;*" and in several other instances. The words rendered "proclaiming," and "proclaim," and "proclaimed," "the name of the Lord," in these passages, literally signify "calling," or "summoning," and "call," etc., "in the name of Jehovah." And it is worthy of remark, that the Arabic word which exactly agrees in all its applications with the Hebrew verb here used is often employed to signify the "calling," "summoning," or "inviting," to the true faith. This Arabic verb is "da'ā;" and its active participial noun is commonly applied to "a religious missionary." The passage to which these remarks relate we therefore regard as the earliest indication that the Bible presents of the existence of idolatry; implying that there were, in the time of Enos, persons, whom we can hardly suppose to have been of the family of Adam, ignorant of the True God.

Another interpretation has been adopted by Jewish writers: " Then a profanation was committed for calling by the name of Jehovah;" that is, applying the name of Jehovah to other objects. This rests only upon an assumption; and in point of probability differs but little from the interpretations in our authorized version.

The Editor of this essay has directed our attention to an illustration of the passage that has occasioned our submitting the foregoing remarks, presented by the words of Amos, in chapter ix. verse

12; observing that the quotation of those words by St. James, given in Acts xv. 17, shows that, instead of "Edom," we should read "Adam," as did the Seventy and Eusebius, and as is found in the Arabic, and in some Syriac manuscripts. These words of Amos we would render, "in order that the remnant of [the sons of] Adam may earnestly seek, and all the Gentiles to whom my name is proclaimed, saith Jehovah, the doer of this:" and the quotation by St. James, as given in the Acts (in the very words of the Septuagint, but with the addition of τὸν κύριον after ἀνθρώπων), "in order that the remnant of men may earnestly seek the Lord, and all the Gentiles to whom my name is proclaimed by them, [that is, by those who are called "the remnant of men,"] saith the Lord, who doeth these things." The Hebrew word "yīreshū," from "yārash," we have rendered "may earnestly seek" for the following reasons: first, on the authority of the rendering in the Septuagint-version and the Acts : secondly, because the Arabic "yerishū," from "warasha," has the same meaning; and these two Arabic words would be in Hebrew, according to analogy, "yīreshū" or "yīresū," or with ē in the place of ī, and "yārash" or "yāras:" and thirdly, because a Hebrew word of a kindred root, namely, "aresheth," signifies "longing," or "desire," or "request;" according to the Septuagint, δέησις. In justification of the rendering "to whom my name is proclaimed," we may adduce several other passages of the Old Testament in which we

CHAPTER II.

think the same verb and substantive and preposition should be rendered in the same manner: namely, Deut. xxviii. 10 ("and all the people of the earth shall see that the name of Jehovah is proclaimed to thee; and they shall be afraid of thee"): 2 Chron. vii. 14 ("my people to whom my name is proclaimed"): Is. lxiii. 19 ("Thou never barest rule over them: Thy name is not proclaimed to them"): and Jer. xiv. 9 ("Thou, Jehovah, [art] in the midst of us, and thy name is proclaimed to us"). And to these might be added some similar instances, of which one will suffice as an example, occurring in 1 Kings viii. 43 ("to know that thy name is proclaimed towards this house which I have built;" agreeably with what is said in verses 29, 30, 35, and 38, of the same chapter). Macknight (Apost. Epistles, Prel. Essay iv., voce ἐπί,) renders the middle clause of Acts xv. 17, "and all the Gentiles among whom my name is invoked by them."—By "the remnant of Adam" spoken of by Amos, and called in the Septuagint-version and the Acts "the remnant of men," may be meant only the remnant of Israel so often mentioned in Scripture; and by "the Gentiles" are plainly meant by St. James all who were not Jews: therefore this passage in the Hebrew we do not cite as an instance of the absolute or unequivocal distinction of the sons of Adam from the Gentiles. But we think it not improbable that these words of Amos may apply, first, to the calling of certain of the Jews, and to that of some of the Gentiles by means of the preaching of those Jews; and, secondly, to the conversion of all that shall remain of the descendants of Adam, and to that of other races, not descended from him, through the preaching of those Adamites.

3. "*And it came to pass, when the Adamites began to multiply on the face of the earth, and daughters were born unto them, that the sons* [or "*servants*"] *of the gods saw the daughters of the Adamites that they* [*were*] *goodly; and they took them wives of all which they chose.*" . . . "*The giants* [or rather (though the Hebrew word, which is "*Nephilim,*" seems to be a gentile appellation,) "*fallen ones,*" or "*apostates,*"] *were in the earth in those days; and also after that, when the sons* [or "*servants*"] *of the gods came in unto the daughters of the Adamites, and they bare* [*children*] *to them; these* [*were*] *the mighty ones which* [*were*] *of old time men of renown.*" . . . . "*And the Lord said, I will destroy the Adamites whom I have created,*" etc. (Gen. vi. 1–7.)

The appellation rendered "the Adamites," in the foregoing paragraph, is "hā-ādām," or "the Adam." This, after the death of the individual to whom it was applied (both thus and without the article) in the manner of a proper name, became a collective patronymic, like as did "Israel," etc.; though it differs from these in being *originally* a generic epithet. Hence it has the article, and is used as a patronymic with somewhat more license than are the names to which we have likened it; but always in a case of this kind, while it retains the article, unless one doubtful instance (in Josh. xiv. 15) must be excepted, virtually retaining, more or less extensively according to the nature of the context, the collective character. Without the article, "ādām" is first found to be applied to the man created in the image of God, and to that man and his wife together; and we think that in these two cases it should be retained in a translation. Afterwards, it is applied to any individual of their descendants, and also to any number of these, and to all of them, and is most properly to be rendered in these later cases "Adamite" and "Adamites," or "[son of] Adam" and "[sons of] Adam," though sometimes, by a synecdoche, or by extension of its proper meaning, applying to all mankind, like as "the Greek" applies in Rom. i. 16 to every man who is not a Jew. This is all that we can learn respecting it from Scripture, the only sure guide in a case of this kind. The assertion that it properly denotes any individual human being, and man and men absolutely, rests only upon the presumption that no human race but that of Adam does, or ever did, exist; that is, upon begging the question which we are discussing. (See Note 3.)

The two phrases which we have rendered "the sons [or "servants"] of the gods" and "the daughters of the Adamites," and which are rendered in the authorized version "the sons of God" and the "daughters of men," most of the commentators have supposed to mean "good men" and "wicked women;" imagining, it seems, that good men were then insnared by the wiles of wicked women; though the most obvious meaning, beyond dispute, is, that the men and women here mentioned were of *different races*, and hence that the former saw in the latter a beauty surpassing that of their own women. Some have even imagined them to mean "angels" and "women." Our rendering of the latter of these phrases we have already sufficiently explained. In vindication of our rendering of the other, the following, also deviating from the authorized version, may be adduced, as less liable to cavil, inasmuch as it presents a plain and consistent statement in the place of one which staggers the reader by its incongruity. "*There was a day when the sons* [or "*servants*"] *of the gods came to oppose themselves* [so in 1 Sam. xvii. 16, and Job xxxiii. 5, and Ps. ii. 2,] *to the Lord, and Satan came also among them*" (Job i. 6, and ii. 1), "*to oppose himself to the Lord*" (ii. 1). The passage may be thus paraphrased: "There was a day when wicked and impious men, the worshippers of false gods, oppugned the moral government of Jehovah, and Satan aided them in their rebellion against Him." If this case could be considered abstractedly, we think that scarcely any candid person would refuse his assent to the correctness of our interpretation of the phrase in question; which we therefore regard as presenting a very strong argument against the unity of origin of the human species, by its occurrence in Gen. vi. The existence of idolatry before the events described in the sixth chapter of Genesis appears to be indicated, as we have already observed, in chapter iv. verse 26 of the same book.— By "sons" are meant "servants" in Deut. xiv. 1, and Ps. lxxiii. 15, and Prov. xiv. 26, etc.

The only instances in which the phrase here rendered "the sons [or "servants"] of the gods" occurs are those which we have cited. An instance nearly the same, only the article being omitted before the word rendered "gods," occurs in Job xxxviii. 7; rendered in the authorized version, "*when the morning stars sang together and all the sons of God shouted for joy:*" in which spirits seem to be intended: but a comparison with Isaiah xiv. 12 ("How art thou fallen from heaven, O Lucifer, [or "O day-star,"] son of the morning!") and the fact that the two verbs in this passage of Job sometimes signify "*crying for aid*" and "*shouting for battle*" show that the meaning is at least doubtful. It is an awful thing to apply to false gods, in a particular instance, a name possibly there meant to denote the true God; but it is equally awful to do the reverse. A literal translation is surely the best in such a case; and a preference of one interpretation may be allowed, without an absolute denial of the other.

To the above-cited passage in the book of Job, there is a very remarkable parallel in the vision of Micaiah: "*I saw the Lord sitting on his throne, and all the host of heaven standing by him* [or "*against him*," i. e. "*opposing him*," as though "*confronting*

THE GENESIS OF MAN. 79

him,"] *on his right hand and on his left*" (1 Kings xxii. 19 : repeated in 2 Chron. xviii. 18). "*The host of heaven*" generally, if not in every case, means *objects of idolatrous worship;* and particularly, *as such, the stars;* and is therefore a very proper appellation for *evil spirits;* whom it may perhaps denote even in Neh. ix. 6, where it is said, "*the host of heaven worshippeth thee;*" for the verb rendered "*worshippeth*" more properly signifies "*acknowledgeth thy superiority or authority.*" (See Ps. xcvii. 7 : "worship him all [ye] gods.") Moreover it seems evident that from "the host of heaven" spoken of by Micaiah, not from among God's holy angels, came forth the "*lying spirit*" that was to persuade Ahab : and thus understood, Micaiah's vision, otherwise incongruous (like the parallel passage in Job as rendered in the authorized version), is perfectly consistent. It bears a near resemblance to the vision in which another prophet saw "Joshua the high priest standing before the angel of the Lord, and *the adversary* [in the Hebrew "*the Satan*"] *standing at his right hand to be his adversary.*" (Zech. iii. 1).

The word rendered "gods" in the passages of Genesis and Job upon which we are commenting is "elōhīm." Thus it is literally rendered, as a plural, in the version of Aquila in the former passage ; and thus it often means in Scripture ; as, for instance, in Ex. xxxii. 1 and 23, and Deut. iv. 28, and Judges x. 14, and xvii. 5, and 1 Kings xix. 2, and xx. 10, and Jer. xi. 12, etc. "Ēlīm" is also thought to signify the same, and is applied to false 'gods (as in Ex. xv. 11, "*Who among gods* [*is*] *like thee, O Lord?*" which compare with Ex. xviii. 11, "*Now I know that the Lord* [*is*] *greater than all the gods*," where the word "elōhīm" is used): and if so, we have the phrase "sons of gods" also in Ps. xxix. 1, "*Give unto the Lord, O ye sons of gods, give unto the Lord glory and strength;*" which compare with Ps. xcvii. 7, before cited ("worship him all [ye] gods"); and again, in Ps. lxxxix. 7, "*For who in the heaven can be compared unto the Lord?* [*who*] *among the sons of gods can be likened unto the Lord?*" As a contrast to this phrase, we find (in Hosea i. 10) "*the sons of the living God.*"

We have referred to several passages in which "elōhīm" certainly means "gods." The context generally shows when it is to be understood in this sense; and throughout the whole of the *distinct record* consisting of the first eight verses of the sixth chapter of Genesis, in which record "elōhīm" occurs twice, the appellation that unquestionably applies to the True God is in every instance "*Jehovah*," though in one instance (the fifth verse) the authorized English version renders it "God." A distinction of some kind must surely be thus intended, and we can see no reason for any other than that which we have made.

The substitution of "*fallen ones*," or "*apostates*," for the "*giants*" of the authorized English version and of other versions, in Gen. vi. 4, is justified by many critics, and is more agreeable with the Hebrew etymology; although we have reason to believe that the people to whom the appellation thus rendered is applied were generally of extraordinary stature. In favour of rendering it "giants," it has been urged that "niphlā" is applied in Chaldee to "the giant in the sky," that is, the constellation "Orion :" Orion, however, is distinguished by the Arabs for its obliquity (see, for instance, Freytag's "Hamasæ Carmina," page 561); particularly, it seems, in respect of the three bright stars of the belt, which form a line oblique to that of its course, as though *falling*. But supposing the word to signify "giants," it is said in the Hebrew, and in the Septuagint-version also, not that " there were giants in the earth in those days," but that "*the giants were in the earth in those days :*" and the most obvious and probable inference from these words, unswayed by a foregone conclusion, seems to be, that the epithet thus rendered is a gentile appellation, like several other epithets which are untranslated in the various versions of the Bible, such as the "'Anākīm" (or "long-necked" people,) the "Hōrīm" (or "cave-dwellers"), the "Amorites" (supposed to signify "mountaineers"), the "Perizzites" (meaning the "villagers"), the "Hivites" (a name thought to have the same signification as "Perizzites"), etc. It occurs only in the passage to which these observations refer and in one other instance, Num. xiii. 33, "*There we saw the Nephīlīm, the sons of 'Anāk of the Nephīlīm;*" which, compared with another passage, shows, if the latter be not a gloss, that the people thus called were either wholly or in part the same who were called the "Rephāīm;" for among the latter also were reckoned the "'Anākīm," as well as those whom the Moabites called "Ēmīm," and those whom the Ammonites called "Zamzummīm;" who are all described as having been of gigantic stature, and *whose pedigrees are not recorded in the Bible.* (See Deut. ii. 10 and 11 and 20, *in the Hebrew;* held by some to be interpolations, but, if so, doubtless of very ancient origin.) Thus we find the Nephīlīm mentioned as existing before the Flood, and also in the days of Moses; and we must not hastily infer from this that they were not a race distinct from the descendants of Adam; for an examination of passages in the Bible hereafter to be cited will show strong reason for believing that people not descended from Adam, if such existed before the Flood, were not among those whom it destroyed. But let it be observed, that we build no theory upon the statement of the spies, in Num. xiii. 33, quoted above. We build upon *other* statements, among which we reckon that in Gen. vi. 1-7 as one of the most remarkable; though we think our view to be *confirmed* by the account of the spies; for it is hardly credible that they condemned themselves by speaking of a people who had no existence, and of their relationship to the well-known 'Anākīm. We are induced to add this by an observation intended to cast discredit upon our arguments, "that it is scarcely safe to build a theory upon a lie." Misrepresentation

THE GENESIS OF MAN. 83

is generally a sign of the weakness of the cause for which it is employed, however good be the motive. (See Note 4.)

If we suppose that the men who are here said to have married with "the daughters of the Adamites" were of the race of Cain, we remove one difficulty: but we have no evidence whatever to show that these were idolaters, though in a manner excommunicated; nor is it probable that they would be mentioned without any reference to their origin: and we should still have to ask,—Who were the wives and husbands of Adam's sons and daughters? Who were the people so dreaded by Cain? Who were the Nephīlīm? etc.

There is an Arabian tradition, which we suspect to be a Jewish forgery, and to be founded upon such a supposition:—that many of the descendants of Seth, in the days of Jared, intermarried with descendants of Cain. We think it probable, however, that a portion of the mixed descendants of Cain returned, about the time of Jared, to the neighbourhood of the race of Seth: first, on account of the preservation of the name of Cain's progeny for several generations; and secondly, because it would seem that Enoch and Lamech of the line of Seth were named after Enoch and Lamech of the line of Cain, and that the father of Lamech of the former line received a name imitative of that of the father of Lamech of the latter; or that the reverse was the case, except as to the Enochs.

Upon the whole, then, we are of opinion that the intermarriages mentioned in the sixth chapter of

Genesis gave rise to a race like that which originated from the intermarriages of the immediate offspring of Cain with descendants of Pre-Adamites.

4. "*By these the isles of the nations became divided in their lands* ([*every*] *man according to his tongue*), *according to their families, in their nations.*" (Gen. x. 5.) And again, "*By these the nations became divided in the earth after the flood*" (last verse of the same chapter). Compare also verses 20 and 31 of the same chapter; and the following very remarkable passage: "*When the Most High gave nations for a possession,* [which may mean either when He gave certain of the sons of Noah nations for a possession (compare Is. liv. 3, "and thy seed shall inherit nations," and other passages), or when He gave nations certain lands for a possession,] *when He separated the sons of Adam,* [literally "*on the Most High's giving nations for a possession, on his separating the sons of Adam,*"] *He set the bounds of peoples according to* [or, perhaps, prospectively, "*even to*"] *the number of the children of Israel.*" (Deut. xxxii. 8.)

These passages, though reconcileable with the general opinion respecting the origination of all mankind, seem rather to indicate the existence of nations not of the same race as the descendants of Adam, and not destroyed by the Flood, and the partition of the lands of the former among certain colonies of the latter; and an argument in favour of this inference may be drawn from the fact that the appellation here rendered "the nations" ("hag-

THE GENESIS OF MAN. 85

gōyīm "), in other instances, which are very numerous, generally, and perhaps always, denotes the nations exclusive of the people of God, or of the Israelites; wherefore it is often rendered in the authorized version "the gentiles" and "the heathen." If so, we may suppose that the confusion of tongues was the *consequence*, not in any manner the *cause*, of the dispersion from Babel: and that the former event was the consequence of the latter seems to be implied in Gen. xi. 7 and 8. The whole of the tenth chapter of Genesis seems to be parenthetic.

A writer to whom we have before referred has expressed surprise that we have quoted the tenth chapter of Genesis to show that the Bible gives intimations of Non-Adamic races who survived the Flood, and have overlooked the nineteenth verse of the ninth chapter, where it is said, " These [are] the three sons of Noah: and of them was the whole earth overspread." According to his mode of reasoning,—to say nothing of the fact that the words rendered "the whole earth" often mean, in the Bible, "the whole known earth," or even less,—it may be argued at some future time, that North America and Australia, and other regions, had no human inhabitants before they were "overspread" by English and other Europeans. And he has added, "If any doubt still remain, we can only refer him to 2 Pet. ii. 5, which it is hoped is conclusive." To this we reply, that if we make κόσμος to signify always "all the inhabitants of the earth," we shall falsify many passages of Scripture. Again, he says that the tenth chapter of Genesis shows "that from the sons of one man have descended tribes in whom all extremes of difference may be traced." We ask him, Where shall we find the Negro? where the Malay? where the Mongolian? where the American Indian? where, in short, any one people whose physical type is not either purely or predominantly Caucasian? Of all the races in a state of barbarism now existing, there is not one whose genealogy can be traced up in the Bible to Noah. The "Cush" of the Bible, as relating to Africa and Africans, is clearly Ethiopia and the Ethiopians, distinct from Nigritia and the Nigritians, or Negroes. Hieroglyphic inscriptions show that in the times of the Eighteenth Dynasty of the Pharaohs, there existed Negroes (who are faithfully represented in accompanying sculptures, and some of whom were dominant,) in "Kish," which certainly applies to Ethiopia, south of Egypt, and is therefore identified with the Hebrew "Cush:" but it does not hence follow that Cush is Nigritia; still less, that it denotes the Negroes; whose proper general appellation in hieroglyphics is "Nahsi." (The ancients, however, not knowing Negroes beyond Ethiopia, often confounded them with the Ethiopians properly so called; as many writers do in the present day.) Cush and Mizraim are represented in the Bible as *brothers*: and the people of Mizraim, we know, were not Negroes; their own paintings and painted sculptures showing them to have been a *brown* people, with *Ethiopian* (*not Negro*) features, like several Ethiopian races in the present day. But the existence of Negroes in Ethiopia, and in Egypt also, before any people of the Caucasian race entered Africa, is a fact without which we are unable to explain African ethnology, as will be seen in future portions of this work.

It should be observed, however, that the rendering of the verb in Gen. ix. 19 in our English Bible is arbitrary and inaccurate, having no other instance to support it. The latter clause of the verse is properly to be translated thus: "*and from these the whole earth was scattered,*" or "*dispersed:*" or "*by these*" etc.: agreeably with the instances in 1 Sam. xiii. 11 and Is. xxxiii. 3, the only other cases in which the preterite of this verb occurs: and by "the whole earth" we are of course to understand either "the people of the whole earth" or "the people of the whole *known* earth," unless the phrase be here used with still more restriction, as it is in several other places. If the meaning be "*from* these" etc., it *may* be virtually the same as the rendering in our authorized version. If it be "*by* these" etc., it is most naturally to be understood as similar to that which we assign to Gen. x. 5 and 32; namely, that the descendants of Noah scattered before them every other people among whom they spread themselves. And certainly it is remarkable that the nations composing what is commonly regarded as the most noble variety of our species, though they have intermixed with some of the others, have scattered all the rest of those among whom they spread themselves to the utmost limits of what was to the former in the earliest historical times *the whole known earth*; dispersing the Mongolian races to the northernmost regions of Europe, and from the rich plains of India; and in a similar manner, in Africa, intruding upon the Negroes.

5. "*Hear ye this, all peoples,* [or "*tribes,*" in the Hebrew "'ammīm," often specially, or at least predominantly, applied to the tribes of Israel, as in Deut. xxxiii. 3 and 19, etc.]; *give ye ear all inhabitants of the world: both sons of Adam* [corresponding to the "peoples" or "tribes" above mentioned] *and sons of man* [*in a general sense,* in the Hebrew "īsh," corresponding to the "inhabitants of the world,"] *together: rich and poor.*" (Ps. xlix. 1 and 2.)

The words here rendered "sons of Adam and sons of man" are converted in the authorized version into "low and high;" and the like is done, in that version, in five other passages, which may be rendered thus: "*Surely vanity* [are] *the sons of Adam: a lie* [are] *the sons of man* " (Ps. lxii. 9): "*They worship the work of their own hands, that which their own fingers have made; and Adamite boweth down like as* [so in Job v. 7, and xii. 11, and xiv. 19, and xxxiv. 3, etc.,] *man* [*in a general sense*] *humbleth himself: therefore forgive them not*" (Is. ii. 8 and 9): "*And Adamite shall bow down, and man shall humble himself,* [in the Hebrew exactly the same as a clause in the passage next preceding, the tense being vague,] *and the eyes of the lofty shall be humbled*" (Is. v. 15): "*Then shall the Assyrian fall with the sword, not of a man; and the sword, not of an Adamite, shall devour him*" (Is. xxxi. 8): "*And with men of the multitude of Adamites* [in the authorized version "of the common sort," but in the margin, "of the multitude of men," *were*] *brought Sabeans* [or, according to the common Hebrew text, "*drunkards*"] *from the wilderness*" (Ez. xxiii. 42).

Among more than seventy instances in which "īsh," or its plural, or a variation thereof, and "ādām" occur in the same sentence, the cases above mentioned are the only ones in which we find them rendered in the authorized version by "high" and "low," or the like; while each of these words in other instances, almost countless, in which one of them occurs without the other in the same sentence, is regarded by the authors of that version as signifying simply "man" or "men," in a general sense, except in a few cases, in which "īsh" is opposed to a woman, or, by extension, to a female, because this word has its proper feminine form (namely "ishshāh"), which "ādām" has not.

For the distinction which has been made, of "high" and "low," or the like, between "īsh" and "ādām," respectively, it is very difficult to find any foundation: but, on the contrary, it is easy to find reasons for a distinction the *reverse* of this: for "God said, let us make ādām in our image" (Gen.

i. 26): "ādām" was also the proper name of the man so made: it was also a name given by God to that man and his wife together (Gen. v. 2): and our Saviour himself is called "the last Adam" (1 Cor. xv. 45). In the eighth Psalm, where David says, "what is man, that thou art mindful of him? and the son of Adam, that thou lookest after him? for thou hast made him less a little (or "a little while") than angels," etc., "the son of Adam" seems to have a double application; the primary application being generic; the secondary, restricted to the Messiah: and its being thus restricted in the second chapter of the Epistle to the Hebrews may be the reason why it is there rendered "the son of *man*." Here, again, "ādām" is apparently a more honourable term than "īsh." But independently of any consideration of superiority implied by either, it is plain that the rules of literal translation require us to regard "īsh" as a general appellation, including "ādām;" and "ādām" as denoting the first man so called, and any, and all, of his descendants, though it may generally be rendered "man" or "men" because the Old Testament seldom speaks of any other human beings than descendants of Adam, unless it do so incidentally and distinctively.

He who asserts that the appellation "ādām" always denotes, in the Scriptures, the whole human species, or any one of that species, when not distinguished from "īsh," should at least consider how often, in every language, words are made to include meanings not *originally* belonging to them. Such is the case, for instance, when *all the believing Gentiles* are called by St. Paul, in a passage which we have already cited, "*Abraham's seed.*" In like manner, therefore, all who have transgressed like Adam may be called "his sons;" and hence *the whole world* may *sometimes* be so called; as all who are not of God are expressly termed "the whole world" in another instance which we have adduced.

We now proceed to offer some observations rendered necessary by the fact that several of the passages of Scripture which we have cited relate to times posterior to the Deluge.

The study of geology, ethnology, zoology, and botany, raises objections so many and so great to the popular belief concerning the Deluge described in Scripture, of its having been universal with respect to the earth, and to its human and other occupants which were excluded from the ark, that it becomes a matter of the highest importance to ascertain what is the true meaning of the narrative of that awful event. The universality of the Deluge with respect to the *earth* has been denied by many very learned and scientific and pious authors: and its universality as to *our species*, with the sole exception of the persons preserved in the ark, has also been denied by several men of science and learning, including the profound naturalist Cuvier, and the members of the school of archæology and comparative philology of which Bunsen and Max Müller are commonly regarded in this country as the leaders; being judged by them to be irreconcileable with the physical differences that are now observed in mankind, and being held by most of them to be inadmissible for various other reasons. But a portion of the Bible professedly conveying a declaration from God, like that in Gen. vi. 7, cannot be really contradictory to nature; nor, in our opinion, can such a statement as that in Gen. vii. 23. If we find any inconsistency between what we certainly know of the *works* of God and what we conceive to be the meaning of a portion of his *word*, we may be sure that we have not rightly understood the latter; and we have not sufficiently emancipated our minds if we cannot accept the revelations of *science*, and use them as means to explain *obscurities* and *ambiguities* in the *Bible*.

Throughout the Scripture-narrative relating to the Deluge, what is rendered "*man*" in our authorized version is invariably "*ādām*," or "*the ādām;*" and of the two words there rendered "*earth*," one very frequently signifies "*land*," or "*country*," or "*region;*" and the other, "*ground*," by which it is rendered in that version in Gen. vii. 23. The denunciation in Gen. vi. 7 (with which the passage in verse 23 of the next chapter exactly agrees) may therefore be strictly rendered thus: "*I will destroy the Adamites whom I have created from the face of the land; from Adamite to beast, to creeping things, and to the fowls of the heaven:*" and all that follows it here and in other parts of Scripture is perfectly consistent with this rendering if we understand what are called the "universal terms" in these cases as universal only with respect to the objects previously named in the denunciation; in doing which, we shall even give them a larger range than they can be allowed to have in some other passages in the Bible; as, for instance, in Ex. ix. 6 compared with 19-21 of the same chapter; and verse 25 of the same chapter compared with 5 and 15 of the next chapter; not to name other cases, far from few, in which it is sufficiently obvious that such terms are not, strictly speaking, universal. It must also be particularly observed that the expression sometimes rendered in the authorized version "*the whole earth,*" or "*all the earth,*" is rendered in other instances in the same version "*the whole land,*" or "*all the land,*" or "*every land;*" and is often applied to a few countries collectively, and even to one country: see Josh. xi. 23; 1 Kings x. 24; Is. vii. 24; x. 14; Jer. i. 18; iv. 20; viii. 16; li. 7, 25, and 49; Dan. ii. 39; Zeph. i. 18; iii. 8 and 19: and in several of these instances (as in 1 Kings x. 24, Jer. li. 7 and 25 and 49, and Dan. ii. 39), where it is rendered "*all the earth,*" and in two other instances (Gen. xli. 57), where it is rendered "*all countries,*" and "*all lands,*" its application only to *portions* of the earth is undeniable. These instances, therefore (beside the fact that the account of the deluge *literally* relates to the *Adamites*), we may adduce in favour of our limiting the meaning of certain passages in which we find the same expression so that they shall not apply to the whole world of unbelievers. Thus we may read, "*The whole region was of one language*" (Gen. xi. 1); as will sufficiently appear from our comparing this passage with 1 Kings x. 24, where we find in the authorized version the words, "*And all the earth sought to Solomon:*" and it should be observed that the words "*they have all one language*" are afterwards said, in the same chapter, verse 6, of "*the sons of Adam*," mentioned in the next preceding verse, and there called in the authorized version "the children of men." In like manner, we may read, "*The Lord did there confound* [or "*mix*," apparently with other languages,] *the language of all the region: and from thence did the Lord scatter them abroad upon the face of all the region*" (verse 9 of the same chapter): or here (as more agreeable with the statement in verses 7 and 8 of that chapter), instead of "*and*," we would rather read "*for*," or "*because;*" as in Gen. xx. 3, "*for* she [is] a man's wife;" and Ps. v. 11, "*because* thou defendest them;" etc.

The whole narrative must be regarded in its relation to the times immediately preceding the events which it describes; and if there existed any race of men not descended from Adam before the Deluge, we must consider them as excluded from the subjects of the narrative by the term "ādām" there employed. That such a race did then exist, we are ourselves fully persuaded: and we believe that the Flood was appointed to destroy none but the Adamites and those who, by dwelling among the Adamites, possessed such knowledge as rendered them alike guilty for sharing in the general depravity. Hence we hold that a portion, at least, of the race of Cain, as well as of that which originated from the intermarriages mentioned in the sixth chapter of Genesis, may be regarded as excluded from destruction: and if so, the original "Kenites," of whom, as of a people existing in the time of Abraham, mention is made in Gen. xv. 19, may have been of his race; "Kenite" and "Cain" having the same radical letters, and the Kenites being called "Cain" in Num. xxiv. 22. It is worthy of notice, that Balaam, in this chapter of Numbers, prophesying the wasting, and carrying away captive, of *Cain*, also foretells the destruction of "Amalek," "the first of the nations;" and, as Onkelos and several others interpret the prophecy, the Messiah's ruling over (not destroying) "all the children of *Sheth*," or "*Seth*," the *brother* of Cain; though by "all the children of Sheth," Onkelos imagines to be meant all the children of *men;* for, in his opinion, all the seed of Cain perished by the Flood.

Hence, also, the meaning of the history of the *Dispersion* would be, that "the children of Adam," exclusively of the rest of mankind, gathered themselves together, in opposition to the plan of Providence, in "a plain in the land of Shinar," and there built " a city and a tower," with the view of remaining together; wherefore the Lord "scattered them abroad from thence upon the face of all the region;" and by confounding their language at the same time, or causing it to be confounded by their mixing with other races, prevented their re-uniting. In their gradual spreading over the globe, they doubtless carried with them the history of their ancestors, originating not a few of those traditions respecting a deluge, more or less agreeing with the Scripture-narrative (though they differ as to place and time and other circumstances), which have been found to obtain in so many regions of the earth, and which afford an argument, but only *primâ facie*, in favour of the opinion that the event in question was universal with respect to all mankind except Noah and his family. The only persons who witnessed the Deluge probably believed it to have spared themselves alone, of all their species; and the traditions handed down by the family of Noah, to their descendants the Jews, would be fully sufficient to account for the manner in which the latter, and the Christians after them, have understood the Scriptural relation which we are now considering. But the memory of the Deluge does not appear to have been preserved even by all of the *early* descendants of Noah; for we do not find any notice of it upon the Egyptian monuments nor in the writings of Manetho, though the contrary has been asserted. It has been plausibly observed, that the Jews are more likely than ourselves, when we differ from them, to understand aright their own Scriptures; but if we should admit it to be so, consistency would require us to take for our guides the Talmud and the Targums, and to adopt the Jewish interpretations of the prophecies respecting the Messiah. It has also been urged, that the belief of the universal Church in past ages should silence him who proposes a new interpretation of any passage of Scripture, opposed to her belief: but to this we have only to reply, that the universal Church, until modern times, believed it to be plainly declared in Scripture that the sun revolves round the earth.

The circumstances of the Deluge, particularly in relation to one of the main sources of the waters, and to the height which the waters attained, suggest that it may have been a miraculous overflowing of the Euphrates and Tigris. "*The great deep*" (spoken of in Gen. vii. 11) may be regarded as a fit appellation of what is called (in Gen. xv. 18, and Deut. i. 7, and Josh. i. 4,) "*The great river, the river Euphrates:*" for the plural of the word rendered "deep" is applied (in Deut. viii. 7) to "*depths* that spring out of valleys and hills" in the promised land; and seems evidently to mean *rivers* where it is said (in Ps. lxxviii. 15), "and He gave drink like *great deeps*." And "the high hills" and "the mountains" which are said (in Gen. vii. 19 and 20) to have been "covered" by the waters appear most probably to have been slight elevations, which are often termed "mountains;" and to be called "high" only because they were the highest of the parts overflowed: for the narrative seems plainly to state (in vii. 20) that the entire rise of the water was "*fifteen cubits*," either from its lowest level, or above the lowest part of the land; or, at least, affords us no warrant for asserting it to have been more than this. That such may have been the case notwithstanding the statement that "all the high hills that [were] *under the whole heaven* were covered," we argue by referring to Deut. ii. 25, and Acts ii. 5, and Col. i. 23; as well as to various expressions in the Bible, upon which we have already remarked, literally, but not really, universal in their import. The lowness of the "mountains" covered by the Deluge seems also to be indicated by the fact that the tree from which was pluckt off the leaf that showed the waters to have abated, and which was evidently upon one of the highest of the parts that had been overflowed, was of a kind which (naturalists have observed) will grow only upon low, or slightly elevated, spots.

This view of the case is perfectly reconcileable with the statement that nearly ten months and a half elapsed, from the commencement of the Flood, before "the waters were dried up from the earth" [or "land"]. Nearly eight months after the commencement of the *natural* rise of the *Nile*, extensive remains of its inundation are found in various parts of Egypt; and in the neighbourhood of the *Euphrates* and *Tigris*, there are extensive tracts which now retain

THE GENESIS OF MAN. 99

water from the *usual* overflowing of those rivers *throughout the whole year*: they are pools and lakes and marshes which would dry up entirely if they were not annually replenished.

Supposing the Flood to have been confined to the region which we have pointed out, it is probable that the waters were kept up by a prevalent wind acting against their current, as is the case in Egypt during the inundation of the Nile; and that the ark was wafted by means of such a wind towards the mountains of Ararat. These, it seems, were the first mountains of which the summits were seen after the ark had rested, and the waters had attained their greatest height, and had decreased during the space of nearly two months and a half.

The tradition which identifies "the mountains of Ararat" mentioned in Scripture with the double mountain now commonly known by that name is of very doubtful authority: but supposing it to be so far true that the latter is a portion of the Scriptural mountains of Ararat, it affords no evidence of the universality of the Flood; for in the statement which, in the authorized version, represents the ark as having rested "upon the mountains of Ararat," the preposition there rendered "upon" may mean, as it does in many other instances, "at," or "by," or "near." The ark, however, when it grounded, could not have been near to any portion of a chain of mountains as high as the spot on which it rested: for it "rested in the seventh month, on the seventeenth day of the month;" and "in the tenth [month], on the first [day] of the month, were the tops of the mountains seen," being so distant that, "at the end of forty days," the dove which Noah sent forth "found no rest for the sole of her foot, and she returned unto him into the ark, for the waters [were] on the face of the whole land" (in the authorized version "the whole earth"). He who asserts that the ark rested on, or near, the highest part of what is now called Ararat must admit that when "the tops of the mountains" were seen from that point an immense portion of Mount Ararat itself must have become exposed, which is inconsistent with the Scripture-narrative.

Hence it appears that the spot where the ark rested was nearly level with "the tops of the mountains" which were seen beyond the reach of the flight of the dove when the waters "had decreased continually" nearly two months and a half; the lowest parts of the land covered by the waters, according to the most obvious meaning of the statement respecting the rise of the flood, being no more than fifteen cubits below the highest level to which the waters attained. This limitation of the total rise of the flood does not involve the necessity of any inconsistency of interpretation throughout the whole record, nor the assigning to any word in it a meaning which it is not well known to have in many other places. But those persons who insist upon straining the terms of the narrative to the utmost, and suppose it to mean that the waters rose fifteen cubits above the tops of the highest mountains of our globe, must be reduced to the necessity of inferring that the ark rested (not upon what *we* call *Ararat*, but) upon the *Himalaya* mountains, and upon a part thereof very little lower than their loftiest summit; "the tops of the mountains" not being then seen; and this inference they cannot maintain without departing from their own principles of interpretation, which require them to read, agreeably with the authorized version, that forty days after "the tops of the mountains" had been seen, "the waters were on the face of the whole *earth*."' As the Bible itself shows that, in this instance (as well as in many others), the word here rendered "earth" cannot have this meaning, nothing can be more uncritical or unfair than to insist that it must have this meaning in other passages of Scripture where it relates to the same event. (See Note 5.)

We have been asked, if the Flood were thus limited in extent, is it not most reasonable to suppose that Noah would have been directed to retire with his family to a neighbouring country? This question is much like that which was asked by Naaman the Syrian, when he said, "Are not Abana and Pharpar, rivers of Damascus, better than all the waters of Israel? may I not wash in them, and be clean?" We hardly feel ourselves justified in attempting to answer objections of this kind. "For who hath known the mind of the Lord? or who hath been his counsellor?" But this we do know; that a most impressive lesson was taught "when once the long-suffering of God waited in the days of Noah, while the ark was a preparing;" and that the saving of him and his household by means of the ark is the only fact in the history of the Deluge affording to his posterity unquestionable evidence of the miraculous character of that event. Moreover, the period occupied by the construction of the ark was undoubtedly longer than would have sufficed for an emigration from the region of the coming Deluge, to a place of safety, even if the appointed limits of that region comprised the whole of Asia; and few of the geologists, we believe, admit its having been of so large an extent. Our own opinion upon this last point we think to be most agreeable with the terms of the Scripture-narrative; but that of the geologists in general (that the Deluge covered a large portion of Asia without extending over the whole of that continent) is obviously one with which all the other opinions expressed in the foregoing pages are equally consistent.

The physical objections to the popular belief respecting the extent and effects of the Deluge have been fully detailed by many writers; and are only to be met by a supposition of a series of miracles to which the Bible makes no allusion. (See Note 6.)

To revert from this necessary digression to the chief subject of our inquiry, we venture to assert that if certain expressions in particular passages of Scripture cited in these observations have the meanings which have been here assigned to them, they

THE GENESIS OF MAN. 103

afford more than a preponderance of evidence in favour of the inference of the coëxistence of two races of men, physically one in species, in the time of Adam (the progeny of Adam being one of these two races); and these meanings are either the most literal that can be allowed, or such as the same expressions indubitably have in many other instances. If we stretch the meanings of these expressions to their utmost possible extent, we may, indeed, reconcile them with the prevailing opinion respecting the origination of all mankind: but this opinion is one which we confidently pronounce inconsistent with physical and other facts hereafter to be mentioned, and involves the admission of God's necessitating, in the marriages of Adam's sons and daughters, the commission, knowingly, of an act which his moral law forbids, and which we regard with a horror generally believed to be instinctive; an act, moreover, which we have shown to be mentioned among certain *abominations that defiled the land* in which they were committed, and for which those who committed them were *abhorred by God, before the promulgation of the Law*. On the other hand, the adoption of *unstrained* interpretations (even when a choice must be made between two or more figurative meanings whichever side of the argument we may take) enables us to discover the necessary harmony of Scripture with facts which have been supposed to impugn it, and also with itself.

It appears, therefore, that Holy Scripture does not

forbid, nay, rather that it requires, a belief in the existence of Pre-Adamites of our species, whose posterity were not destroyed with the unbelieving Adamites by the waters of the Deluge. We read of a time, described in Gen. ii. 5 and 6 (strangely misinterpreted in our authorized version), when *"no shrub of the field was as yet in the earth, and no herb of the field did as yet sprout forth; for the Lord God had not caused it to rain upon the earth; and there was no Adam for tilling the ground: then a vapour went up from the earth, and watered the whole face of the ground:"* after which we find immediately added, *"and the Lord God formed the Adam [of] dust of the ground;"* although we most certainly know that several successive creations of animals as well as plants intervened. We are left to supply the omissions from other parts of the Bible, and from the endless discoveries of science and learning: and among the subjects here to be supplied, we include the ancestors of the persons with whom the sons and daughters of Adam intermarried, of those men whom Cain at one time so much dreaded, and of those whose intermarriages with the daughters of the Adamites produced that corruption which occasioned the destruction of Adam's unbelieving posterity by the Deluge, perhaps a people of the same race as the Nephīlim whom we find mentioned both before and after that event. The saying that "there was no *Adam* for tilling the ground" seems to imply that there was no tilling of the ground *before* Adam : and recent geological researches have brought to light unexpected evidences of the existence, at a period immeasurably remote, of a race of men whom (judging from their rude implements of stone) we may infer to have been ignorant of agriculture, and to have either led a kind of nomadic or Arcadian life, or sustained themselves by hunting, fowling, and fishing, and by the spontaneous productions of the earth. These and other indications of the immense antiquity of man will be considered in subsequent chapters.

CHAPTER III.

PHYSICAL OBSERVATIONS.

A GENERAL view of the present geographical distribution of the varieties of man immediately suggests the inference that Providence has adapted them to the climates and other physical conditions of different regions of the earth. It is found in general to agree very nearly, in some cases exactly, with that of the inferior animals, and that of plants; and hence it would seem that the geographical distribution of all organic beings might be reasonably inferred to have been regulated by the same general laws. From this analogy, some philosophers have argued, that as each of the principal zoological and botanical regions of the earth has its peculiar species, and even genera, of animals and plants, so it has its peculiar species of man, sprung from a stock that had its origin therein: but for "species" of man, we must substitute "variety," unless we oppose a great majority of men of science, who support their opinion of the unity of our species by arguments almost, if not quite, amounting to demonstration.

There is, however, another analogy which requires

our consideration. As the earth in different successive periods has had its peculiar genera and species of animals and plants, may it not in different successive periods have had its peculiar varieties of man, adapted rather to peculiar conditions of these periods than to such conditions of particular regions, though the latter periods are but subdivisions of the last of the former? Even of the *existing* species of animals and plants, it is probable that most originated at different periods as well as in different centres; and that some have partially superseded others in consequence of changes in the forms and climates of the islands and continents, and in the general physical conditions of the earth. That *many* of the existing species originated in different ages has been established by geological researches.

Let us first consider the inference drawn from the former analogy; that Providence has adapted the varieties of man to the climates and other physical conditions of different regions of the earth. If this inference be true, when, and how, was the adaptation effected? Are the differences in the physical characteristics of man in different regions of the earth attributable to the mutability of those characteristics in consequence of migrations from one centre of origin? And is a peculiar conformation or complexion necessary to fit a people to live and flourish only in a particular region of the earth?

Those who hold that all mankind are descended from Adam are generally of opinion that the assumed adaptation, by modifications of form and colour, was effected gradually, by the agencies of climate, soil, food, mode of life, occupation, and the like; and by artificial means, such as aboriginal American tribes, and modern Greeks, employ for the purpose of altering the natural conformation of the skull.

But there are very strong objections to be urged against this idea of progressive change as adequate to the exigencies of the case. The alterations of form effected in human beings by the natural means above mentioned are extremely slow. Those of colour, on the contrary, are sometimes very great even in the case of a single individual; for we all have, in the *rete mucosum* of our skin, whether it be demonstrable or not, a substance, or matter, which renders it, like photographic paper, capable of becoming darkened by the sun's rays: but no length of exposure to the fiercest sun, in the present condition of the earth, seems to be sufficient to produce the deep black tint of the Nigritian.

Several of the most eminent ethnologists, unwilling to abandon their belief that all mankind are descended from Adam, have adopted the opinion that he was created many thousands of years before the earliest period which the book of Genesis, considered as historically true, can be held to indicate: and among them are included writers who are constantly cited as leading authorities in favour of what is commonly regarded as orthodox ethnology; many of the

PHYSICAL OBSERVATIONS. 109

advocates of which have either been ignorant of this very important fact or have wilfully suppressed it. But to say nothing of the hardness of this condition which the theory of the unity of origin of our whole species has been held to demand,—requiring us to surrender our faith in that which should be the main foundation of all ancient history, sacred and profane, —we cannot persuade ourselves to believe that *any* period would suffice to produce, in the descendants of a single pair, of a high type (such as we must believe that of Adam to have been), the varieties that are now found to exist.

In Nubia, a portion of the very hottest region of the earth, we find, in ascending the Nile, first, a race of which the prevailing colour is nearly black, descendants of the Beni-l-Kenz, who are said to have come from the adjacent desert on the east and southeast, and whose residence on the banks of the Nile is historically traced back by Eastern writers through at least seven centuries: and then, hemmed in between these and equally dark races which extend to Abyssinia, various tribes of the Nūbeh (from whom the country is named), exhibiting, like the Abyssinians, complexions of many shades of brown, the lightest nearer to white than it is to black. The Beni-l-Kenz originated from the intermarriages of Arabian settlers with families of the Bejā, or Bujā, the southern branch of the great Ethiopian tribe of which the common modern appellation is "Bishārīs"; and their descendants are now called the "Kunūz."

(See Note 7.) The race of which we have spoken as being termed "Nūbeh" (among which are many small tribes mainly descended from Arab and other foreign settlers) are those whom we have constantly heard to call themselves by this appellation, and who are strongly marked with genuine Ethiopian traits, although, like all the Nubians, having an admixture of Arabian blood, many of them claim to be Arabs. We have distinguished among the race calling themselves "Nūbeh" many persons of a clear, and very light, brown hue, both in their native country and in Egypt. The various hues of the Abyssinians are particularly remarkable, considering their being mostly of a decided and fine Caucasian type; and seem to indicate a partial mixture of their race with Negroes, or rather with peoples allied to the Negroes, but not to a degree sufficient to impart to many of them any permanent Negro characteristic of feature or form. And it is further remarkable that the Abyssinians are hemmed in by other races, the Bishārīs on the north, the Gallas on the south, and various Nubian tribes on the west, all largely partaking of the Negro characteristics of features and hair, as well as complexion. With these or similar neighbouring races we must suppose them to be in some degree mixed, unless we suppose a strange anomaly. In the Gallas we see most obviously a link between the Caucasian and the Negro in respect of form and hair and colour, but never the intensity of the Negro complexion, notwithstanding their nearness to the Equator: and many of these are mingled among Abyssinians of the Caucasian type without any assimilation of either of the two races to the other, except in rare instances, doubtless the effects of mixture of the sexes; while a similar mingling is also observed in the northern parts of Abyssinia. We likewise find that numerous other tribes have continued from time immemorial conterminous in their territories, and even intermixed, with the aborigines of Nigritia, not only differing widely from the true Negro in physical conformation, but without assuming his intensely black hue. By such tribes (exhibiting in their persons the physical characteristics of the Negro blended with those of the inhabitants of South-western Asia, and thus presenting indications of mixture, which are confirmed by several of their languages,) we find the true Negroes to be completely hemmed in on the north and east: and although the region which the latter occupy contains extensive alluvial tracts, it is for the most part elevated and mountainous, and not hotter, nor, except in the neighbourhood of the Atlantic Ocean, more humid, than are most of the countries occupied by the former. Again, in the Malayan region, we find several conterminous and intermixed races very widely differing in complexion, hair, and features. India, also, exhibits a population in which two very distinct types are observable under the same circumstances of climate, descendants of Caucasian immigrants (the Aryas), and of earlier inhabitants, of the

CHAPTER III.

Mongolian type, with whom the former are historically known to have intermarried during the course of many centuries.

It appears, therefore, that climate does not in the course of many centuries produce even the *hue* of the Negro race; much less does it, in such a lapse of time, produce the *physical conformation* of that race. Nor do the mixtures of other races with Negroes produce either of these effects. In general, when one parent is of the Negro race and the other is white, and almost always when the white parent is the father, more than half of the Negro hue is lost in the transmission to their children. The offspring in this case is commonly tawny, with more physical resemblance in most respects to the white parent than to the black; and by marriage with the white, produces an offspring nearly as fair as the European: by one more admixture of the blood of the white, every trace of the Negro's complexion is generally lost; the peculiarities of his form also disappearing with his hue. And even after repeated additions of the blood of the Negro in several successive generations, traces of a single white ancestor are still apparent in the hue or type, or in both of these characteristics, though often in very different degrees in children of the same parents; whence it is that we find, in Africa and Arabia, many families and tribes whereof every one exhibits in itself great diversity of colour and features. It seems, indeed, that nobility of type and hue, together, never become finally

PHYSICAL OBSERVATIONS. 113

and totally extinct in mixed races: that if either, or both, disappear in a very few individuals or generations, the type, at least, reappears more or less in descendants of these. It has been argued, with truth, that almost every shade of complexion is observable among the Jews of different countries in the present age; but this is a fact which the Bible-history would lead us to expect (see Ezra ix. and x., and Neh. xiii. 23 —27, etc.); and the practice of concubinage with Negresses and other Gentile women is notorious as obtaining among modern Jews in Eastern countries, in spite of frequent edicts against it; though *most* of that people in the Turkish empire exhibit little or no evidence of their being imbued with Negro blood. (The same practice obtains among the Arabs, by whom such concubinage is held to be lawful.) It is a fact of great importance in ethnology, and one which appears to have been generally unknown to writers on that science, that very many of the Jews in Eastern countries, who are not known to have had any ancestors resident in other regions, are characterized by reddish or yellowish hair, and blue, gray, or yellowish-hazel eyes, as well as by a very fair complexion. It has been falsely supposed that such Jews are only found in Europe. The high antiquity of these characteristics, in people known to the ancient Egyptians, will be shown hereafter, in our fifth chapter. Writers have often pointed to the people called "the black Jews of India" as showing that a black race may originate from white ancestors: but

8

the people thus called are well known to be descendants of proselytes. The Falashas, or so-called "black Jews of Abyssinia," whose type is said to be like that of the Abyssinians in general, are also doubtless descendants of proselytes to the Jewish faith; as were many of the people of the same religion among the pagan Arabs, for so history tells us. The Arabs differ in their physical characteristics more than the Jews in Eastern countries, and are generally much darker, by reason of the extreme heat of their country and their having mixed more with darker races. There are gray-eyed Arabs who pride themselves in being of purer origin than the generality of their nation. And there are many families almost black, who are called "the black Arabs," and are affirmed by their countrymen, if not always acknowledged by themselves, to be descendants of Arab men by Negro women. When men of this mixed race are unable to obtain fairer women for their wives, which is often the case, they take women like themselves, or Negresses; and then, the common custom of cousins' intermarrying results in the production of many generations of so-called "black Arabs." But when they intermarry with fairer women and their children do the same, the modified Negro characteristics of colour and feature nearly or entirely disappear.

Thus we see that Providence has ordained rapid means of effecting a change from the form and hue of the darkest of our species to the form and hue of the fairest, by a mixture of races. Cases are recorded, moreover, in which Negroes have gradually become less and less dark from the influence of a cool climate, to a degree hardly credible; and other cases are mentioned in which the progeny of Negroes permanently residing among Caucasians are asserted to have become, in successive generations, more and more assimilated to the latter in *form and hair*, without any ascertainable or suspected mixture. But the contrary change, even in respect of *colour*, is never complete: it is in most cases only a change from fair to tawny, or light brown; in other cases, at the most, amounting to a blackish brown, produced in the course of many generations, partly by a hot climate, but in a great measure attributable with the highest degree of probability, if not with certainty, to mixtures of races, save only in some extraordinary instances of particular individuals, in whom the complexion of some dark ancestor reappears, if we may judge from all the cases of which we have heard, or read, or had ocular proof. The Abyssinians, hemmed in as they have been from time immemorial, on every side except that on which the sea is their boundary, by races largely partaking of the physical characteristics of the Negroes, exhibit a sufficient proof that pure Caucasians can never become even of a *modified Negro type*, though they may assume various shades of *colour*, from tawny to dark, and perhaps even blackish, brown. The proof is of a most convincing kind, as it cannot be reasonably doubted that the Abyssinians have partially intermixed with the neighbouring races.

Hence it has been supposed by some eccentric philosophers that Adam and his wife were Negroes! Dr. Prichard asserts (in his "Natural History of Man," third ed., p. 85), that "instances are not unfrequently observed in different countries in which Negroes gradually lose their black colour, and become as white as Europeans;" and the fact of the frequent births of Albinoes (persons entirely destitute of colour in the skin and hair, and often having blue eyes,) from Negroes, we cannot but regard as favouring the supposition that the brown and tawny races have sprung from the black. But the wide differences of physical conformation which distinguish the Negro from the Caucasian, with other considerations hereafter to be mentioned, forbid, in our opinion, the deriving of the latter of these two varieties from the former without an intermixture with a race of distinct origin. To attribute so great a transformation to physical laws operating upon a single race during a vast lapse of ages prior to historical times would involve an enormous difficulty in conceding, but far greater in denying, the existence of a Pre-Adamite race of men: the former difficulty affecting the *creation* of Adam and Eve; and the latter, the *age* of their creation, and consequently the authenticity of a great portion of the book of Genesis.

Others have suggested that Adam and Eve may have been brown. This hypothesis would *apparently*

PHYSICAL OBSERVATIONS. 117

lessen the difficulty of our question, and the name of Adam might be urged in its favour, though we know that the epithet "red" as applied to a man is adopted in Eastern countries in preference to "white" because the latter is used to signify "leprous:" but still this supposition, as we have already shown, is attended with difficulties which seem to be insuperable.

One of the greatest of the difficulties that beset us when we endeavour to account for the commonly-supposed descent of all mankind from a single pair, that pair being Adam and Eve, even if we adopt the last of the hypotheses mentioned above, lies in the fact of our finding, upon Egyptian monuments, mostly of the thirteenth and fourteenth and fifteenth centuries before the Christian era, representations of individuals of numerous nations, African, Asiatic, and European, differing in physical characteristics as widely as any equal number of nations of the present age that could be grouped together; among these being Negroes, of the true Nigritian stamp, depicted with a fidelity, as to colour and features, hardly to be surpassed by an accomplished modern artist. That such diversities had been produced by natural means in the interval between that remote age and the time of Noah, probably no one versed in the sciences of anatomy and physiology will consider credible. In confirmation of this opinion, as far as the Negroes are concerned, we may refer to an assertion of Cuvier, mentioned in Note 6 to the present work. But we find even earlier, much earlier, representations of races foreign to Egypt very widely differing from the Egyptians, as we purpose to show in another chapter.

It has therefore been argued by a late writer (the Rev. Dr. Hamilton, of Mobile, in his work entitled "The Friend of Moses," pp. 444, *et seqq.*), that as the dispersion of the descendants of Noah from Babel was miraculous, they were then miraculously adapted, in their physical organization, to live and flourish in the several different regions which they were destined to occupy. But this argument is not founded upon any express declaration in the Bible, nor even upon any intimation therein; and is in a great measure, if not entirely, fallacious; for it is inconsistent with facts which we have already mentioned, and with others which we have yet to adduce.

Shortly after the remark that "a general view of the present geographical distribution of the varieties of man immediately suggests the inference that Providence has adapted them to the climates and other physical conditions of different regions of the earth," we mentioned another analogy, the consideration of which we proposed by the following question: "As the earth in different successive periods has had its peculiar genera and species of animals and plants, may it not in different successive periods have had its peculiar varieties of man, adapted rather to peculiar conditions of these periods than to such conditions of particular regions, though the latter periods are but subdivisions of the last of the former?"

Now the idea that a peculiar physical conformation, or even hue of skin, is necessary to fit a people to live and flourish only in a region of the earth distinguished from all other regions by its physical condition, or is necessarily produced by the peculiar physical condition of a particular region, we have shown to be false in many instances. From the former of the two hypotheses mentioned above, we therefore turn to the consideration of the latter; and we find that the different varieties of our species are evidently suited *rather* to different *periods* than to different *regions;* for the ways of Providence prove that this is the case by placing one variety throughout a range of climates differing in the utmost degree, and gradually supplanting it by another; *the darker being always supplanted by the fairer,* whenever the change is on a large scale. The true Negro is perhaps the most remarkably adapted to the particular regions in which alone he is naturally found. But we have before mentioned that numerous tribes have continued from time immemorial conterminous in their territories, and even intermixed, with the aborigines of Nigritia, not only widely differing from the true Negro in physical conformation, but without assuming his intensely black hue; and we have adduced other similar facts, evident instances of the intrusions of races into seats not their own by inheritance, and of their expelling, or blending with, the older inhabitants. The Malayan variety is found to be intermixed with tribes of which some are evidently descended wholly or in part from Negro ancestors; the latter generally occupying localities which plainly indicate that the former have encroached upon them. The Australian race, mostly black, or very dark, occupies a vast region extending nearly equally to the north and south of the southern tropic, and is being supplanted by the fair Caucasian. The neighbouring dark Tasmanians are believed to have already been entirely so supplanted. The Mongolian variety in Asia and Europe ranges from within the tropical zone to the most northern limits of the habitable earth; and this, too, has been partly supplanted, and partly encroached upon, by Caucasians: the older of the races of India are all of the former variety; the chief bulk of its inhabitants (according to their own histories and traditions later settlers) are mainly of the latter, and are distinguished by their castes according to the degrees in which they partake of the blood of the earlier stock. The American race (which is considered by some of the best authorities, and, as we hold, justly, to be a branch of the Mongolian variety,) extends from within the limit of constantly-frozen ground throughout every other zone of climate, and, like the Australian race, is being supplanted, or rather has already to a very great degree been supplanted, by the Caucasian, which seems to be destined (as many ethnologists have predicted) either to supersede, or, by gradual intermixture, to assimilate to itself, every other variety throughout all the regions of the globe. In a country wherein pure Caucasians cannot live and flourish for many successive generations, they are found to produce a race perfectly adapted thereto by intermarriages with aboriginal inhabitants: and in many cases, Caucasian settlers, dispossessing inferior races, have adapted the regions which they have chosen to their own peculiarities of constitution, by felling forests, by draining swamps, and by other conquests over nature.

Thus in many cases, analogously with the course of nature prior to the present geological period, a variety of man is planted upon the earth, flourishes and multiplies for many centuries, we know not how long, and then is extirpated from a large portion of its original region, and supplanted therein by another variety. We cannot, therefore, reasonably suppose that mankind were stamped by a miracle with those physical characteristics by which we find them to be distinguished, since it appears that such a miracle would have been needless. Nor can we suppose that they were miraculously made to differ in order to keep them apart, since Providence has made them all of one species, that is to say, capable of intermarriages productive of prolific offspring.

The facts here adduced, and a multitude of circumstances connected with them, all tend to establish the theory of successive productions of varieties of man, at periods separated by long intervals of time: and as we have formerly shown that the existence of human beings before Adam appears to be plainly indicated in several passages of Scripture, we have what seems to us to be an amount of testimony sufficient to produce a moral certainty of the truth of this theory. On no other principle have we been able to explain, to our own satisfaction, the difficulties attendant upon the case which we are discussing. We will therefore proceed with the consideration of the theory here advanced; endeavouring to develop it by stating the following propositions, and testing and illustrating them by some further observations, in subsequent chapters, partly suggested by our own researches made during travels among African and Asiatic peoples, and during several years of residence in a country where numerous races of different varieties were always found to be congregated.

1. That man came into existence as soon as the condition of the earth had become such as to fit it for his habitation; consequently, at an unknown period, probably never to be defined, but which, we shall show, may have been many thousands of years before the creation of Adam. That the first stock of man was created in the equatorial region of Africa, where uninterrupted summer prevents the necessity of clothing, and where every want of nature is easily supplied by the luxuriance of vegetation; or, in other words, that the true Negro, the aboriginal inhabitant of Nigritia, is the primary variety of our species. And that branches from this stock gradually spread throughout the basins and lower regions of the Nile and other rivers, through the tracts on the south of their original seat, through the southern parts of

Asia, into China, and through most, or many, of the islands of the Malayan variety.

2. That from the Nigritian stock, in regions nearly equidistant from the equator, sprang the Hottentots and the Chinese; whose striking mutual resemblance has been remarked by the accurate Barrow; and the former of whom are regarded by Dr. Knox as a branch of the Mongolian race (to whom they also seem to have some analogy in language, as will be seen in the last chapter of this work), and as particularly resembling in face, except in the greater thickness of their lips, a particular family of the Mongolians, namely, the Calmucks, a tribe having the same facial angle as the Negro. And that from the Chinese, or from this great family together with collateral tribes, originated all the Mongolian, or Turanian, races, extending from the limits of the Malayan region, through Asia and Europe, to the coldest limits of the habitable earth, and throughout the American continents, pervading every zone of climate: for, as we have before stated, we hold the American races to be justly considered as a branch of the Mongolian variety.

3. That the Malayan variety, judging from physical and philological evidences together, originated from a branch of the Mongolian, or Turanian, stock, nearly allied to the Chinese; and by degrees entirely supplanted, or, by repeated intermixtures, assimilated to themselves, the older Negro settlers eastward of the African continent, except in a few instances.

The most remarkable of these exceptions are, first, the mountainous parts of the Malayan Peninsula, together with some islands, including Luzon in the north and Tasmania in the south, where we find a race, which has been termed Negrito, and Negrillo, very nearly resembling the Nigritian in features, and almost as dark, with short woolly hair: secondly, parts of New Guinea, with several neighbouring islands, where a few Malayans appear to have mixed with Negroes, and so produced a race, the Papuans, or Papuas, having a form of skull and a cast of features in which the Nigritian type greatly predominates, with crisp, frizzled, and bushy hair, but without the true Negro's deep hue of skin : and lastly, the interior of New Guinea, New Britain, New Ireland, and some other islands, inhabited by the degraded and persecuted Haraforas, Alfoërs, Alforas, or Alfourous ; with the whole of Australia; where the Nigritian features and hue are more preserved, but the hair is more like that of the Malayan. The scattered Malayan family extends from Madagascar to the western coast of North America.

4. That we may suppose the first (or Nigritian) variety to have commenced with a single pair. If we believed the condition of the first of our species to have been like that of Adam and Eve, we should rather hold the opinion that they consisted of two pairs, and that the children of one of these pairs intermarried with those of the other; because the marriage of brothers with sisters is contrary to a law

of the Creator, to whose moral government we have no right to impute inconsistency. But supposing that mankind commenced with a single pair whose sons and daughters were in a mere state of nature, and without a language sufficiently advanced to make them acquainted with their mutual relationship, we see nothing improbable in the inference that those sons and daughters may have consorted in marriage. In succeeding generations, the distinction of families must have become known by improved means of communicating ideas, and by experience; and then, nature itself, we believe, must have taught the unlawfulness of such consorting, and have caused it to cease among the better sort, such as were willing to "do by nature the things contained in the law," and to "show the work of the law written in their hearts;" for even races that possess no trace of revelation generally regard it with abhorrence. Evil example, however, being often stronger than nature, customs indisputably unnatural not only prevail among certain races, but are held by them to be commendable: and if mankind commenced with a single pair, in circumstances such as we have here described, the marriages of brothers with sisters in ignorance of their relationship may have been taken by some of the less ignorant as examples to be followed. Hence, perhaps, the sanctioning of such marriages by the oldest nation with whose institutions we are acquainted, namely, the ancient Egyptians, who, as we shall hereafter show, appear to have been closely connected with a Negro people in race and religion and language; and hence, probably, the marriages of half-brothers with half-sisters, by the father's side, among the Athenians, who were, according to an old tradition, a colony of Egyptians. Or the custom in the case of the Egyptians may have been founded upon an imitation of those irrational animals which were objects of their religious veneration, and which they therefore regarded as incapable of doing wrong.—Since the generality of naturalists, in common with most of the believers in the Bible, hold that all mankind are the offspring of only one original pair, we have not argued for three distinct creations to account for the origins of the Nigritian and Mongolian and Malayan varieties. Various facts, of which not a few remain to be noticed, seem to us most plainly to indicate *two* creations of man, originating the two extremes of type and colour. We have also various evidences, beside those which we have already adduced, that the lower types of man are more ancient than the higher. And upon the whole, in the present state of physical knowledge, we think that we have the strongest reasons for the inference of a succession of gradual natural modifications from one primitive pair, during a long series of ages, down to the period of the origination of the most noble variety by a new creation; judging from what we now see, and making due allowance for the probable effects of later intermixtures. Very great changes produced by such intermixtures have indu-

PHYSICAL OBSERVATIONS. 127

bitably taken place in the populations of extensive regions of Africa, and also in at least two great families of the Mongolians, namely, the Indian and the Turkish. The Chinese, too, if we may credit their own traditions, are a mixture of two races, the earlier of which may be reasonably supposed to have been similar to the Oriental Negroes called Negritoes and Negrilloes, while some of the later may perhaps have received a tinge of Caucasian blood. And it is well known that Caucasian traits are conspicuous in many of the Malays; a probable consequence of their commercial intercourse with the Arabs, in many of whom Malayan traits are alike observable. But a gradation may be traced from the Negroes to the Mongolians, and from the latter to the Malays. And hence we are of opinion that wanderers from Africa, spreading into Central Asia, and subjecting themselves to various hardships, gradually assumed what we term the Mongolian type; that several tribes of these then settled in the south of that continent, and displaced other African immigrants, that had not thus improved; and that some of them, mixing more or less with the Negroes of the Malayan Peninsula and of the Islands, originated the Malayan variety. The striking resemblances of many of the Mongolians to the Hottentots may be reasonably attributed, at least in a great measure, to the similar migrations to cooler climates, and the similar nomadic lives, of the ancestors of both these races during many generations. The greater advance of the former towards civilization may be accounted for by their intercourse with races superior to themselves.

5. That the Caucasian variety (characterized by the form of head which is now found to be predominant throughout the south-western parts of Asia and nearly the whole of Europe, and originally by a fair complexion, brown, or light, hair, and probably what is commonly termed the blue eye,) was brought into existence after various regions of the earth had been peopled by tribes of Nigritian origin; proceeding, first, from Adam, the man created in the image of God; and then, from a union of his immediate offspring, Cain excepted, with Non-Adamites. For we hold that the race of the exile Cain degenerated by his own and his children's marrying with descendants of the primitive stock, and so became in a greater degree Non-Adamite than Adamite; while that of Adam's other sons and of his daughters, though themselves deteriorated by one intermixture of the blood of the primitive race, may be reasonably presumed, on religious as well as other grounds, to have set the example of the intermarriages of cousins, followed by many of their posterity, and thus to have produced that progeny which may more properly be termed the Adamite race. This latter alone we therefore regard as the true Caucasian variety; holding the race of Cain to have been an intermediate variety between the Caucasian and the Pre-Adamite families, and so the race of which the origin is recorded in the sixth chapter of Genesis, apparently as the com-

mencement of a corruption, physical as well as moral, of a large portion, not improbably the majority, of Adam's progeny. What is related in that chapter suffices, in our opinion, to show that three varieties of our species existed before the Flood, which, we believe, did not extend to any but Adamites (in the more proper sense) and some others remaining among these: and that at least one branch of the intermediate variety remained wholly or partly distinct after the Flood is perhaps indicated in Gen. xv. 19 and Numb. xxiv., as we have remarked in page 95. If an objection be raised against our opinion of the double origin of the Caucasians on the ground of their wide difference from every other variety now existing, we think that it will be seen to have no solid foundation when it is considered that our most exalted ideas of the physical beauty of Adam and Eve are purely imaginary, and may be very far below the truth. It should also be considered that an advance towards a higher type, in several regions of the earth, during a long lapse of ages prior to the creation of Adam, is involved in our theory.

Thus we hold that *one blood* pervades the whole human species, although in a very large portion thereof intermixed with *another* blood, the blood of a nobler stock, the physical characteristics of which have become predominant in that portion, as we always find to be the case in the offspring of two distinct varieties. All the arguments that are commonly adduced in favour of the descent of all mankind from a single pair, without any second creation, whether they be physical, chronological, historical, or philological, apply to the case which we have here put; and in most respects, with far greater force. But, as we have already shown, we have no wish to insist on this hypothesis of general consanguinity: the main point that we desire to establish (because we are firmly convinced of its truth) is, that the Caucasian is of later origination than any other variety of man; and that it proceeded first from Adam, and then from the intermarriages of certain of his immediate offspring (Cain excepted) with descendants of an earlier stock.

The fact of a succession of new species of animals and plants that have superseded others of the same genera, in like manner as Caucasians have already superseded, in many regions of the earth, other varieties of man, cannot be doubted by any one acquainted with geology: and this fact is, by itself, in our opinion, one from which we may reasonably infer the probability of there having been more than one creation of man. We might further urge the tenet held by many eminent naturalists, that an entire species is not in every instance, if in any, referable to one common origin; but we do not desire to build upon disputable ground. Dr. Hitchcock, in his "Religion of Geology and its connected Sciences" (Lecture I.), states it to be a "well-established fact, that there have been upon the globe, previous to the existing races, not less than five distinct periods of organized existence; that is, five great groups of animals and plants, so completely independent that no species whatever is found in more than one of them, have lived and successively passed away before the creation of the races that now occupy the surface." And he shortly after adds, "The slow change from warmer to colder appears to have been the chief cause of the successive destructions of the different races; and new ones were created better adapted to the altered condition of the globe." So we may suppose that the Nigritians and their unmixed descendants were best adapted to the condition of the earth during one period, and that the Caucasians have been so during a later period. And this supposition is more nearly analogous to facts revealed by geology than it would seem to be from the words of Dr. Hitchcock cited above. We have no evidence to show that any species was entirely destroyed before the production of another that was to supersede it. On the contrary, abundant remains of many still-existing species are found in several tertiary deposits of different ages, which tell of the extinctions of other (successive) species: and remains of microscopic insects of many species now existing are found even in secondary rocks; at least, in the chalk, of which they form a main constituent. We have, therefore, strong reason for inferring that, during the succession of many species, there has been no sudden destruction of the whole of any one of them (however extensive the destruction may have been, short of being universal to that species,) before the creation of another or others by which it was to be superseded. And to such a succession of distinct species we may justly compare a succession of distinct varieties of man, whether all of these varieties have originated from distinct creations, or, as we think most probable, only the first and last of them. If an altered condition of the earth be a sufficient reason for the creation of new species of animals, it may surely be regarded as a sufficient reason for the creation of a new variety of man, destined, as it appears from history and from passing events, gradually to spread over the whole earth, exterminating, for the most part, every other variety, and, by intermixture, assimilating to itself the rest.

CHAPTER IV.

CHRONOLOGICAL OBSERVATIONS.

GEOLOGICAL investigations are generally held to have established beyond all reasonable doubt that man has existed only during a portion of the alluvial period. This period has been limited by some to about thirteen thousand or fourteen thousand years; but the latest and most accurate researches have shown it to have been more than seven times this length.

"At the meeting of the British Association at Southampton, in September 1846, Mr. [now Sir Charles] Lyell delivered a discourse, marked by his characteristic comprehensiveness and perspicuity, upon the Delta of the Mississippi, a narrow promontory projecting into the Gulf of Mexico. This is known to have been, and still to be, increasing and advancing, from the constant action of the river in bearing down mud and other matter of deposit. Observation and comparison, made during more than one hundred years, had directed attention to the progress of deposit, and the consequent gain of land advancing into the sea. But never before had the requisite talents, the result of science and experience, been employed for the resolution of the question. Mr. Lyell had the concurrent investigation, and assent to his conclusions, of several American men of science. The conclusion of the whole is, that the alluvial plain from which the portion of land projects, with that portion itself, after making great deductions to satisfy the most excessive caution, has required [for its formation] *more than one hundred thousand years.*" (Dr. Pye Smith's "Relation between the Holy Scriptures and some parts of Geological Science:" edition of 1852, pp. 390 and 391.)

It has been asserted that human remains are only to be found within a few feet of the surface of the alluvium; and hence it has been argued, that man cannot have been an occupant of the earth more than a few thousand years. But the experiments that would suffice to establish this assertion never have been made, and probably never will be; and a similar assertion, respecting anthropomorphous apes, has within the last few years been proved to be false by discoveries in several quarters of the globe. Moreover, if we concede the truth of the assertion respecting man, upon which this argument is founded, we may be only justified in inferring from it that in the earlier ages of his existence he did not inhabit the *low* tracts in which the alluvial deposit is now found to be of great thickness, nor the beds of any of the occasional torrents down which the deposit descended. This, indeed, is what we should infer, without experiment, supposing man to have existed many thousands of years, from the consideration that the places of these low tracts, in general, for vast lengths of time after the commencement of the alluvial period, must have been occupied by the waters of rivers, lakes, estuaries, or the open sea; and that the beds of the occasional torrents above mentioned must have been known to be insecure places for habitation. If we must admit the lapse of an enormous portion of the alluvial period before *any* part of the earth may be supposed to have become fitted, by its vegetable produce and other physical conditions, for the habitation of man, still it is evident, if the Bible do not forbid the deduction, that man may have existed many thousands of years before the highest date which chronologers who believe in the historical truth of the book of Genesis assign to the creation of Adam.

But so remote an age as we have here stated to be possibly that of man's first appearance on the earth is not required to render credible the existence of Pre-Adamites. We might therefore argue thus: according to the common opinion, the temperate regions of the earth have been fit for the habitation of man about six, or seven, thousand years, or a little more; and if the alluvial period began more than one hundred thousand years ago, we cannot reasonably deny that those parts of the warmer regions where vegetation is most abundant, and most rapid in growth, may have been fit for man's habitation (at least for the habitation of a race like the Negroes)

CHAPTER IV.

for *some* thousands of years before the temperate. (See Note 8.)

Thus we argued in the first edition of this work. We now venture to urge some apparent positive evidences of a much higher antiquity of man than that for which we have contended in the preceding remarks; namely, the arrow-heads and other implements of flint found in cave-deposits, mostly of the newer pliocene period, with the teeth or bones of extinct species of the elephant, hippopotamus, rhinoceros, bear, hyæna, and tiger or lion. We might suppose that a man lived and died, or that his dead body was deposited, in a cavern in which had been found remains of species of animals that became extinct long before his creation : and in either case, —in the former naturally, and in the latter agreeably with known ancient usages,—we might expect to find, with his remains, the remains of some of his weapons and utensils ; but we should also expect to find that he, or those who buried him, had removed those *other* remains, of extinct species of animals. Or we might suppose that a wild beast of a still-existing species occasionally dragged a man into a cavern, and there devoured him, leaving his bones mingled with those of some more ancient species; but we cannot by any supposition of this latter kind reasonably account for the presence of remains of *weapons* or *implements* mingled with those of animals of species that were extinct long before man began to be. The only obvious and probable inference from the fact above mentioned seems to us to be this:—that man was contemporary with those animals of species now extinct, with the remains of which his own remains and those of his weapons or implements are found; and therefore, that the origin of man is very far more ancient than it is commonly believed to be, though the extinction of those species of wild beasts may, perhaps, be somewhat less ancient than it is held to be by the geologists; for all the beasts above mentioned belonged to a period in which several still-existing species are found to have lived. It is, moreover, a most remarkable fact, confirmatory of our theory of the succession of the varieties of our species, that the forms of human skulls found in caves with the remains of animals of extinct species, in various countries,—Germany, Belgium, and France, —are described as being of a modified Negro type, or of a variety resembling the Mongolian.

These bone-caves, often found to contain knives and arrow-heads of flint, much more rude in make than those of the so-called "Celtic period," and never any implement of metal, have attracted increased attention since the foregoing remarks were written; and the opinion that man was coexistent with the animals of extinct species whose remains are found therein has of late been rapidly gaining ground, to such a degree as to have drawn forth some reluctant concessions of the strength of its foundation from Sir Charles Lyell, whose cautious reserve respecting the inferences to be deduced from evidences of this kind must have been manifest to all the readers of his works. At the meeting of the British Association at Aberdeen which has just terminated (we wrote this in September 1859), Sir Charles delivered an address from which (as reported in the "Athenæum," No. 1665,) we here insert some extracts.

He began by saying,—"No subject has lately excited more curiosity and general interest among geologists and the public than the question of the antiquity of the human race; whether or not we have sufficient evidence to prove the former coexistence of Man with certain extinct mammalia, in caves and in the superficial deposits commonly called drift or 'diluvium.' For the last quarter of a century, the occasional occurrence, in various parts of Europe, of the bones of man or the works of his hands, in cave-breccias and stalactites [or stalagmites?] associated with the remains of the extinct hyæna, bear, elephant, or rhinoceros, have given rise to a suspicion that the date of man must be carried further back than we had heretofore imagined. On the other hand, extreme reluctance was naturally felt on the part of scientific reasoners to admit the validity of such evidence, seeing that so many caves have been inhabited by a succession of tenants, and have been selected by man, as a place not only of domicile, but of sepulture, while some caves have also served as the channels through which the waters of flooded rivers have flowed, so that the remains of living beings which have peopled the district at more than

CHRONOLOGICAL OBSERVATIONS. 139

one era may have subsequently been mingled in such caverns and confounded together in one and the same deposit. The facts, however, recently brought to light during the systematic investigation, as reported on by Falconer, of the Brixham Cave, must, I think, have prepared you to admit that scepticism in regard to the cave-evidence in favour of the antiquity of man had previously been pushed to an extreme. To escape from what I now consider was a legitimate deduction from the facts already accumulated, we were obliged to resort to hypotheses requiring great changes in the relative levels and drainage of valleys, and, in short, the whole physical geography of the respective regions where the caves are situated—changes that would alone imply a remote antiquity for the human fossil remains, and make it probable that man was old enough to have coexisted, at least, with the Siberian mammoth."

Next he remarked upon "another class of proofs" " advanced, in France, in confirmation of man's antiquity,"—"the discovery, in the volcanic district of Central France, of portions of two human skeletons (the skulls, teeth, and bones), imbedded in a volcanic breccia, found in the mountain of Denise, in the environs of Le Puy en Velay, a breccia anterior in date to one, at least, of the latest eruptions of that volcanic mountain." The main result of his examination of a specimen of these remains, and of the mountain in which they were found, he thus stated: —" I feel that we are, at present, so ignorant of the precise circumstances and position under which these celebrated human fossils were found, that I ought not to waste time in speculating on their probable mode of interment, but simply state that, in my opinion, they afford no demonstration of man having witnessed the last volcanic eruptions of Central France. The skulls, according to the judgment of the most competent osteologists who have yet seen them, do not seem to depart in a marked manner from the modern European, or Caucasian, type, and the human bones are in a fresher state than those of the *Elephas meridionalis* and other quadrupeds found in any breccia of Denise which can be referred to the period even of the latest volcanic eruptions."

He then added, " But while I have thus failed to obtain satisfactory evidence in favour of the remote origin assigned to the human fossils of Le Puy, I am fully prepared to corroborate the conclusions which have been recently laid before the Royal Society by Mr. Prestwich, in regard to the age of the flint implements associated in undisturbed gravel, in the north of France, with the bones of elephants, at Abbeville and Amiens. . . . The stratified gravel resting immediately on the chalk in which these rudely-fashioned instruments are buried belongs to the post-pliocene period, all the fresh water and land shells which accompany them being of existing species. The great number of the fossil instruments which have been likened to hatchets, spear-heads, and wedges, is truly wonderful. More than a thousand of them have already been met with in the last ten years, in the valley of the Somme, in an area 15 miles in length. I infer that a tribe of savages, to whom the use of iron was unknown, made a long sojourn in this region; and I am reminded of a large Indian mound, which I saw in St. Simond's [or St. Simon's] Island, in Georgia—a mound 10 acres in area, and having an average height of five feet, chiefly composed of cast-away oyster-shells, throughout which arrow-heads, stone axes, and Indian pottery are dispersed. If the neighbouring river, the Alatamaha, or the sea which is at hand, should invade, sweep away, and stratify the contents of this mound, it might produce a very analogous accumulation of human implements, unmixed perhaps with human bones. Although the accompanying shells are of living species, I believe the antiquity of the Abbeville and Amiens flint instruments to be great indeed if compared to the times of history or tradition."

It was to be expected that these bold affirmations would meet with some opposition. The Rev. Dr. Anderson, arguing against them, urged, with respect to man, " that his first appearance was characterized by many proofs of high intellectual condition which our sacred beliefs attach to his origin, and that he was not primarily the ignoble creature that arrow-heads and flint knives and ossiferous caverns would so lamentably indicate." And certainly the belief in the immense antiquity, and the original low condition, of man, as indicated by the remains found in bone-caves and drift, if unaccompanied by the belief in the existence of Pre-Adamites of our species, does appear to us to be utterly incompatible with the spirit, as well as the letter, of the history of Adam and his descendants in the book of Genesis. Implements of stone were doubtless sometimes used in early historic times by races considerably advanced in civilization, and gradually superseded by blades of metal; for stone arrow-heads are occasionally found in the tombs of ancient Egyptians; but their blades for weapons and other implements were mostly of bronze. We find it extremely difficult to believe that knives and axes and arrow-heads of flint alone have ever been in common use among any people not wholly or mainly of Pre-Adamite origin : and no one, we feel assured, would doubt that the implements of this kind found in bone-caves and in drift indicate the antiquity of man to be immense, were it not for the prevailing belief in the origination of all mankind from Adam.

Some men of science and learning, holding the common belief that Adam was the first of our species, have confessed themselves to be compelled, by geological and other considerations, to adopt an opinion to which we have adverted in our third chapter; namely, that he was created twenty thousand years, or more, before the Christian era ; and the early Biblical history has been enormously distorted to accommodate it to this belief. But our own opinion,

CHRONOLOGICAL OBSERVATIONS. 143

that the Bible itself indicates the existence of Pre-Adamites, relieves us from the necessity of requiring a more extended Biblical chronology than that which appears to be advocated by most of the best judges in the present day; we mean that of the Septuagint; the authority of which, at least as giving with approximative accuracy the date of the Deluge, we regard as deserving of the highest respect.

The following table shows the chronology of the Septuagint (neglecting small variations in different copies) to the birth of Abram, and the disagreements therewith in the present copies of the Hebrew text and in the Samaritan version, by stating the age of each of the ancestors of that patriarch, according to these three authorities, at the time of the birth of the next, who was not in every instance the eldest son. The commas in the table denote figures agreeing with those of the Septuagint.

CHAPTER IV.

	Age of each when the next was born.			Years of each after the next was born.			Total length of the life of each.		
	Sept.	Heb.	Sam.	Sept.	Heb.	Sam.	Sept	Heb.	Sam.
Adam . . .	230	130		700	800		930	,,,	,,,
Seth	205	105		707	807		912	,,,	,,,
Enos	190	90		715	815		905	,,,	,,,
Cainan . . .	170	70		740	840		910	,,,	,,,
Mahalaleel.	165	65		730	830		895	,,,	,,,
Jared . . .	162	,,,	62	800	,,,	785	962	,,,	847
Enoch . . .	165	65		200	300		365	,,,	,,,
Methuselah	187	,,,	67	782	,,,	653	969	,,,	720
Lamech . .	188	182	53	565	595	600	753	777	653
Noah . . .	502	,,,	,,,	448	,,,	,,,	950	,,,	,,,
Shem . . .	100	,,,	,,,	500	,,,	,,,	600	,,,	,,,
2 yrs. after the Flood	2264	1658	1309						
Arphaxad .	135	35	,,,	400	403	303	535	438	
Cainan* . .	130	—	—	330	—	—	460	—	—
Salah . . .	130	30	,,,	330	403	303	460	433	
Eber	134	34	,,,	270	430	,,,	404	464	,,,
Peleg . . .	130	30	,,,	209	,,,	109	339	239	
Reu	132	32	,,,	207	,,,	107	339	239	
Serug . . .	130	30	,,,	200	,,,	100	330	230	
Nahor . . .	79	29	,,	129	119	69	208	148	
Terah . . . Abram.	70	,,	,,	135	,,,	75	205	,,,	145
	1070	290	940						

* This second Cainan is found in the Septuagint-version in Gen. x. 24 and xi. 12, and also in Luke iii. 36; but most critics hold it to be an interpolation in all these instances. It is omitted in the Vatican copy of the Septuagint-version itself in 1 Chron. i. 24, and in all the other ancient versions and targums, as well as in the Hebrew; and by Philo, Josephus, and other ancient writers; and Origen, in his copy of the Septuagint-version, marked it with an obelisk, to show that he regarded it *as doubtful.*

This table suggests a chain of observations on some points of great importance.

1. It is obvious that the Jews from whom we have received the existing copies of the Hebrew Scriptures, or the Jews to whom we owe the Septuagint-version, have *designedly* altered many of the numbers, for a chronological purpose. The most esteemed of our chronologers in the present day generally agree with most of the early Fathers, and with the Eastern Churches in every age, in preferring the authority of the Septuagint in this case; and suppose that the later Jews made alterations in the numbers which fix the chronology in order to bring the birth of Christ from the sixth millenary to the fourth, and so to induce the belief that, at the birth of Jesus, the time of the coming of the Messiah had not arrived (as He was expected to appear in the sixth millenary because Adam was created on the sixth day); while they followed an original generally agreeing with the Septuagint-version, or not very widely differing therefrom, in the cases of the other numbers, *mutatis mutandis*; and that a similar proceeding was adopted in a portion of the Samaritan version.

It has also been objected against several of the Hebrew numbers in the second and third of the three main divisions of the table, that they make Shem, as well as Salah and Eber, not only to have lived at the time of the building of the Tower of Babel, but even to have outlived Abraham; which is hardly reconcileable with circumstances of the times.

The Samaritan numbers are rendered suspicious in three points by the fact of their making Jared and Methuselah and Lamech to die in the same year (the year of the commencement of the Flood); but a providential reason for their all dying in that year may perhaps be deemed not improbable.

2. As two of the three sources must have been corrupted, we may reasonably doubt whether any one of them be preserved in its genuine state.

3. As either the later or the earlier Jews have designedly altered the numbers, we can hardly believe that they regarded the passages which contain them as being of a higher authority than a mere historical document introduced into the Word of God, in separate portions, as an illustration, or a supplement. And this inference is rendered more probable by the fact that these passages form three distinct fragments, the first and last with particular titles ("the book of the generations of Adam," and "the generations of Shem"), and by the general admission that the Bible is not altogether free from illustrative interpolations or glosses.

We therefore think it doubtful whether the numbers originally existed in any correct copy of the Bible; that is, whether the portions in which we find them consisted originally of much more than is contained in the former half of the first chapter of the first book of Chronicles, which presents the complete genealogy of Abraham from Adam, with the names of collaterals of some of his ancestors, for the most part agreeing *verbatim* with that in the tenth chapter of Genesis, with very small omissions, but without any statement of the lengths of generations, or of lives from first to last.

But we are fully convinced that these genealogical tables in the book of Genesis are historically true, so far as that they contain a complete list of all the male ancestors of Abraham, in the direct line from Adam, because we find the same names not only in the first book of Chronicles, but also in the Gospel of St. Luke.

4. If it is probable that the later Jews designedly altered the numbers for a chronological purpose, it is not unreasonable to suppose that the earlier Jews may have done so for a like purpose, or may have been the first to insert them, if any cause for either of these acts existed. Now such an alteration or addition may have appeared to the authors of the Septuagint-version to be demanded, to render credible the genealogies, by some of the monuments of the country in which they were dwelling (for it cannot reasonably be doubted that they dwelt in Egypt); to say nothing of the notices which the Bible itself contains respecting populous kingdoms in the time of Abraham. For they may have found it impossible to reconcile the existence of those monuments, and hardly possible to reconcile the existence of those populous kingdoms, with a chronology less extended than their own, agreeably with the universal opinion of the Jews, that none but the eight

persons who were saved in the ark escaped destruction by the Flood.

Reasons of this kind are the strongest that have been urged in favour of the chronology of the Septuagint from Adam to Abraham; and we regard it with a most decided preference. We do so partly for these reasons, and partly for the near agreement therewith of the Samaritan chronology of the postdiluvian period; but more especially because, although it may be said (and not without reason) that its numbers are uncertain, and probably exaggerated, we think it may be supposed with equal reason that they have been altered, or originated, and apportioned, to make up a known period, or a period which can hardly be conceived to have been not known approximatively, in the age in which the Septuagint-version was made, nearly up to the time of the Deluge; and that the names of females have been omitted in the lists of the ancestors of Abraham.

Yet, while we so decidedly prefer the chronology of the Septuagint, we think that its uncertainty should be admitted by every one who desires to uphold the credit of the Bible. This is a point of which the consideration has, during the last few years, rapidly become more and more important and imperative; and a few more years of research may probably decide it. Already monumental evidence has shown that the foundation of the kingdom of Egypt must be referred to a period long anterior to the Hebrew date of the Deluge, and barely reconcileable, as post-diluvian, with the Septuagint-chronology; and the means of settling the question are far from being exhausted. The monuments of Babylonia and Assyria, moreover, are restoring to us the history of a most interesting portion of the ancient Eastern World, and may perhaps reveal to us the existence of nations coeval with, and surviving, the Deluge, and bordering upon the region which may have been the sole scene of that event. We should therefore beware, lest, in trusting too much to passages which have come down to us in three forms, all widely differing, we injure the cause which we desire to uphold, and become in the condition of those who "give heed to fables and endless genealogies, which minister questions, rather than godly edifying."

5. A strong argument against the correctness of the generations of the Septuagint, and of the Samaritan version in the period after the Flood, may be said to be presented by Abraham's words (mentioned in Gen. xvii. 17), "shall [a child] be born unto him that is a hundred years old?" and by St. Paul's saying (in Heb. xi. 12) that he was then "as good as dead;" seeing that, according to those versions, among all his ancestors, except three, up to Adam in the Septuagint-version, and up to Noah in the Samaritan, there was not one whose age did not considerably exceed a hundred years at the time when he is said to have begotten a son. But this may be answered by the supposition of the omission of fe-

CHAPTER IV.

males, and of consequent extension of the lengths of single generations.

As to the opinion of some, that Abraham had many children after this, by Keturah, it is founded upon a passage which should literally be rendered, "And Abraham added and took a wife, [or rather, "concubine," as we find her termed in 1 Chron. i. 32,] and her name was Keturah" (Gen. xxv. 1); and many critics, with good reason, understand it as meaning that he took an additional wife, or concubine; that is, a wife, or concubine, in addition to Sarah, during her life-time; holding the event to be mentioned after the account of the death of Sarah for the purpose of avoiding an interruption of the main narrative.

Another cause for want of perfect confidence in the accuracy of the chronology of the Septuagint-version is the existence of extreme uncertainty as to what was the genuine text of that version, and what were the characters and the literary qualifications of its authors.

6. What is most extraordinary in this table is the enormous age assigned to Noah at the time of the birth of his son Shem. It is said in "the book of the generations of Adam" (Gen. v. 32) that "Noah was five hundred years old; and Noah begat Shem, Ham, and Japheth:" and in "the generations of Shem" (Gen. xi. 10), that "Shem was a hundred years old, and begat Arphaxad two years after the Flood."

CHRONOLOGICAL OBSERVATIONS. 151

If the numbers in these two statements, which are the same in the existing Hebrew text and in the versions, be interpolated, they may, perhaps, be mainly founded upon three passages which we find in Gen. vii. 6 and 11, and viii. 13: "Noah was six hundred years old when the flood of waters was upon the earth:" and "in the six hundredth year of Noah's life, in the second month, the seventeenth day of the month, the same day were all the fountains of the great deep broken up, and the windows of heaven were opened:" and "in the six hundredth and first year," etc.

The age thus assigned to Noah at the time of the birth of Shem is not only very far from having any parallel, but is not supported by any other statement respecting him, except that which gives the sum of the years to which he is said to have attained at the time of his death; and a mistake in the statement of his age at the time of the Flood may have occasioned one in that of the total length of his life. Now if we suppose a single letter (lāmedh) to have been accidentally dropped, in a standard-copy of the Hebrew text, from the middle of the word signifying "six," in one of the three passages mentioned above, in Gen. vii. and viii., and afterwards intentionally in the others, the age of Noah, at the time of the Flood, becomes reduced to *three hundred* years. An omission of a letter in the middle of a word is not of rare occurrence, and is therefore not improbable. But such an omission at the *beginning of a word is less* improbable; and if we suppose a single letter (vāv) to have been accidentally dropped before the latter of the two words rendered "six hundred" "and six hundredth," the age of Noah at the time of the Flood becomes reduced to *a hundred and six* years (in the Hebrew it would be "six and a hundred years," though the usual Hebrew idiom is either "six years and a hundred years" or "a hundred and six years"), without the necessity of any other alteration to effect this change of meaning. For if it be objected that the latter of the two words is written in the plural form in our copies of the Hebrew text, it may be replied that we find an instance of its being thus written when used as a singular, in 2 Chron. xxv. 9; and that a double reason may have suggested the writing it in the usual plural form in the instances in question; for we find it, as a plural, written in a form which, divested of the modern points, is exactly the same as the singular, in two instances in "the book of the generations of Adam."

The admission of either of these suppositions would require the inference that "the book of the generations of Adam" and "the generations of Shem," in the Hebrew and the translations, are incorrect in many of their numbers which cannot be *proved* to be erroneous: but as so many of the numbers *are indisputably* incorrect, such an inference does not seem to us to be unreasonable.

The dropping of a letter by accident is much more

likely than its accidental insertion; and many emendations have been proposed and approved by Christian Biblical critics and divines, and (what is more to the point) by leading doctors of the Jews, differing far more from the existing text of the Bible than these. If the letter were accidentally dropped in the first of the three instances, and not in the others, the latter may have been probably thought to be mistakes, and altered accordingly. The multiplicity of the various readings in the Hebrew copies of the Bible is a fact of immense importance to our faith: in many cases they have doubtless arisen from accident: in some, as we have remarked above, they have been occasioned by design.

7. Even the latter of the two reductions here suggested would leave us to infer that the longevity of Adam and his descendants, nearly to the time of Abraham, was enormous in comparison with the greatest length of life known to have been attained in later times; the total age of Noah, as found by adding the number of years which he lived after the Flood, according to what we find in Gen ix. 28, to a hundred and six, being four hundred and fifty-six years, instead of nine hundred and fifty, the sum mentioned in the next verse. But these two verses, the former of which is absolutely necessary to define the total length of the life of Noah, belong to the same category as "the book of the generations of Adam;" or rather they constitute a portion of that book, like "the generations of Shem;" the three

pieces forming one complete document, which presents the entire genealogy of Abraham; and as this document has come down to us in three widely-different states, we should look to other evidence, not liable to suspicion. Such evidence we have, though it leads only to a very vague conclusion: that the longevity of Jacob's ancestors was in a high degree extraordinary is shown by his saying to Pharaoh (as is related in Gen. xlvii. 9), "The days of the years of my pilgrimage [are] a hundred and thirty years: few and evil have the days of the years of my life been, and have not attained unto the days of the years of the life of my fathers in the days of their pilgrimage." (See Gen. xxv. 7 and 8, and xxxv. 28 and 29.)

Extraordinary longevity, indeed, is what we should expect to find in these cases; and it may be argued that its degree is not to be limited by the consideration of the causes of decay pointed out by modern physiology, which is founded upon the observation of subjects infected by the diseases of countless ancestors. Adam must be held to have been created without any morbific affection (for we can hardly believe God to have created a being with any taint, physical or moral); and it is a common opinion, which seems to be sanctioned by Scripture, that he was created without any germ of decay, and became subject to natural as well as spiritual death by eating the forbidden fruit; that this fatal fruit, while engendering new and unholy ideas and passions, introduced into his frame the first seed of disease, and consequently eventual death; and that the eating of the tree of life would, as its name indicates, have cured that incipient malady. Disease, then, being once introduced, and successively increasing in those by whom it was inherited, until checked by the providence of God and by the curative means prepared and made known by Him, might be supposed, agreeably with the analogy of nature, to have gradually reduced the length of human life to its general term. For decay and death, it is well known, are mainly caused by a process of consolidation, which commences at the first moment of growth, and continues to the last moment of life; and this, being rapid or slow according as the subject is more or less diseased, may be inferred to have been incalculably slow where scarcely any disease existed. But this argument is so much weakened, except in relation to Adam and his immediate offspring, by the moral necessity, in which we are placed, of believing that the latter intermarried with a different race,—though, in many instances, a child appears to inherit the healthy constitution of one parent without any malady of the other,—that it seems most reasonable to look mainly to the special providence of God as the cause of Jacob's ancestors' living so long as we must infer that they did from his words which have been cited above.

Our main concern, however, is not with the lengths of the lives of the patriarchs, but with the *chronology* before the time of Abraham; and particularly in relation to the dates of the Deluge and the Dispersion.

The common opinion which refers the date of the Dispersion to the time of Peleg (who was born, according to Ussher's Hebrew chronology, in the year B.C. 2247, but according to Hales's chronology, chiefly based upon the Septuagint, B.C. 2754, though he places the Dispersion two centuries later), being founded upon the *name* of Peleg, may be erroneous; for it is held by some authors of good repute, that Peleg may as probably be supposed to have been so named from the opening of a chasm in the earth in his time as from the division and dispersion of the descendants of Noah.

It is, perhaps, worthy of remark, that, according to Manetho, in the reign of the first king of the Second Dynasty of the Pharaohs, apparently somewhat more than two centuries and a half after the accession of Menes, the founder of the first Pharaonic kingdom, a chasm in the earth opened at Bubastis, in Lower Egypt, and many persons in consequence perished. Seldom is a tradition of this kind without foundation; and as Lower Egypt is not subject to earthquakes, except when they are far more violent in the regions lying to the north-east or north of that country, this tradition suggests the probability of the occurrence, at the same period, of an earthquake of extraordinary violence in Syria, or in a more distant country occupied by early descendants of Noah.

But whether this be considered probable or not,

CHRONOLOGICAL OBSERVATIONS. 157

the date of the Dispersion is obviously founded upon a very unsure basis by those who hold it to have happened in the time of Peleg. It may therefore, perhaps, be referable to a period much nearer to that of the Deluge, which, according to Ussher, was in the year, B.C. 2348-9, but according to Hales, B.C. 3155. Preferring the latter authority, we suppose that the Dispersion may have taken place neither much later nor much earlier than the middle of the twenty-eighth century B.C., which happens to be almost exactly the period to which Hales refers the birth of Peleg.

With this date the chronology of Egypt appears to be reconcileable, as we shall have to show hereafter; and for this reason, rather than for any other, we believe it to be nearly correct. If the Dispersion were proved to have been but a century, or even half a century, later, in which case its date would be far anterior to that assigned by Ussher, the principal question which we are endeavouring to solve in the present work would be placed almost beyond dispute; for then it would be impossible, or extremely difficult, to reconcile with that date the Egyptian chronology without conceding the existence of people not included among the Adamites; that is, without conceding that there existed nations not in any degree descended from Adam, or, at least, that the race of Cain, or some similar race, was not included among the Adamites who were destroyed by the Flood; and even that some of the Pharaohs were anterior to

Noah, as Arabian traditions assert them to have been. But the establishment of a Biblical chronology much less extended than that of the Septuagint we regard as scarcely within the bounds of probability; though we consider an acknowledgment of its *possibility* as a concession which no impartial critic can withhold after noting the many intentional alterations which we have mentioned, and as one which is perfectly compatible with faith in the Scripture-history, notwithstanding the consequences indicated above.

The foregoing observations on chronology we have found it necessary to make in order to prepare the way for testing our inference from the Bible respecting the existence of Pre-Adamites by considering its relation to historical facts and traditions.

CHAPTER V.

HISTORICAL OBSERVATIONS.

THE inquiry which we have thus far pursued had led us to form an opinion which we have already expressed, respecting the origination of the human species, without our foreseeing that we should find that opinion to be confirmed to us by some very remarkable historical facts which seem to be unexplainable by any other theory; though this result suggested itself immediately afterwards.

We have inferred that man came into existence as soon as the condition of the earth had become such as to fit it for his habitation; for otherwise there would be a seeming inconsistency in the works of God. And we have argued that he may have existed many thousands of years before the creation of Adam.

We have also inferred that the first stock of man was created in the equatorial region of Africa, where uninterrupted summer prevents the necessity of clothing, and where every want of nature is easily supplied by the luxuriance of vegetation; or, in other words, that the true Negro, the aboriginal inhabitant of Nigritia, is the primary variety of our species.

This inference implies that we consider the first of mankind as living in a state of nature, but not as possessing no knowledge of God, though without any express revelation; for man in his natural state must always have had a knowledge of God sufficient for the condition in which he had been placed. Although God " in times past suffered all nations [or rather all " the Gentiles" (πάντα τὰ ἔθνη)] to walk in their own ways, nevertheless He left not Himself without witness, in that He did good, and gave us rain from heaven, and fruitful seasons, filling our hearts with food and gladness." "For the invisible things of Him, from the creation of the world, are clearly seen, being understood by the things that are made, [even] his eternal power and godhead." But the people of whom we are speaking "changed the glory of the incorruptible God into an image made like to corruptible man, and to birds, and four-footed beasts, and creeping things," "and worshipped and served the creature more than the Creator, who is blessed for ever." Thus arose that strange superstition which is known by the term *Fetishism*, consisting in the worship of animals, trees, rivers, hills, and stones, and found to obtain in every region through which the Nigritian race has spread itself: some of these objects of worship being local and tribal, and some being peculiar to households or individuals, like the *Lares* and *Penates* of the ancient Romans, and the Phœnician Πάταικοι, or *Patæci*, a word remarkable for its resemblance to *Fetish*. The word *fetish*, however, is said to be derived from the Portuguese *fetisso*. It appears to be properly applied to a charm, or spell, and an amulet; but is used to denote an object of idolatrous worship of any of the kinds mentioned above.

If this race originated in the equatorial region of Africa, we must suppose its first seat to have been in a part where alluvial soil had been deposited in a quantity sufficient to produce the necessary vegetable food; most probably, near the sources of the Nile, not only the greatest, but the most fertilizing also, of all the African rivers, and on this account held sacred by the ancient Egyptians, as the upper portion of the main Abyssinian branch of that river, and the tributary Takazzé, are said to be still by the Agows of Damot and of Lasta, and like as the Ganges has been by the Indians to the present day. As the race multiplied, we suppose it to have spread over the increased alluvial soil; some of its more extended branches (having learned, by the invention of simple clothing, to accommodate themselves to changes of climatic temperature unknown in their original seat) advancing over the basin of the Nile, and then along the narrow and winding valley through which that river pours its waters into the sea; thus giving rise to the aboriginal, pre-historic, *Egyptian People*.

Throughout these tracts, no agricultural art was necessary; no tilling of the ground; but the simple scattering of the seed, and treading it into the moist earth, after the rainy season or the subsiding of the inundation. And even this light labour was probably not needed by the first inhabitants of Egypt. The date-palm, the lotus, a great variety of cucumbers and melons, and numerous other productions of the soil, together with the fish of the Nile, an abundance of wild fowls, and several species of animals of the chase, must have supplied food that may well be believed to have been sufficient, during many generations, for the early inhabitants of a country which, by cultivation, is capable of supporting a dense population.

We formed this idea respecting the first peopling of Egypt without reflecting that the history of Herodotus contains a passage expressing a similar notion. He says (in Book II. chapter 15), "I think the Egyptians not to have originated with what the Ionians call the Delta, but ever to have been, since the race of man was; and as the land advanced, many of them to have remained, and many to have descended by degrees. Thus, of old, Thebes (which has a circuit of six thousand and one hundred and twenty stades) was called Ægyptus." And Diodorus Siculus, in his account of the Ethiopians, relates a tradition of that people, to the effect that the land of Egypt was gradually formed by the Nile, that the Egyptians were an Ethiopian colony led thither by Osiris, and that most of their customs, and even their hieroglyphical characters, were of Ethiopian origin. Hence these characters have been called, by some ancient writers, "the Ethiopian letters."

The opinion in which we have thus been anticipated, as to the main assumed fact, by the most celebrated of the Greek historians, who had probably heard the tradition afterwards related by Diodorus, appears to us to indicate the only way in which we can reasonably account for several very remarkable peculiarities which distinguished the ancient Egyptians under the Pharaohs. It may also be regarded as explaining the origin of the tradition mentioned by Manetho, that Gods, Demigods or Heroes, and Dead ones (Νέκυες, by some rendered "Manes"), reigned in Egypt before the accession of Menes, the first of the Pharaohs, with whom apparently commenced the civilization of the nation, and certainly its veritable history, and before whom we find a dynasty of Gods in the Turin Papyrus of Kings, but without any other dynasty intervening. A tradition somewhat similar to this obtains in India: that the dominion of that country, in primeval ages, was divided between two families, who were called the family of the Sun, and that of the Moon.

In the former of the two traditions last mentioned above, as we find the appellation of "Dead ones" applied to certain kings who reigned during a period next before that of the historical dynasties, and as all the kings of these dynasties were dead in the time of Manetho, that appellation must have a peculiar sig-

CHAPTER V.

nificance, more restricted than its literal meaning. It seems to import that the kings thus called were of a race which, in Egypt, had become *extinct;* and reminds us of the "Rephāīm," whose name, after they had entirely passed away, appears to have been used as synonymous with "mēthīm" (or "dead ones"); as in Isaiah xxvi. 14 and 19. The tradition, therefore, may have been (and we think that it was) founded upon the following facts:—that the first Asiatic settlers in Egypt found there a race of whom some intermixed with them and the rest gradually retired: and that this earlier race, on arriving in that country, found it to be inhabited only by wild animals, among which were included many of the objects of their religious worship; that is, that they found it to be under the dominion of their *gods.* These facts, if facts they be, required but little dressing up in order to be presented in the garb in which they are exhibited by Manetho; with Vulcan (occupying the first place as being the creative power, or demiurgus), Helios (placed next as the source of light), Agathodæmon, Osiris, and other similar divinities, in lieu of the sacred animals (the beetle, hawk, etc.,) which were *the emblems of these gods.*

Believing that the chronology founded upon the Septuagint-version of the Bible is approximatively correct, we see no cause to doubt that the first Asiatic settlers in Egypt were postdiluvians, of the race of Ham the son of Noah. But as a shorter chronology is preferred by many of the learned, we

HISTORICAL OBSERVATIONS. 165

think it desirable to offer a few remarks on the *possibility* of there having been an earlier immigration, into Egypt, of a portion of the race of Adam.— First, we must observe that Egypt is called in the Bible "the land of Ham;" and "Mizraim" and "Cush," which are said to be the names of two of the sons of Ham the son of Noah, are applied to Egypt and Ethiopia, and to the Egyptians and Ethiopians. Hence the prevailing opinion that the Egyptian and Ethiopian nations *originated* from two sons of Ham the son of Noah. But as one of the sons of Noah was *prophetically* named "Japheth" because his posterity were to be widely spread, in like manner another of his sons may have been named "Ham" because Egypt was to be the chief inheritance of his offspring: or, as we think more probable, the name "Ham" may have been substituted for another name when the descendants of him to whom it is applied had settled in that country, in order to indicate their principal destination: and for a like reason, which seems to hold in several other instances, the names of "Mizraim" and "Cush" may have been applied to two of his sons. If so, Egypt and Ethiopia may have been *peopled* before the time of Noah either wholly by Non-Adamites or partly by descendants of Adam. Egypt is called in hieroglyphics "Kem," "Chem," "Kam," or "Cham," which is probably identical in its radical signification with the Hebrew "Ham;" though the former is said to signify "black," and the latter is not known to have had this meaning, but signifies "hot" or "warm." Both of these appellations of Egypt may mean "black," as characteristic of the soil; or "hot" or "warm," as characteristic of the climate: or the latter may have been substituted in Hebrew for the former as being similar to it in sound, and equally appropriate.—Secondly, we have to consider the terms employed in the denunciation of the Flood, "I will destroy *the Adam*" etc. (Gen. vi. 7); together with the fact that the appellation "Adam" is applied to the *Egyptians,* where Isaiah says (xxxi. 3), "the Egyptians [are] *Adam,* and not God; and their horses, flesh, and not spirit." Now it is clear that "the Adam" in the former instance means "the *race* of Adam;" and "Adam" in the latter instance, "beings of the *nature* of Adam." And it should also be observed that if the nation spoken of in the latter instance originated from the intermarriages of Adamites with an aboriginal Non-Adamite population of Egypt, it may have been with strict propriety excluded from "the Adam" in the former case, and included among "Adam" in the latter; and may therefore have originated before the Flood. As we are firmly persuaded that there were antediluvian races partly of Adamite blood—as that of Cain, and that which was produced by the intermarriages mentioned in the sixth chapter of Genesis, —not necessarily to be regarded as included among the people against whom the Flood was specially denounced, we see no necessity to limit such races to

HISTORICAL OBSERVATIONS. 167

Asia, though as yet we see no substantial reason for inferring their extension into Egypt, or the origination of any such mixed *antediluvian* race in that country.—It will be seen that the correctness of the remarks that here follow does not depend upon the validity of our assumption that the first descendants of Adam that settled in Egypt were of the race of Ham the son of Noah, nor upon the correctness of the particular scheme of Biblical chronology to which we have given the preference.

The settlement of the descendants of Ham is generally supposed to have taken place soon after the Dispersion, which, as we have before remarked, we do not think it reasonable to refer to a period much higher than about the middle of the twenty-eighth century B.C. Now according to the Egyptian chronology of Mr. Stuart Poole, founded chiefly upon an arrangement of the dynasties of the Pharaohs which he has proved to be correct in many points by monumental evidences of synchronisms and by other means, and to the correctness of which Sir Gardner Wilkinson has testified his assent, the first of the Pharaohs, Menes, began his reign in, or about, the year B.C. 2717. And between three and four centuries later, in the age in which the most famous pyramids were built, the Memphite kings and their subjects are shown by painted sculptures of contemporary monuments to have been as distinct in their general *Physical Characteristics* from their neighbours in Asia as were the Egyptians of later, but ancient, times, at least down to the age of the last of the Pharaohs. In almost all the sculptures and paintings of the Pharaonic ages, except such as represent foreigners and a few of those that are designed as portraits of particular individuals, the form of the head, and the features of the face, are of a modified Caucasian type, approaching to that which is known as the Syro-Arabian, but inclining in the general cast, and particularly in the nose and lips, and in the soft and languid expression of the eyes, to the Negro character, as in several Ethiopian races in the present day. A similar degree of resemblance to the Negro is also observable in the body and limbs, more particularly in the legs and feet. The complexion of the men is denoted by a dark red pigment; and that of the women, generally, by a light shade of red, or, on the more ancient monuments, by a deep yellow. The hair, though often long, and capable of being drawn straight, is shown, in the instances in which the head is not represented as shaven or as covered, to have been extremely crisp, by its being generally divided into a number of small plaits, or twists, like cords; exactly as the similar hair of many tribes on the east and south of Upper Egypt, and that of some of the Papuans also, is dressed, by means of grease, in the present day: for which reason, in sleeping, a neck-rest (in the form of a crescent supported by a foot, generally of wood,) was used in ancient Egypt, and is still used by Ethiopians and by Papuans. The beard is very small, and artificially dressed and trimmed: we therefore cannot judge of its natural character: but it was probably short and scanty; for many of the beards appear to have been false. Such were the principal physical characteristics of the ancient Egyptians as shown by their own monuments, which present more certain criteria than the mummies (as many of these are Greek or Roman, or from remote countries whence the Romans drew their foreign legions, or from Asia or Ethiopia, and none of them can show the complexion), and even than the testimony of the accurate Herodotus, who (in Book II. chapter 104) speaks of the Colchians as resembling the Egyptians, "because they are black," or "swarthy" (μελάγχροες), "and crisp-haired." Like every other mixed race, the ancient Egyptians of historical times comprised individuals and families differing considerably from the general type: some inclined more to the Caucasian; and some, to the Negro: but the instances in which their sculptures and paintings exhibit, as Egyptians, individuals with no trace of the Negro characteristics are extremely rare.

All the physical peculiarities indicated as characteristic of the ancient Egyptians in general by their sculptures and paintings, as described above, are exactly what are now found to be produced by the mixture of Caucasian and Negro races in the same country; and if the first Noachian settlers for the most part mixed with aboriginal natives of Nigritian ancestry, they must have produced a race perfectly such as the ancient Egyptians under the Pharaohs are thus shown to have been by their own monuments, in general neither more nor less approaching to the Caucasian type; for the more noble type is always found to predominate in the offspring of persons of two different varieties. Their monuments exhibit to us none of the supposed aborigines; but as their sculptures and paintings of the first twelve centuries after Menes, to the times of the Eighteenth Dynasty, are few, and none representing a human figure has been ascertained to belong to the first quarter of this period, and as the mixed race was evidently that which was dominant, this is what we might reasonably expect to find. It does not disprove the assumption (which on other grounds we must consider as probable in the highest degree) that Egypt continued to comprise for some centuries after the settlement of the sons of Ham an unmixed aboriginal population, which assisted in the enormous labour of constructing the Pyramids and other great works, and (like the aborigines of the Spanish settlements in South America) became gradually more and more blended with the race of their rulers. Indeed, a contemplation of the Pyramids, and reflection upon the nearness of their age to that of the Dispersion, have convinced us that such must have been the case: and we have little doubt that there existed in Egypt, long before it was entered by the sons of Ham, rude, but massive, structures, not much inferior to many still found in Haurān; some of which a traveller who has recently examined and described them (the Rev. J. L. Porter) inclines, apparently with good reason, to ascribe to the Rephāīm, whom we number among the races of Pre-Adamite origin. But we think it most probable that many of the prehistoric Egyptians were troglodytes, whose rough-hewn caves may have served as the beginnings of not a few of their successors' rock-temples and tombs. We may readily conceive the willing submission of such aboriginal inhabitants to a superior race of settlers, introducing among them for the first time the arts of civilized life. And this observation suggests what we think a probable explanation of the remarkable fact, that the subjects of the sculptures and paintings in the tombs of the ancient Egyptians are generally the arts of civilized life (mostly husbandry), and sports; for it seems reasonable to suppose that the custom of thus decorating the walls of their tombs originated from the first civilized settlers' thus commemorating their own useful innovations. Diodorus Siculus relates (in Book I. chapter 45) that a curse was inscribed against Menes, or, as he calls him, Menas, [the first of the Pharaohs,] in the temple of Jupiter [or Amen-Ra] at Thebes, by Tnephachthus, the father of Bocchoris the Wise, for his having changed the original simple manners of the Egyptians; but this, if there be any truth in it, was a condemnation only of luxurious living, and of him who introduced it; not of useful arts.

The first of the Pharaohs laid the foundation of

his kingdom in Upper Egypt; the city of This being his capital: and hence it would seem that the first Asiatic settlers found the whole extent of Lower Egypt occupied by a population too numerous to allow of their immediately establishing themselves in that more desirable region: but when their own number and power had increased, a portion of them succeeded in doing this, and founded a second kingdom, the Memphite, which eclipsed, without supplanting, the former. Afterwards arose other kingdoms, during the continuance of the first and second; and contemporary dynasties held rule for many centuries in different parts of the country. Manetho relates, that the first king of the First Dynasty (Thinites) made *a foreign expedition:* and that in the reign of the first of the Memphites, *the Lybians revolted from the Egyptians*, but, being terrified by a sudden increase of the moon, returned to their allegiance.

That the first Asiatic settlers in Egypt found there an aboriginal population, by mixing with which their Caucasian characteristics became modified in their posterity, is not a notion here for the first time put forth. A high authority, before mentioned, Sir Gardner Wilkinson, thus pronounces his opinion on this subject. "The origin of the Egyptians is enveloped in the same obscurity as that of most people; but they were undoubtedly from Asia; as is proved by the form of the skull, which is that of a Caucasian race, by their features, hair [?], and other evidences;

and the whole valley of the Nile throughout Ethiopia, all Abyssinia, and the coast to the south, were peopled by Asiatic immigrations. . . . At the period of the colonization of Egypt, the aboriginal population was doubtless small [?], and the change in the peculiarities of the new comers was proportionably slight; little variation being observable in the form of the skull from the Caucasian original. Still there was a change: and a modification in character as well as conformation must occur, in a greater or less degree, whenever a mixture of races has taken place."—With these observations, as to the main points, we perfectly agree. (We cite them from their author's recent work, "A Popular Account of the Ancient Egyptians," vol. i. p. 302.) One statement which they comprise, that of "little variation being observable in the form of the skull from the Caucasian original," does not require the inference that the aboriginal population must have been small, as appears from a physical fact before mentioned (that the more noble type is always found to predominate in the offspring of persons of two different varieties), and from the probability that the mixed race, once produced, generally intermarried among themselves, and gradually superseded the unmixed aborigines. Nor must it be understood as meant to imply that little variation is observed in other respects; for the same author has abundantly shown in other places that this was far from being the case.—We must subjoin some additional remarks on this point, as it is one of great importance.

The sculptures and paintings upon the monuments of the ancient Egyptians, beside their exact representations of that people, exhibit a very remarkable confirmation of the conviction which we have expressed respecting their double origin, by proving that wide differences of feature, complexion, etc., distinguished them from their contemporaries in Asia. This is manifest to every one who, like ourselves, has studied those monuments, or has examined the plates in the great and accurate works of Champollion and Rosellini and Lepsius, or the engravings, equally accurate, though smaller, with which Sir Gardner Wilkinson has enriched his valuable writings.

If the Egyptian nation were solely of Asiatic origin, they must have preserved for many generations a near physical resemblance to their eastern neighbours. Of the truth of this assertion we have living evidences in the descendants of Arabs who have settled in Egypt at various times during the last twelve centuries. For, among the bulk of the modern population of Egypt, produced from the ancient stock with a large admixture of other races, mostly of Arabs, whose religion and blood have generally pervaded the nation in the course of the period above mentioned, we find that, although the prevailing national type still bears a considerable resemblance to that of the Pharaonic ages, the genuine Arabian features are conspicuous in numerous individuals and

HISTORICAL OBSERVATIONS. 175

families who count long lines of ancestors resident in that country. But Egyptian sculptures in the peninsula of Mount Sinai, of the same age as those in Egypt which exhibit the earliest examples of the Egyptian type, that is, of the age in which the most famous pyramids were built, according to the most moderate probable calculation (that of Mr. Stuart Poole) the period between the years 2400 and 2300 B.C., represent enemies of the Egyptians with features very widely differing from those of the latter race, as may be sufficiently seen from two examples (though each is copied on a very small scale) given by Lepsius in his "Denkmäler," Abtheilung II. Bl. 2, fig. c., and 39, fig. f. Next in the order of time, in the reign of Sesertesen (or Osirtesen) II., about two thousand years B.C., we find the well-known representations, in one of the grottoes of Benī-Hasan, of persons whose physiognomy is so remarkably Jewish that they have been supposed to be Hebrew bondsmen; which their age, now known, shows that they cannot be. They have a reddish yellow complexion, with black eyes, full black hair, and a black beard. In the Tombs of the Kings at Thebes, and upon other monuments, of the period between the fifteenth and twelfth centuries B.C., we find numerous other representations of races foreign to Egypt, and, among them, examples of a race apparently the same as that of the persons last mentioned above: in one instance, with a similar physiognomy, light pink complexion, blue eyes, and full black hair and beard: in another, with a similar physiognomy, light red complexion, yellow eyes, denoting a peculiar yellowish hazel which is one of the most remarkable characteristics of many of the modern Eastern Jews, and full yellow beard, which is also a characteristic of many among that people in Eastern countries—a fact of great importance in ethnology, as we have before observed, in our third chapter. Among the other races which these monuments exhibit to us, we find examples as widely differing from the Egyptian, and unquestionably Asiatic or European, in which the nose is generally prominent and aquiline; and where the colours are still preserved, the complexion is pink or yellow, the eyes are often blue, and the hair is of a reddish brown or black. In almost all the instances with which we are acquainted, the enemies of the Egyptians are represented either as Negroes or as bearded, and in the latter case, where the colours remain, light-complexioned.

The evidences which we have thus adduced as indicative of the double origin of the ancient Egyptians of monumental and historical times (and which are of the greatest importance as showing the very early physical distinctions of nations) are confirmed by our finding that their *Religion* was in like manner a compound of Asiatic and Nigritian elements. With Nigritian fetishism, the lowest kind of nature-worship, it combined the higher kinds of that worship, which prevailed in Babylonia and other parts of South-Western Asia soon after the Deluge, and, if we may

HISTORICAL OBSERVATIONS. 177

believe tradition, even before that event; together with some of the grandest principles of the religion of the Bible.

The lowest kind of nature-worship which was the most remarkable characteristic of the religion of ancient Egypt is too well known to need our giving any account of it in these pages; but its identity, or near agreement in almost every respect, with that still obtaining among the Negroes has never, we believe, been pointed out. This will be sufficiently shown, together with other very striking points of agreement between the ancient Egyptians of historical times and the modern Negroes, in religion and in religious institutions, by the following extracts from the valuable work of Dr. Prichard on the Natural History of Man (third edition, pp. 525-539), a work respecting which we may here mention that we have carefully examined it without finding in it anything that is not either confirmatory of our opinion respecting the originations of the varieties of our species or perfectly reconcileable therewith.

"The excellent missionary Oldendorp, who appears to have had rare opportunities, and to have taken great pains to become accurately acquainted with the mental history and character of the Negroes, assures us that he recognised among them an universal belief in the 'existence of a God,' whom they represent as very powerful and beneficent. 'He is the maker of the world and of men: he it is who thunders in the air, as he punishes the wicked with his bolts. He regards beneficent actions with complacency, and rewards them with long life. To him the Negroes ascribe their own personal gifts, the fruits of the earth, and all good things. From him the rain descends upon the earth. They believe that he is pleased when men offer prayers to him in all their wants, and that he succours them in dangers, in diseases, and in seasons of drought. This is the chief God who lives far from them on high; he is supreme over all other gods.' 'Among all the black nations,' says Oldendorp, 'with whom I have become acquainted, even among the utterly ignorant and rude, there is none that did not believe in a god, which had not learned to give him a name, which did not regard him as the maker of the world, and ascribe to him, more or less clearly, all the attributes which I have briefly summed up. As, however, the Negroes always designate God and the heaven by the same term, [as the Chinese, also, are by many held to do,] it is doubtful whether they do not regard heaven itself as the Deity: but, perhaps, their notions are not so clear as to have led them even to contemplate this distinction.

"' Besides this supreme beneficent divinity, whom all the various nations worship in some way or other, they believe in many gods of inferior dignity, who are subject to the chief Deity, and are mediators between him and mankind. Such are the powers which they reverence in serpents, tigers [?], wolves, rivers, trees, hills, and large stones. The more stupid

HISTORICAL OBSERVATIONS. 179

of the Negroes certainly imagine the serpent, the tiger [?], and the stones, to be themselves gods; that the tree understands them, and the tiger [?] gives them rain: on the other hand, the more intelligent look upon these objects as representations of the inferior gods, and imagine that local deities dwell unseen under certain trees, or on particular hills.'
. . . . The objects of their worship are either national or domestic."

"'Sacrifices constitute the most important part of their worship, which are always performed in sacred places by consecrated persons. The sacred places are those where one of their divinities dwells, visibly or invisibly, particularly buildings, or hills, or trees, remarkable for their age, height, and strength. They have also sacred groves, [as the ancient Egyptians had, as well as *models* of such groves,] which are the abodes of a deity, which no Negro ventures to enter, except the priests. The oblations of the Negroes consist of oxen, cows, sheep, goats, fowls, palm-oil, brandy, yams, etc. Human sacrifices are offered by some nations. [And the Egyptians, in early times, are related by Manetho, as cited by Plutarch and Porphyry, to have offered such sacrifices. Their common oblations, also, were similar to those of the Negroes; being oxen and other beasts, geese and other fowls, vegetables, fruits, flowers, grain, wine, etc.] . . . The priests and priestesses are the sacred persons upon whom the divine service of the Negroes depends, and who, as they suppose, have confidential intercourse with the gods, and interpret their will. They alone understand by what means the wrath of the deity may be appeased. To them it belongs to present the offerings to the gods, and to be the intercessors between them and the people. They convey the questions of the people to the gods, who reply by the mouths of the priests. . . . . The priests of the Negroes are also the physicians, as were the priests of Apollo and Æsculapius. . . . Some priests are likewise sorcerers; but among several nations, the Sokko and Watje for example, the latter office is distinguished from the former.'"

" 'The Negroes believe, almost universally, that the souls of good men, after their separation from the body, go to God, and the wicked to the evil spirit. . . . They believe that the souls which go to the evil spirit become ghosts and re-appear; and, because they preserve their disposition to do evil, torment those whom they dislike in sleep; and, besides, flutter about in the air, and make noises and disturbances in the bushes.' . . . The Karabari, and several other black tribes, believe in the doctrine of the transmigration of the soul from one body to another, and imagine that the soul of a dead person revives in the body of the next child born after his death. It is fully established, by the assurances of the Negroes, that [like the ancient Egyptians] they believe in the transmigration of a human soul into the body of a bird, fish, or other creature."

In most of these particulars, we see what we might

reasonably suppose to be characteristics of a primeval people destitute of revelation. We see in them the ruder elements of most of the religions of the ancient pagan world; together with a kind of priesthood exercising functions and influence and authority similar to those of the priests and priestesses of ancient Egypt, as well as of the Bonzes of China, the Shamans of Northern Asia, the wizards of the Finns and Lapps, the Angekoks of the Esquimaux, the "medicine-men" of the American Indians, the Druids, the Brahmans, and the Magi; and also of those vagrants who pervade Turkey and South-Western Asia, and, under the cloak of religion, impose upon the credulity of every class. And here we may observe, that the rite of circumcision, obtaining among the pagan Negroes in various parts of Africa, appears to have been practised by none beside them, except by races physically resembling them in Africa and Polynesia and other parts, and by races who have been socially connected with them, either immediately or mediately, as the ancient and modern Egyptians, the Abyssinians and other inhabitants of Ethiopia, the Arabs, the Israelites, and, it is said, some of the ancient Canaanites. This rite we therefore suppose to have originated in Africa; and we infer from what is said in Josh. v. 9 that it was imposed upon the Israelites, partly at least, to remove from them "the reproach of Egypt;" whence we may also infer that it was imposed upon Abraham for the same, or a like, reason, as well as for "a token of the covenant" that God made with him when He gave him that name. But the most remarkable features of the Negro religion are the *veneration of irrational creatures, and that of trees and rivers and hills;* differing in different parts of the same country; the kind of nature-worship which most prominently characterized the religion of ancient Egypt, and the origin of which, in that religion, has hitherto, we believe, never received any explanation in the smallest degree approaching to probability. Is it credible that the descendants of the Noachian settlers in Egypt, necessarily acquainted with revealed religion, invented this monstrous system in the very early age in which we know it to have existed among them? We doubt not that they found it prevailing in that country among a more ancient, aboriginal, Negro population. The name of "Athothis," the second of the kings of Egypt, meaning "son of Thoth," or "Hermes," to whom the ibis was sacred, and also the cynocephalus (not a native of Egypt, but of more southern regions), favours the inference to be drawn from very ancient sculptures, that animal-worship obtained among the Egyptians in the earliest age of their historical existence; and we know how the Israelites were led into idolatry by mixing with their heathen neighbours. But it may have been adopted by the Noachian settlers in Egypt *gradually*, though *soon*; for Manetho relates that in the reign of Cæëchôs, the second king of the Second Dynasty, the bulls

Apis (in Memphis) and Mnevis (in Heliopolis), and the Mendesian goat, were called gods. In the Egyptian sculptures in the peninsula of Mount Sinai, we have evidence of the worship of Thoth in the age of the Great Pyramid: and we find, also, monumental evidence of the worship of Apis in the earlier times of the dynasty under which that pyramid was constructed.

We should not expect to find in Ethiopia any monuments of religious *art* presenting trustworthy evidences of their being more ancient than those of Egypt. For the ages of the ancient works of barbarous races, of whatever kind those works may be, such as grotesque paintings and sculptures, rude pottery, rough-hewn excavations, erections like those of the Druids, and cyclopean structures, cannot be determined; and with respect to Ethiopia and Egypt, we know that the arts of civilized life travelled from the latter country to the former, except, according to a tradition related by Diodorus Siculus, which we have before mentioned, the art of hieroglyphic writing, the least artificial mode of representing to the eye what one would say, and practised, in a rude manner, by more than one uncivilized people. But we might reasonably look for some *natural* monument indicating the spreading of nature-worship through the former country to the latter; and as such, we think, may probably be regarded "the Sacred Mountain," as Jebel Barkal is called in its own hieroglyphic inscriptions. Such also, perhaps, was the sacred sycamore at the place (in Lower Ethiopia) called after it, " Hierosycaminon," where a sculptured representation of it still remains, a work of Roman times.

Beside adopting this grossest kind of superstition, and making many of its objects to be representatives also of imaginary gods, the ancient Egyptians had a higher kind of nature-worship, the worship of the heavenly bodies. This the Noachian settlers in Egypt probably found in that country or brought with them from Babylonia. A proof of its very early existence in a neighbouring country is given by the Bible, in the saying of Job (ch. xxxi. vv. 26-28),

> " If I beheld a sun when it shined,
> Or a splendid moon progressing,
> And my heart were secretly enticed,
> And my hand touched my mouth,
> Surely this [were] a depravity of judgment,
> For I should have denied God above."

The Egyptians of the Pharaonic ages had also a still higher kind of nature-worship: they *personified* the powers of nature; and with these they associated personifications of various divine attributes; generally representing their gods by human figures with the heads of inferior animals, and thus seeming to connect the very lowest kind of nature-worship with the highest.

Hence, *alone*, we might infer that they were not without some knowledge of the true God: but that they had such knowledge plainly appears from our finding that they combined with their three-fold system of nature-worship some of the grandest doctrines of *revelation*. This fact is fully established by the following observations, which we extract from the article "Egypt," by Mr. Stuart Poole, in the edition of the Encyclopædia Britannica now in the course of publication.

"Osiris is the most remarkable personage in the Egyptian Pantheon, and was probably more highly reverenced than any of the other gods. His usual form is that of a mummied figure holding the crook and flail, and wearing the crown of Upper Egypt, generally with an ostrich-feather on each side. He was regarded as the personification of physical and moral good, and hence one of his commonest names, Un-nufre, signifies 'the opener' or 'revealer of good things.' *He is related to have been on earth*, instructing mankind in useful arts, *to have been slain* by his adversary Typhon, by whom he was cut in pieces, to have been bewailed by his wife and sister Isis, to have been embalmed, *to have risen again, and to have become the judge of the dead, the righteous among whom were called by his name and received his form*, in which indeed they are always represented. Although in this extraordinary story we may possibly trace a physical meaning, yet the moral meaning is far more prominent; and the intention appears rather to point to the struggle between moral good and moral evil, than between physical good and physical evil. In-

deed, although the opponent of Osiris personified both physical and moral evil at a comparatively late period, there is strong reason for supposing that such was not originally the case; and it is therefore not probable that the story of Osiris was intended to typify the opposition of good of both kinds to evil of both kinds. Admitting, then, that it teaches the doctrine of the conflict between moral good and moral evil, it is to be inquired why this doctrine was embodied in so remarkable a narration. Considering all the points of resemblance—bearing in mind that mankind must have been granted a primeval revelation, and what evidence of there having been such a revelation is afforded by the great doctrines of the immortality of the soul, the resurrection of the dead, judgment to come, and future rewards and punishments, all so closely interwoven with the story of Osiris—carefully weighing all this, it seems an unavoidable conclusion that this story is derived from some prophecy of the remotest times respecting the future Saviour of mankind. The discovery of this remarkable analogy was made some years since by Mr. Lane, aud a careful comparison of all the hieroglyphic documents which bear upon it in our hands has afforded it a complete confirmation. . . . .
The only representation that we find of moral evil is that of an enormous serpent called Apep, which was, in the Greek form, Apophis. The gods are portrayed in the mystic subjects on the walls of the Tombs of the Kings at Thebes engaged in warfare with this

monster, whom they ultimately destroy. Moral evil being represented by a serpent, affords another link in the argument that much of primeval revelation was retained, more or less distorted, by the ancient Egyptians."

The opinion which we have advanced respecting the double origin of the Egyptians of the Pharaonic ages, first as being suggested by their physical characteristics, and next as being confirmed by the principles of their religion, is further confirmed by their *Language.* But this important subject we reserve for examination in the next chapter.

A still further confirmation of the same opinion we find in the remarkable agreements, never, we believe, hitherto explained, in religious and other usages of Ancient Egypt and of *India,* more particularly in animal-worship and tree-worship and river-worship, which, with metempsychosis and other superstitions, the Caucasian settlers in India, as well as the ancient Egyptians, may be reasonably supposed to have learned from a race of Negro origin: for we have shown that the extension of the Negroes in remote times, to the eastward of Africa, even beyond the Indian Ocean, may be traced in the Negritoes, or Negrilloes, and other races, inhabiting parts of the Malayan Peninsula, and islands in the western portion of the Pacific. In India, moreover, as in Egypt, the powers of nature were *personified;* and thus arose a philosophic, poetic, fantastic, and monstrous mythology, which, while in many respects it resembled the Egyptian, in others more nearly agreed with the Greek, the Roman, and the Scandinavian.

Having mentioned India, we may here observe, that the Caucasian settlers in that country, the Aryas, or Arians, found there, according to their own historical traditions, an aboriginal population, whom they represent sometimes as monkeys, and sometimes as giants, or savages, and with whom they evidently, more or less, intermixed; whence the division of the former into castes, originally distinctions of colour; for "colour" is the proper meaning of the Sanskrit term (varna) which we render "caste." The descendants of the latter for the most part occupy the Deccan, south of the Vindhya chain; their complexion is generally darker than that of the Aryas (many of whom are as light in hue as people of the southernmost parts of Europe); their predominant type is Mongolian, more or less approaching to the African Negro in colour and in features; and their dialects, agreeably with their type, are of the Turanian stock. Branches of the same race are also found in the north-eastern parts of India, whither their ancestors retreated from the invading Aryas; and the speech of these also is Turanian; and their physiognomy, Mongolian.

In *Arabia*, as in Egypt, descendants of Noah appear, from the Bible, to have settled very soon after the Dispersion. The southern and more fertile parts of the former country were chosen by the family of Joktan, generally supposed to be the same whom the

Arabs call "Kahtān:" colonies of Cushites, also, established themselves in the same and other parts, next the ocean, and probably intermixed with Himyerites and other branches of the Joktanites: the rest became the abode of later Noachian settlers, chiefly of the family of Abraham by Hagar and Keturah. Beside these, however, Arabian writers make mention of several extinct tribes, to whom, probably taught to do so by the Jews, whose religion spread widely in their country, they likewise assign a Noachian origin, but whom we rather incline to regard as aboriginal inhabitants. We possess no veritable ancient history of any of these races, either of the extinct or of the surviving; nor any very ancient monuments, except, perhaps, a few in the southern parts, bearing Himyeritic inscriptions, and some of the inscribed rocks in the peninsula of Mount Sinai, recording, in a Semitic dialect, visits of pagan and Christian pilgrims. But thus far we know, that the religions of the Joktanites and Ishmaelites, and the language also of the former, were such as can hardly be explained without the supposition of their having intermixed in early times with other races. With the worship of the true God, they combined that of angels, and of idols, and the higher kind of nature-worship which seems to have originated either in Africa or in Babylonia, or to have been learned by the people of the latter region from some neighbouring Asiatic nation with whom the founders of the Babylonian kingdom are supposed by us to have intermixed; namely, the adoration of the sun, moon, and stars. And to all this they added the lowest Negro fetishism, the worship of trees, and of stones, or masses of rock; still surviving, in a manner, in the practice, common among the Arabs and their modern co-religionists, of decking certain trees with votive offerings or memorials of pious visits, and in the veneration of the Black Stone of the Kaabeh. And here it is worthy of remark, that tree-worship may be traced from the interior of Africa not only into Egypt and Arabia, but also onward, uninterruptedly, into Palestine and Syria, Assyria, Persia, India, Thibet, Siam, the Philippine Islands, China, Japan, and Siberia: also, westward, into Asia Minor, Greece, Italy, and other countries: and in most of the countries here named, it obtains in the present day, combined, as it has been in other parts, with various forms of idolatry. We may also add, that the Arabs have an old tradition (similar to one which we have already mentioned as preserved by the Aryas of India), that the earth was inhabited before the time of Adam by genii. They believe, moreover, that the Tempter in Paradise was one of these genii, and that he was sentenced to be banished thence for refusing to acknowledge his inferiority to Adam, but obtained a promise that his life should be prolonged to the day of resurrection. (See Sale's Korân, chapters vii. and xviii.)

The *Chinese* are one of those nations that deserve particular notice for the apparent evidences which they present, in their traditions as well as in their language, of a very remote antiquity. Reserving the subject of their language to be considered in the next chapter, we shall here only speak of their traditions, which refer the foundation of their empire to a period many thousands of years before the Christian era; relating that their country was then invaded, from the mountainous region on the northwest, by a race of conquerors, who found it occupied by barbarous tribes, and partly extirpated these aboriginal inhabitants, compelling those whom they spared to adopt their language and customs. The conquerers, we think, may be most reasonably supposed to have been a race of the same origin as the people that they subdued, but altered in their physical characteristics, during many successive generations, by a nomadic life in the deserts of Central Asia. It would seem that they gradually absorbed or exterminated the aborigines. And if their civilization be not as ancient as they pretend it to be, it may, perhaps, have been learned from wanderers of the race of Cain, whose first journeying is recorded to have been eastward, and from whom sprang the first persons known as originators of arts. The Arabs in their nomadic state have ever been remarkable for their backwardness in arts; and so have the Mongolians; but the Arabs have become equally remarkable for the facility with which they have learned arts from others, and for their having made these arts exclusively their own by a peculiar and admirable development; and so, as it appears from their own traditions, have the Mongolians who compose the population of China. Rude kinds of sculpture and painting are common among barbarous peoples; but very different from such arts are those which are peculiar to the Chinese, a people eminent for imitative skill, and also the inventors of printing, of the magnetic needle, of gunpowder, of silk fabrics, and of porcelain.

Even independently of their chronology, which may be greatly exaggerated, it is clear that the Chinese traditions favour the belief in the existence of Pre-Adamites: for we can hardly suppose a people to have *sunk* into a state of barbarism like that of the traditional aborigines of China (a state into which the Arabs are not known to have ever become degraded), and then to have attained a signal proficiency in arts through the influence of a foreign race of invaders.

The same may be said of the traditions of many other nations, and particularly of those of the ancient *Greeks* and *Romans*.

According to the concurrent testimony of antiquity, the Hellenes, whom we call the Greeks, were not the first inhabitants of their country: yet they seem to have settled there very soon after the dispersion from Babel. Their legends represent them as descended from Hellen, a son of Deucalion and Pyrrha, who were saved from a great flood; and they were long divided into four tribes; namely, the Dorians,

Æolians, Ionians, and Achæans; said to be the progeny of Dorus and Æolus the sons of Hellen, and of Ion and Achæus the sons of Xuthus the son of Hellen. Hence alone we would not venture to infer that the Hellenes were early descendants of Noah; nor from Plutarch's mention of the dove which Deucalion sent forth from his ark. But we have stronger reasons for doing so: the Ionians (called by Homer, Il. xiii. 685, 'Ιάονες,) are generally held to be the "Javan" (pronounced "Yāvān") of the Bible: the Æolians are identified by Josephus among the ancients, and by several of the moderns, with descendants of "Elishah" the son of Javan; or Elishah, according to some, denotes "Elis," an Æolian settlement: and as the "Dodanim" of our English Bible is "Rodanim" in the Samaritan and Septuagint versions and according to Jerome, and the d and r are so nearly alike in Hebrew, and sometimes, in the most ancient known alphabet of that language, even identical, the right reading may perhaps be "Doranim;" and the people meant thereby, the Dorians. But to establish that "Javan" denotes the Ionians would alone suffice; for the latter appellation is often applied to *all* the ancient Greeks; and variations thereof are generally, if not always, so applied in the languages of neighbouring peoples on the east and south; in the ancient Egyptian and the Arabic, the Syriac, the Sanskrit, and the old Persian. According to common consent, "Javan" means "Greece" in Dan. viii. 21, and Zech. ix. 13, and other passages in the Bible; and "the Greeks" are meant by "the sons of the Javanites" in Joel iii. 6.

There appears, therefore, to be at least a preponderance of probability that the Hellenes were among the earliest Noachian emigrants from Babel: and if so, their traditions clearly point to an ante-diluvian people not destroyed by the deluge of Noah; for they represent Greece, before the Hellenic immigration, with part of Asia Minor and Italy, as mostly, or wholly, occupied by the Pelasgians. Of the origin of this earlier race, of which the Arcadians are said by Pliny to have been the most ancient, and with which other races appear to have been intermixed, we naturally find no credible or uniform accounts: in some of the traditions, they are said to be autochthons, offspring of the soil: in others, nomadic immigrants. They are generally represented as a rude and barbarous people; but in Greece they became gradually blended with the Hellenes (mostly, it seems, with the Ionians, who are called by Herodotus, in Book i. chapter 56, a Pelasgian people, while the Dorians, apparently from their having kept more apart, are called by him Hellenes); and hence, Pelasgian elements are found to characterize the language and the religion of the later race. Thus the mixed origin of the Greeks of history, and of their dialects and mythology, appears to be well established: and numerous roots which are common to the Greek and Hebrew languages lend support to the traditions which state that the Greeks received

HISTORICAL OBSERVATIONS. 195

colonies from Phœnicia, whence they obtained their alphabet, and also from Egypt, of which the language, as we shall show in our concluding chapter, was partly Semitic, and of which the religion was in many respects analogous to the Greek.

The three principal stages in the progress of false religions, exclusive of astrolatry, to the third of which belongs the idolatry of the Greeks, are, by Epiphanius (a writer of the fourth century of our era, quoted by Cory in his "Ancient Fragments," pp, 53-55), termed "Barbarism," "Scythism," and "Hellenism." The first, according to him, extended from the days of Adam to those of Noah; during which period, he says, every one "was at liberty to follow the dictates of his own inclination." But, according to our own view, the first form of religion mentioned by him was the nature-worship of the Negroes, and of those who inherited from them this superstition. The appellation which he applies to it (being radically identical with the existing name of a great race of Northern Africa, whence "Barbary," and also with that of the two principal races of Nubians inhabiting the valley of the Nile above Egypt, with that of a district of Upper Nubia, with that of a place on the African shore of the Gulf of Aden, and with a name applied by the ancient Egyptians to a race of Africa, apparently Negroes,) strongly confirms our opinion of its proper application. The second stage, "Scythism," he asserts to have extended from the days of Noah to those of

Peleg and Reu; and among the nations bordering upon Europe, to the age of Terah, and afterwards; and he says that the Thracians were of this religion. He represents it as a kind of demonolatry; and thus it correctly applies to the Shamanism of Mongolian tribes. The third stage he describes as that of the worship of pictures and images of honoured ancestors. He says "that the Egyptians and Babylonians and Phrygians and Phœnicians were the first propagators of this superstition of making images, and of the mysteries: from whom it was transferred to the Greeks [Hellenes] from the time of Cecrops downwards. But it was not till afterwards, and at a considerable interval, that Cronus and Rhea, Zeus and Apollo, and the rest, were esteemed and honoured as Gods." (Cory's Transl.) These three kinds of religion Epiphanius thus represents as originating, successively, before Judaism and Christianity, and as, with them, constituting five stages of progress. The heresy which emanated from Arabia, mainly a compound of the last two of the above-named religions, may be mentioned as the only great retrograde movement. But in speaking thus of five stages of progress, let us not be supposed to hint the impious opinion, that Judaism was a *natural* advance from an older form of religion, and Christianity a *human* improvement of Judaism; though we believe that there was a time when all mankind, like the greater portion of them in later ages, possessed nothing higher than *natural religion*; when the Supreme Being was only "understood by the things that are made;" these things being the first in the progressive series of his manifestations of "his eternal power and godhead."

The traditions of the Romans respecting the nations that preceded them in the occupation of their country are similar to those of the Hellenes respecting the earliest occupants of Greece; but more vague and uncertain; particularly as to the Etruscans; of whose origin the most discordant opinions still obtain; whose language is almost unknown; whose religion was the model after which that of Rome was in a great measure framed; and who are famous for their progress in various arts, from a rude and barbarous backwardness to a very high degree of proficiency, which, in painting and sculpture, was chiefly attained by imitation of the Greeks. Nature-worship, which is more conspicuous in the religions of ancient Italy and Sicily than it is in the religion of Greece, the Bible warrants us in regarding as having originated with men who had no express revelation; as we have shown in speaking of the Negroes.

Of the origins of other European nations we have no trustworthy information beyond that conveyed in the Bible, showing that those nations comprise descendants of Japheth. But their general physical characteristics, while agreeable with a near relationship to the known Shemites, are such as, in our opinion, indicate that they have mainly sprung from a mixture of Noachians (doubtless Japhethites) with older races, of which latter the Finns and Lapps are almost entirely pure remnants.

Such, we believe, are the principal ethnological facts and traditions which monuments and books have made known to us respecting the earliest historical ages and the times preceding them; and all concur to confirm the inference which we have drawn from the Bible of the existence of Pre-Adamites.

CHAPTER VI.

PHILOLOGICAL OBSERVATIONS.

The principal results of the latest researches in comparative philology, considered as illustrative of ethnology, have been amply and ably exhibited by Baron Bunsen, in his work entitled "Outlines of the Philosophy of Universal History, applied to Language and Religion;" and though many of the opinions expressed in it are inconsistent with our own, it is a work from which we have derived much valuable information respecting the intricate and difficult subject that we have now to consider, and of which we shall therefore largely avail ourselves in this concluding portion of our inquiry.

The following scheme (distinguishing three kinds of speech, the monosyllabic, the agglutinate, and the amalgamate,) will show our view of the mutual relations of the families of language to which the observations that we are about to offer will chiefly apply. The term "agglutinate" is employed to denote languages in which the significations of roots are varied by affixes or prefixes, but not by internal modification: "amalgamate," languages in which the significations of roots are varied by internal modification as well as by affixes or prefixes.

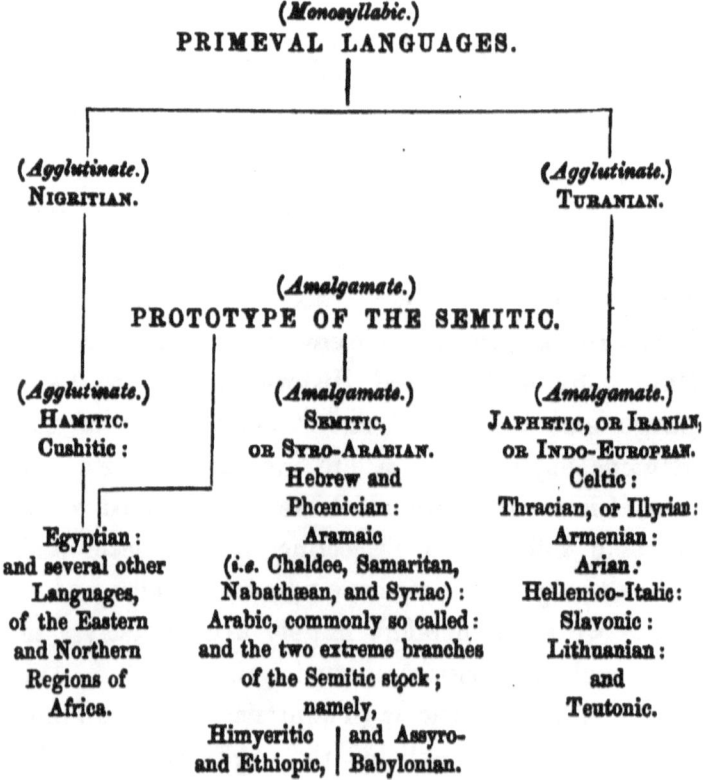

This scheme is at variance with the opinions of Baron Bunsen in two very important points: first, in representing the Semitic stock as in no way derived from a primeval language, though it may have received many Turanian roots; whereas he regards it as having probably a common origin with the

Turanian and Iranian: and secondly, in representing the Egyptian, which he terms "Khamitism," or "Chamitism," as being, from the first, collateral to the Semitic (properly so called); while he regards it as being "Ante-historical Semitism." If he be right respecting these two points, we must infer, as it appears to us, either that there have existed Pre-Adamites of our species, or that the portion of the Bible which relates to the ante-diluvian period consists of faulty and vague traditions: for his theory requires an enormous extension of the longest chronology that is consistent with the historical truth of the book of Genesis. If our own opinion respecting them be correct, then the former inference without the latter seems to us to be inevitable, though not at first sight so strikingly obvious.

"Languages compared together and considered as objects of the natural history of the mind, and when separated into families according to the analogies existing in their internal structure," says the late venerable author of "Cosmos," "have become a rich source of historical knowledge; and this is probably one of the most brilliant results of modern study in the last sixty or seventy years. From the very fact of their being products of the intellectual force of mankind, they lead us, by means of the elements of their organism, into an obscure distance, unreached by traditionary records. The comparative study of languages shows us that races now separated by vast tracts of land are allied together, and have migrated from one common primitive seat; it indicates the course and direction of all migrations, and, in tracing the leading epochs of development, recognises, by means of the more or less changed structure of the language, in the permanence of certain forms, or in the more or less advanced destruction of the formative system, *which* race has retained most nearly the language common to all who had emigrated from the general seat of origin." ("Cosmos:" Otté's Transl. vol. ii. p. 471.) This is clearly true, with some restriction. Comparative philology enables us to trace *many* races, but certainly *not all* the races of mankind, to one seat of origin.

We generally find that physical and philological characteristics agree in their indications of the relations of different divisions of mankind. In most of the instances in which it is known that they do not thus agree, history explains the reasons of the exceptions to the general rule.

More than one half of our species consists of nations of whose origins we possess no authentic record; and by far the greater portion of this large division of mankind consists of races which are physically similar, composing what is commonly called the Mongolian variety, and speak either monosyllabic or agglutinate languages; both of which kinds of language are distinguished by characteristics from which they may be inferred to have originated with artless, uncivilized, illiterate races; while forms of speech more rude and inartificial are found to obtain among races living almost in a state of nature, whose physical characteristics connect them very nearly with the Nigritians. All the races of these varieties, and all others in a state of barbarism or semi-barbarism, exhibiting no evidences of any past intermixture with civilized nations, appear to be distinguished by inferior linguistic progress, as well as physically, though in different degrees, from nearly all the rest of mankind, inasmuch as their most advanced languages known to us display but small approaches, if any, towards amalgamation.

The languages of almost all the nations renowned in history compose two widely-distinct families, both of them amalgamate, and characterized by very high degrees of refinement; namely, the Semitic, or Syro-Arabian; and the Japhetic, or Indo-European, also called Iranian and Arian: and part of a third family; namely, the Hamitic; comprising the Egyptian, which is composed of elements found in the first, and of other elements which are found in the second and appear to be traceable to an African origin. The first and second are the languages of nations of one predominant physical type, and generally distinguished by their superior civilization above every other people : the most famous language of the third family was spoken by a nation (that of ancient Egypt) in which we have shown that the same type was blended with one of a much lower character: and sacred and profane history, combined with monuments and other evidences, elucidate the originations of these three remarkable families of language.

If every people always retained the original character of its language, we might most reasonably infer that all races distinguished by monosyllabic languages are of earlier origin than any of those whose languages are agglutinate; and that all those races whose languages are agglutinate are of earlier origin than those whose languages are amalgamate. But as they do not always retain that character, much caution should be exercised in drawing such inferences. It is, however, a most remarkable fact, that the amalgamate languages are wholly confined to races purely or predominantly of the Caucasian variety, except in instances in which persons of other races are known to have *adopted* such languages. We might suppose that all mankind were originally of the highest type; and that, during the progress of speech from the monosyllabic to the amalgamate, some families or tribes branched off from the main stock, and degenerated by physical and other causes: but we have shown, in another chapter, that physical facts are strongly opposed to such a hypothesis.

Identity or similarity in the languages of two or more peoples in different countries, when their physical characteristics are the same or similar, obviously affords a strong presumptive evidence that they have originated from a common stock. But identity or similarity in the languages of two or more physically-distinct races inhabiting the same country indicates that one has imposed its language upon the other or others. Thus, for instance, the Arab settlers in Egypt gradually imposed their language upon the Copts.

Difference of the essential characters in the languages of two or more peoples in different countries, when their physical characteristics are the same or similar, affords no evidence of their having originated from different stocks, but is attributable to an intermixture of some of them with foreigners whose language or languages they have adopted, or modified, or remodelled, and enriched with new words. Thus, languages essentially different from those of Nigritia are spoken by Negroes who have mixed with Europeans; English being spoken by the Negroes of the Republic of Liberia, as well as by those of the United States of America; and French by those of Hayti.

A mixed language obtaining in one country indicates a mixture of races; and the *grammar* of that language, by its being unmixed or mixed, is an index to the number or power of one race in comparison with the other at the period of the formation of the mixed language; a great superiority of number or power in the intruding race being necessary to enable them to abolish altogether, or even partially, the grammar of the race among whom they have settled, though they easily and necessarily introduce a multitude of new words. Teutonic tribes changed the grammar of the Latin in forming the Spanish, Portuguese, Italian, Wallachian, and French, languages.

but the language of England, though made Teutonic in grammar by the Saxon invaders, has retained this grammatical character in spite of the Norman conquest.

It is in those cases with respect to which both history and monuments are silent, that comparative philology affords the most valuable illustrations; and we shall therefore now employ it as a test of the correctness of the opinions which we have advanced concerning the originations of the principal varieties of mankind.

In the passages of the Bible in which we are told, according to our authorized version, that "the whole earth was of one language, and of one speech," until the Dispersion from Babel, and that "the Lord did there confound the language of all the earth," we believe that the word rendered "earth" means, as it does in many other instances, "land," or "region," and applies only to the part occupied by the descendants of Adam, through Noah. We think that this will be evinced to the satisfaction of an unprejudiced mind by facts to be mentioned in the course of the following observations, though the fact of the Dispersion itself is one without which the originations of the languages of almost all the nations famous in antiquity can hardly be explained.

All competent judges agree as to two points, which are, indeed, indisputable; that the Semitic languages compose a distinct family, very closely united among themselves; and that the Iranian languages compose another distinct family, though not so closely united. But many of the most accomplished scholars of the present age, among whom Bunsen and Max Müller hold prominent places, maintain that all the languages of the world have most probably originated from one; and hence they argue that all mankind have descended from a single pair. Others hold, with ourselves, that the Semitic languages cannot with any just reason be supposed to be derived, through the medium of any other language or languages, from a rude primeval form of speech: and further, that the Iranian languages cannot be derived from the Turanian, nor the Turanian from a still earlier language, such as the ancient Chinese.

The opinion of the latter party, so far as it relates only to the Semitic languages, obviously favours the belief in the existence of Pre-Adamites: and as relating to other languages, it has been urged in confirmation of the hypothesis that man is of many independent origins. One of the latest of the writers who have advocated this view of the origins of languages, M. Ernest Renan, after having adduced and reviewed the opinions of many distinguished scholars, in his "Histoire Générale et Système Comparé des Langues Sémitiques" (p. 475), states in the following manner the principal ethnological conclusions to which his studies of comparative philology, aided by history, have led him :—

"La philologie comparée, aidée par l'histoire, arrive, non pas certes à résoudre, mais à circonscrire le problème des origines de l'espèce humaine. Elle établit avec une entière certitude l'unité de la grande race indo-européenne ; or cette race étant évidemment destinée à s'assimiler toutes les autres, avoir établi l'unité de la race indo-européenne, ce sera, aux yeux de l'avenir, avoir établi l'unité du genre humain.—Elle rattache d'une manière très-vraisemblable à la race indo-européenne la race sémitique, inséparable de la première dans l'histoire de la civilisation.—Elle permet de rapporter à la même famille les races chamites et couschites, et arrive ainsi à montrer comme possible l'unité de toutes les races qui ont fondé la civilisation dans l'ouest de l'Asie, dans l'Europe, dans le nord et l'est de l'Afrique.— Elle fixe avec une vraisemblance presque égale à la certitude le point de départ de la race arienne dans l'Hindoukousch ou le Belourtag, et elle rattache volontiers à ce même point le berceau de la race sémitique.—Elle répugne à en faire autant pour la race chinoise, et surtout pour les races inférieures qui durent former la première couche de la population du globe.—Elle établit d'une manière approximative l'ordre chronologique selon lequel ces races diverses sont entrées dans l'histoire, et la date relativement moderne de l'apparition des races civilisées. —Enfin, elle attend sur tous ces points des lumières nouvelles de l'étude encore si peu avancée des idiomes de l'Asie centrale et de l'Afrique, prête à renoncer devant les faits à toute hypothèse préconçue, et persuadée que, dans l'état actuel de la science, tout système ne peut être que provisoire, si l'on compare le peu que l'on sait à la masse énorme de ce qu'il est encore possible de savoir."

It is particularly remarkable that the statement which we have here quoted, in assigning a higher antiquity to the barbarous than to the civilized races, as well as in several other points, agrees with inferences drawn by Baron Bunsen and others from their opinion that all languages are connected by unity of origin; though M. Renan's opinion of languages (which is urged with much learning, but not always with sound criticism,) is decidedly opposed to the notion of their being all thus connected. On both of these opinions we must offer some observations; but more particularly on the former of them, for two reasons: first, because it has often been urged in support of the tenet that all mankind are of one origin, though obviously consistent with the theory of their production by several successive creations: secondly, because we hold it to be correct as to the doctrine that monosyllabic languages preceded agglutinate, and that agglutinate languages preceded amalgamate. This we shall do chiefly in the form of an examination of the facts and arguments adduced by Bunsen in his "Outlines," as far as they affect the main question discussed in the present work: and first we shall exhibit his classification of languages (founded upon his own and others' researches), and the manner in which he holds them to be traceable to one common origin.

The languages of the "SEMITIC STOCK" compose a group which, with the Egyptian, a language but partially belonging to that stock, Bunsen thus arranges:—

"A. *Chamitism*, or Ante-historical Semitism: the Chamitic deposit in Egypt; its daughter, the Demotic Egyptian; and the Coptic, its end.

"B. *The Chaldee*: first, the original Babylonian, or the ancient sacred language of Babylonia and mother of historical Semitism; secondly, the Chaldee of Babylonia and Mesopotamia, or the most ancient North Semitic stock; thirdly, its latest phasis, the Jewish and Christian Chaldee in the book of Daniel and the Targum, and in the Christian Chaldee or the Syrian (Aramæan).

"C. *The Arabic*, or South Semitic stock, in its two branches: the Himyaric, with its Abyssinian deposit; and the language of Northern Arabia, with the Amalekite [?] dialect of the Sinaitic inscriptions.

"D. *The Hebrew*, or the language of the Bible from the Mosaic records to the age of the Maccabees, with its dialect, the Canaanite language (Phœnician and Carthaginian). It forms the younger branch of the North Semitic stock." (Vol. i. pp. 183 and 184.)

Here, at the outset, we feel compelled to differ from Baron Bunsen, not only with respect to the Egyptian language, as we have before shown, but also with respect to the relation of all the principal dialects of this stock; for we regard them as standing to each other in the relation of *sisters;* that is to say,

PHILOLOGICAL OBSERVATIONS.   211

as deriving their common elements from one parent or prototype, and severed, nearly simultaneously, in consequence of the Dispersion from Babel. And we must further observe, that the language which Bunsen calls "the original Babylonian" appears to have originated in *Assyria*, and is found to have been *preceded* in the kingdom of *Babylonia* by a language of a kind analogous to the *Turanian*: we therefore term it the *Assyro*-Babylonian."

Of the "IRANIAN STOCK," Bunsen says, "Eight more or less extensive historical families or single nations have been ascertained to constitute one great Asiatic-European stock, of which even the remotest members speak original languages, more intimately connected with each other than with any third tongue, or family of tongues, in the world. We have called this stock the Iranian, according to a terminology which recommends itself by many advantages. [In terming it also "Japhetic," we must express our belief that several of its members, though modified and developed by Japhethites, *originated*, as distinct languages, in Pre-Adamite times, or, at least, before the Noachian Deluge; holding this event to have taken place about the period to which it is referred by the Septuagint-chronology, whereas Bunsen refers it to a period about seven thousand years earlier.]

"The *first* great branch of this stock are the *Celts*, once spread over Asia Minor (Galatia), Spain, France, Belgium, Helvetia, a great part of Germany, and throughout the British Isles: it lives still in the

Kymric (of which the Bas Breton is a corrupted form), as the language of Wales, and in two cognate forms, the Gaelic and the Erse, as the native tongue of the Highlands of Scotland, and of the whole of Ireland. This family we consider as representing the most ancient formation of the whole stock. . . .

"The *second* branch is the *Thracian* or *Illyrian*, once spread on the Dnieper, the Hellespont, and in Asia Minor, in which countries it was followed, and partly supplanted, by the *Pelasgian*, or ante-historical formation of the Hellenic. [But the comparative antiquity of the Pelasgic language is extremely uncertain, as we know very little of its character. According to Herodotus (lib. i. cap. 57), the inference to be drawn from the general speech of the Pelasgi of his time is that the Pelasgic was "a barbarous language:" and Mr. Grote (in a note in vol. ii. p. 356 of his "History of Greece") affirms that "we have no means of deciding whether the language of the Pelasgians differed from the Greek as Latin or as Phœnician."] . . . The languages of the Epirots and Macedonians belong to this family, which is now represented in those countries by the Skipetarian, the language of the Albanians or Arnauts.

"The *third* is the *Armenian*, the language spoken during the historical age in the country which, according to the most ancient traditions of the Semites, was the cradle of mankind, and again the primeval seat of man after the deluge of Noah.

"The *fourth* formation we propose to call the

Arian, or the Iranian stock as presented in Iran Proper. Here we must establish two great subdivisions. The one comprises the nations of Iran Proper, or the Arian stock, the languages of Media and Persia. Its most primitive representative is the *Zend*. We designate by this name both the language of the most ancient cuneiform inscriptions (or Persian inscriptions in Assyrian characters) of the sixth and fifth century B.C., and that of the ancient parts of the Zend-Avesta, or the sacred books of the Parsees, as explained by Burnouf and Lassen. We take the one as the latest specimen of the western dialect of the ancient Persian and Median (for the two nations had one tongue), in its evanescent state, as a dead language; the other as an ancient specimen of its eastern dialect, preserved for ages by tradition, and therefore not quite pure in its vocalism, but most complete in its system of forms. The younger representatives of the Persian language are the Pehlevi (the language of the Sassanians) and the Pazend, the mother of the present, or modern Persian tongue, which is represented in its purity by Ferdusi, about the year 1000 [of our era]. The Pushtu, or language of the Afghans, belongs to the same branch. The second subdivision embraces the Arian languages of India, represented by the Sanskrit and its daughters.

"The *fifth* branch is the *Hellenico-Italic*, or the Greek and Roman, and all the Italic languages, with the doubtful exception of the Etruscan, which at all events was a mixed language, having a groundwork kindred to Greek and Latin, with a great barbarian admixture. Under Italic tongues we understand the languages of Italy Proper, south of the Apennines [or Alps ?], and of the Italic Isles.

"The *sixth* branch is that of the *Slavonic* nations in their two great branches; the eastern, comprising the old Slavonic of the Bible and of Nestor, the Russian, Servian, Croatic, and Wendic; and the western, the languages of the Tschekhs (Bohemians) Slovacs, Poles, and Servians [?]. These languages, once prevalent in the north of Germany, are now spoken from the Adriatic to the Dnieper. In the ancient world, this great, powerful, and much-divided family is represented by the *Sauromatæ* of the Greeks, or the *Sarmatæ* of the Romans, a nation living on the Don and near the Caspian Sea. . . .

"The *seventh*, nearly allied to this and the next branch, that of the *Lithuanian* tribes, among which the ancient Prussian represents the most perfect form, is in some points nearer to the Sanskrit than any other existing tongue.

"*Finally*, last but not least, the *Teutonic nations* in their two families, the Scandinavian and the German. The first has preserved its most ancient form in the Icelandic; the Swedish and Danish are the modern daughters of the old Norse language of Scandinavia. The second is the German, now the language of the whole of Germany, and almost the whole of Switzerland. Its northern or Saxon form has received a peculiar individuality in the Flemish and Dutch tongues, and, by the emigrations which took place in the fifth century of our era, has become (mixed with French words since the Norman conquest) the prevalent and leading language of the British Isles, and is becoming now, by the emigrations which began in the seventeenth century, and are still continuing, that of the northern continent of America. The southern German tribes have successively formed, with a greater or less infusion of words into the Latin groundwork, the Italian, French, and Spanish languages." (Vol. ii. pp. 6-9.)

Respecting the "TURANIAN STOCK" of languages, Bunsen quotes the following observations of Professor Max Müller:

"The very absence of that close family likeness which holds the Semitic and Arian [or Iranian] languages together seems to form a distinguishing mark of these nomadic dialects. There is, however, one positive principle which pervades the whole Turanian speech, from its lowest to its highest manifestations, and which cannot be better expressed than by the name of 'agglutination.' This principle, which consists in the mere juxtaposition of material and formal elements, may seem so simple and purely mechanical as hardly to offer a distinctive attribute on which to establish a family of languages; still it forms so broad a line of demarcation, that neither in Turkish and Finnish, where the Turanian approaches nearest to the formative principles of Arian grammar, nor in the Tungusic and Taï dialects, where it verges towards Chinese simplicity, does it fail to keep the nomad type distinct from that of family or state languages. There are many ways in which the principle of agglutination can be applied; and the greater or less perfection to which it has been brought furnishes the best scale by which the close or distant relationship of Turanian languages can be determined. There is, however, besides this formal, a material relationship also between the members of this worldwide family; only that, owing to the very nature of these languages, its traces must be sought for in radicals only, and not, as in Greek and Sanskrit, in derivatives.

"The separation of the Turanian stock took place long before the ancestors of the Arian family left their common home; for wherever these Arian colonists penetrated, in their emigrations from east to west, they found the land occupied by the wild descendants of Tur. Through all periods of history, up to the present day, by far the largest share of the earth belongs to Tur; and the countries reclaimed by Shem and Japhet, although they mark the high road of civilization, and comprehend the stage on which the drama of ancient and modern history has been acted, are but small portions if compared with the vast expanse of the empire of the Turanian speech. [These remarks should be considered in connexion with the account of the migrations of the descendants of Noah, in the tenth chapter of Genesis, to which they obviously relate.] The Arian [or Iranian] and Semitic languages occupy but four peninsulas—India, Arabia, Asia Minor, and Europe: all the rest of the primeval continent of Asia belongs to the descendants of Tur.

"The chief branches of the Turanian stock all radiate from a common centre; though they are not, like the members of the Semitic and Arian families, descended from one common parent. Their geographical distance from China seems to indicate the successive dates of their original separation; and the different degrees of grammatical perfection to which they have each attained may likewise be measured by their distance from Chinese monosyllabism.

"There are two divisions, the Northern and the Southern.

"The northern division comprehends the Tungusic, Mongolic, Tataric, Samoïedic, and Finnic branches.

"The southern division comprehends the Taï, Malaïc, Bhotîya, and Tamulic branches.

"In the northern division the Tungusic and Mongolic, in the southern the Taï and Malaïc branches, are the nearest neighbours to the Chinese, not only in geographical position, but also by the low degree of their grammatical development.

"Next follow the Tataric in a northern, and the Bhotîya in a southern direction; the former spreading through Asia toward the European peninsula and the seats of political civilization, the latter tending toward the Indian peninsula, and encircling the native land of the Brahmanic Arians.

CHAPTER VI.

"The most distant branches of the Turanian stock, and therefore probably the first to attain an independent growth, are the Finnic in the north, and the Tamulic in the south. The regularity and settledness of the grammar of these languages bear witness to an early literary cultivation; of which in India nothing remains but tradition, owing to Brahmanic encroachment, while in the fens of Finland oral tradition has preserved up to our own time the songs of Wäinämöinen, and of his sacred home, Kalevala.

"Besides these regular radii of Turanian speech, there are still several sporadic clusters of dialects, equally belonging to this family, but severed from the rest by mountains or deserts. In their seclusion, and debarred from the severe attrition which every dialect experiences in the intercourse with other languages, they have each produced the utmost variety of grammatical forms, and revel in a luxuriance of verbal distinctions which small and secluded tribes alone are able to indulge in. These are the Caucasian languages, spoken in the impenetrable valleys of Mount Caucasus; the Basque, in the Pyrenees and on the very edge of Europe; and the Samöiedic, in the still less accessible Tundras of the North of Siberia.

"That all these branches of speech on the Asiatic continent form a historical unity in themselves and as opposed to Semitic and Arian races, is a conviction which has been gaining strength from year to year; and the connecting links of several branches have now been laid open by the skill of comparative philologists. Much, however, remains still to be done before the mutual relation of all these branches can be considered as finally settled. A further extension of this nomadic family of speech has been hinted at, not only with regard to America but even to Africa. In the former case, the bridge on which the seeds of Asiatic dialects could have been carried to the New World is clearly indicated by the researches of physical science; in the latter all is still conjecture, except this, that, besides the Semitic type of some African languages north of the equator, there is another grammatical character impressed on African idioms, such as the Hottentot, which, by its mechanical perfection and somewhat artificial complication, invites a comparison with the grammatical system of the descendants of Tur." (Vol. ii. pp. 17-20.)— This last remark confirms the inference drawn from physical resemblances, that the Chinese and the Hottentots are branches of early origination from the Nigritian stock. The language of Bornū, also, is particularly remarkable, as bearing considerable resemblance to Mongolian dialects, more especially to the Turkish, in having affixes to denote the cases of its nouns, the persons of its verbs, its plurals, and its possessive pronouns, and having, like the Coptic, negative verbs. Some further particulars respecting African languages will be found in future pages of this chapter.

Referring to the investigations upon which these

classifications of the three main stocks of language are founded, and in which he has examined the Iranian stock first, then the Semitic, and lastly the Turanian, Baron Bunsen makes the following general observations:—

"Adopting the principle of the strictest philosophical criticism, and the severest method of establishing the proofs of physical and historical kindred, we examined the languages of the nations of Asia and Europe in three great groups. Starting from the analysis of the Germanic and the classical languages, and examining those families which are incontestibly connected with them, we arrived by overwhelming evidence at the proof of the immediate unity in blood of by far the greater half of the civilized nations of the world.

"We then examined the languages of another great family, second in its importance to the civilization of mankind only to that first, generally called the Indo-Germanic stock, and we laid before our readers the documents which self-evidently establish the following facts. First, that the Semitic languages, commonly so called, form a most closely connected family among themselves. Secondly, that the Egyptian language, or the tongue of Kham, belongs to the same stock, but points, however, to a considerably more ancient period of mankind. Thirdly, that the cuneiform inscriptions of Babylonia exhibit to us a language in the transition from primordial to historical Semitism. (Here we rupt our extracts to observe, that the evidences upon which these remarks are founded seem to us to establish the inferences that the earliest known Egyptian language and the earliest Semitic, properly so called, occupy nearly synchronistic places, and that both intervene chronologically between the prototype and the known dialects of the Semitic. But this is not what is meant by Bunsen, as will be seen from what follows.]

"But, at the same time, we could not help seeing from an evidence which is similar in its character to that founded upon natural facts, that these two families, as they appear together in the same part of the earth, really belong to one and the same stock, and that Iranism and Semitism represent only members of one and the same family. [This we cannot admit; holding that the Semitic became allied to the Turanian only by the adoption of some, perhaps many, Turanian roots, and, not improbably, idioms also.]

"Now, following the same method, we discovered, in the third place, that all the remaining nations of Asia and Europe, which are neither Iranians nor Semites, form among themselves a third family, which is the greatest in extent, and reaches up to the most ancient formations. But, moreover, we found that this family, which in my Lecture of 1847 I had ventured to call Turanian, was intimately connected with the Iranian, and stands to it in a similar position as Khamitism to Semitism. It is primitive Iranism, one-sidedly and wildly modified and particularized. [Here we object to the inference that Khamitism is primitive Semitism; admitting only that the Egyptian language contains elements of the Semitic derived from the prototype of this latter, and holding that the Semitic elements found in other Hamitic languages are in like manner exotic.]

"Thus we arrived at two great historical facts: first, that the four great families of the historical times, reduce themselves to two, the Iranians and the Semites; the one having its primordial roots [or rather many of them] in Turanism, and the other in Khamitism; secondly, that by a more close and methodical investigation both prove to be originally, and, therefore, physically cognate among each other; or, in other words, that, as far as the organic languages of Asia and Europe are concerned, the human race is of one kindred, of one descent. [We shall have to offer some remarks on this inference in future pages.]

"Now the question arises, if those two great families are thus united, is not their unity represented by some positive primitive formation? All the facts hitherto examined lead us to assume, that this formation must have differed from even the most ancient historical Turanism, or Khamitism, in a similar manner as inorganic nature differs from the first organic formations.

"Those strata of organic structure are, therefore, necessarily underlaid by an inorganic, or as it were crystalline language, which according to all probabilities is preserved in the ancient Chinese, on which the Turanian formations are bordering internally, as they do geographically. This development requires a period of time which may appear very long according to the traditional ideas of the extent of human history; but, in fact, is very short and recent if we look back upon the history of the earth and of her lower productions." (Vol. ii. pp. 3-5.)

Pursuing the same course of reasoning, Baron Bunsen says, in a later portion of his work,

" Our historical researches respecting language have led us to facts which seemed to oblige us to assume the common historical origin of the great families into which we found the nations of Asia and Europe to coalesce. The four families of Turanians and Iranians, of Khamites and Shemites, reduced themselves to two, and these again possessed such mutual material affinities as can neither be explained as accidental nor as being so by a natural external necessity, but they must be historical, and therefore imply a common descent.

"The philosophical inquiry showed us that the monosyllabic or particle language on which the most ancient of these formations border, both the Turanian in the East and the Khamitic in the West, is the formation which must be supposed theoretically to have preceded the organic or formative language. Every word was a sentence before it could become a specific part of speech; and either every language separately must once have been like the Chinese, or the Chinese itself is the wreck of that primitive idiom from which all the organic (or Noachian) languages have physically descended, each representing a phasis of development. Such a phasis itself would, under the latter supposition, be a necessary element in the evolutions of the idea in time, a link in an uninterrupted chain of development." (Vol. ii. p. 99.)

That forms of speech of the same kind as the ancient Chinese preceded the agglutinate languages, we are fully persuaded; and now we must proceed to consider whether the former may not have been preceded by languages yet more simple. This is a point which cannot at present, and which perhaps never will, be certainly established; but we have strong reason to think that it was the case. The ancient Chinese language, simple as it is, appears to us to be too conventional and systematic to have originated, as the first form of speech, from a people living in a state of nature; and the facts of its being composed of a small number of monosyllabic words (said to be only four hundred and fifty), and varying the senses of these words by two, three, or four differences of tone, or accent, suggest that it may be reasonably supposed to have been preceded by languages commencing with almost inarticulate sounds. Now it is very remarkable that a language of the rudest conceivable kind appears to obtain in the present day; and it is also remarkable, as agreeing with our opinion of the successive productions of the varieties of man, that it obtains among a secluded race whom we have mentioned as very nearly resembling the Nigritians in features and in complexion and in having short woolly hair. Dr. Pickering, in his valuable work entitled "The Races of Man" (Bohn's edition, p. 305), quotes an account of this "so-called Original People," of the Malayan Peninsula, "from a printed sheet obtained at Singapore," "derived partly from the Malays and partly from people of neighbouring tribes," in which it is stated that "their language is not understood by any one; they lisp their words, the sound of which is like the noise of birds, and their utterance is very indistinct." He remarks that "what is stated of their language is the more worthy of note when it is considered that the dialects of the neighbouring and closely-related tribes belong to the Malay class," whose language, we have before mentioned, is one of those dialects of the Turanian stock least advanced beyond the stage of Chinese simplicity; and he adds that in the condition of "the Wild People of Borneo," who are described as "living absolutely in a state of nature," "treated by the Dayaks as wild beasts," "building no habitations of any kind, and eating nothing but fruits, snakes, and monkeys," yet procuring excellent iron, and making blades sought after by every Dayak, "it seems questionable whether a language of words is really needed." (See Note 9.)

Without supposing a very rude commencement, and a very slow development of the languages of the first separate branches of mankind, we can hardly account for the great variety, combined with a kind of general family-likeness, found to subsist in almost all the languages of barbarous and semi-barbarous races with which we are acquainted, unless we adopt the theory that those races originated from several different pairs in different regions, and that the analogies in their languages have resulted partly from a kind of common instinct and partly from intermixture. But in supposing that the first form of speech was of an extremely rude kind, corresponding to an extreme simplicity and paucity of thoughts, we do not entertain the opinion that the primeval man was essentially inferior in nature to his descendants, and that he thus in some degree resembled the most intelligent of the brutes; for we regard the first of our species, like the more advanced of his progeny, as endowed with a faculty of speech proportioned to his necessities. Our admiration must increase as we consider languages of higher and higher degrees of excellence; but the rudest conceivable kind of speech is marvellous enough to exalt the nature of man immeasurably above that of the brute creation, and a language adequate to the wants of a people is to that people a *perfect* language. It seems, then, that we should find the character of the first form of speech most nearly represented by the rudest language spoken by a people in a state of nature : not by the ancient *Chinese* language, which was adapted to the wants of a nation considerably advanced in civilization, even without the principle of agglutination, which we find to have been adopted in its modern dialects.

Hence it appears to us to be most probable that the agglutinate languages were preceded by forms of speech of the same kind as the ancient Chinese; and these by a yet more simple kind, which (as such a language is found to belong to a people who seem to be evidently a very early offshoot from the Nigritian stock) may be probably inferred to be of African origin, and, by reason of its excessive rudeness, to be of the primeval class. An additional argument for this inference will be found in a statement some pages later, respecting the languages of the various races resembling the Nigritians in features or in complexion, or in both of these characteristics, in many of the islands between the Indian and Pacific Oceans.

It does not necessarily follow that those parts of the globe in which we now find languages of the supposed earliest kind were the first seats of the human race. Bunsen, arguing that the ancient Chinese is probably the primeval form of speech, observes, that "colonists may either preserve the ancient form, or become the instruments of a great change. The early languages of Northern Asia, which, according to Chinese tradition, is the land of their earliest recollections, [or rather the land from which their country—previously occupied by barbarous tribes—was invaded by the race that established there the first dynasty of their kings] may have been preserved by the colonists who formed the Chinese empire, while Thibet and Mongolia developed the inorganic language into organic structures." (Vol. ii. p. 102.) And in like manner, we may suppose that emigrants from Nigritia, scattering themselves throughout the Malayan region, retained a form of speech of the earliest kind, while the parent stock, remaining together, naturally improved and developed their language. Physical indications of relationship, which, in the absence of history, are our surest guides in the application of comparative philology to the illustration of ethnology, lead us to this inference.

Having now reached the highest point to which these philological investigations can ascend, let us pause to consider whether their necessary consequences agree, or disagree, with Sacred History.

If we regard Adam as the first of all mankind, this general view of the origin and development of language, supposing it to be admitted, obliges us to reduce a great part of the history of the book of Genesis to the category of faulty and vague traditions, as we have before observed. It has induced Baron Bunsen to assert, "that a concurrence of facts and of traditions demand for the Noachian period about ten millennia before our era, and for the beginning of our race," which he evidently commences with Adam, "another ten thousand years, or very little more" (Vol. ii. p. 12): and though this vast period of about twenty thousand years may be considerably reduced by refusing our assent to his derivation of the Semitic languages from the Egyptian, still there will remain, according to his estimate, about ten thousand years to set against the few antediluvian generations in the Bible.

Now we will not insist upon the probable correctness of this estimate, when thus reduced; yet we cannot make such a further reduction as would much lessen the difficulty arising, in the present case, from the small number of the generations that intervened between Adam and Noah, even on the supposition (which we think reasonable) that females are omitted in the line of Noah's ancestors. For it is a necessary consequence of the theory under examination that the full growth and development of the Turanian class of languages, requiring a very long succession of ages, must have preceded the origination of the ancient Egyptian, which can be traced, on monuments, up to a time not more than about three centuries later than the earliest date assignable to the Dispersion from Babel, consistently with belief in the historical truth of the book of Genesis. We say that this is a necessary consequence of the theory under examination, because the ancient Egyptian language exhibits a manifest improvement on what is termed Turanism; occupying an intermediate place, as to its vocabulary and grammar, between a language of a kind resembling the Turanian (with elements of Iranian) on the one side and the Semitic languages on the other.

But if we have correctly rendered those passages

in the Bible which we regard as indications of the existence of Pre-Adamites, then the history of mankind as far as it is exhibited in the Scriptures, and the history of language as far as we are able to elicit it by the strictest and surest methods of critical investigation, not only agree, but signally confirm each other. In order to show this more plainly, we will now retrace our steps, and consider the principal phases of speech from the monosyllabic (which claims to be regarded as the earliest of all) down to the two most perfect classes.

It is our opinion, as we have already stated, that the first form of speech was of an extremely rude kind, commencing with almost-inarticulate sounds: and the natural progress of every language we believe to have been one from confusion and incongruity, which necessarily occasioned division into different dialects, like varieties of a species; these, in process of time, becoming more or less modified, and generally simplified in structure, by foreign influences.

But let us once more consider the peculiar nature of the ancient Chinese language, and its asserted claim to be regarded as the earliest form of speech.

"If language," says Bunsen, "exhibit a principle of development by a gradual increase of the sensibility of the single words in reference to the whole of the sentence, and by conglomerations or compositions arising out of this sensibility, such a development points to, rather than excludes, a state of language where there was no such sensibility at all, not even so far as to give, by the unity of accent, a certain organic union to two rigidly separate words into one. Such an insensibility then would be normal, primitive, not a consequence of decayed organization. Do not the phenomena of the old Chinese look very much like such a formation? and as no less than a third part of mankind speaks in tongues of this nature, will it not be worth our while to consider well its original and peculiar character before we pronounce for or against the genealogical unity of the human race? We must, at all events, allow that the phenomena present no difficulty in assuming that a given inorganic language may have passed through such a state as the old Chinese represents compared with the modern. On the contrary, the Chinese phenomenology confirms the supposition that the law of secondary formation in language is universal. The process of dissolution, which prepared in the Chinese the very first germ of development and the approach to organic language, is one and the same with that observable and traceable in all other languages." (Vol. ii. p. 70.) Again, speaking of "that great monument of inorganic structure, the Chinese," he says, "We have already intimated, that it may be joined on to the other families of human speech, by the least developed Turanian. There is no scientific proof that it cannot: the law of analogy says, it must; philological and philosophical arguments combine to show the method of verifying the fact." (Vol. ii. p. 119.) And again, "The study of the

CHAPTER VI.

Tibetan or Bhotîya language, and that of the Burmese, offers the nearest link between the Chinese and the more recent formations; but even a comparison with Sanskrit roots is indicated by our method. For it is the characteristic of the noblest languages and nations that they preserve most of the ancient heirlooms of humanity, remodelling and universalizing it at the same time with productive originality." (Vol. ii. p. 120.)

Thus from the ancient Chinese to the Indo-European languages, we may trace distinct stages of improvement, which we regard as corresponding to stages of mental and social advancement: and if the first of mankind enjoyed a condition like that of Adam, we could hardly attribute to him a form of speech less perfect than that which Bunsen supposes to have been the parent of all other languages. But facts, in our opinion, point to a condition of primeval humanity much less enlightened than that of Adam; a condition in which a language like the ancient Chinese would have been beyond the wants of man, and therefore unnatural.

Certain scattered and isolated tribes of Negroes, and of races very nearly allied to the Negroes, living almost, if not absolutely, in a state of nature, appear to be the rudest of all mankind in their forms of speech. The ancient language of an outlying and isolated portion of the Mongolian variety, namely, the Chinese, is, as we have before observed, adapted to the wants of a nation considerably advanced in civilization, but is of a more simple kind than are the languages of the rest of that variety: so, too, though in a less degree, are the modern spoken dialects of the Chinese. And the languages of an isolated branch of the Indo-European stock, far removed from the place of origin, namely, the Celts, are, according to those whom we esteem the best judges, more ancient than the other languages of the same stock. Supposing, then, that the Negro race originated in Africa, we might, from analogy, reasonably expect to find their modern languages in that region to be more advanced than the form of speech which the ancient Chinese (that most exclusive nation) either originated or inherited and preserved: and this is the case.

The *African* languages are known to us chiefly through the recent researches of the Rev. S. W. Koelle and other missionaries: as yet, very incompletely; but sufficiently for our forming a correct opinion of their principal characteristics. They are generally of the agglutinate kind; and though most of them display great richness in the modifications of the significations of the verbs by means of prefixes or affixes (either in a manner somewhat like the Arabic or in a manner nearly resembling the Turkish), in other respects they exhibit a striking backwardness and poverty, expressing many of the most simple ideas by circumlocutions. They consist of numerous distinct groups; most of which, however, are pervaded by a general family-likeness; and of those that are known to us, all that are spoken by the *true Negroes*, together with several others, are entirely *alien from the Semitic*: but in the languages of countries on the east and north of the central region, in which countries the Negro type is modified by *Caucasian* traits, we find *an admixture of Semitic elements*, distinguishing them from those branches of the main African stock to which they are chiefly allied. The Ethiopic and the Punic, the latter a dialect of Phœnician, both of them Semitic in the strict sense of the term, were certainly spoken by races predominantly of the Caucasian variety; like as are now the Arabic dialects that have for many centuries obtained in Egypt and throughout the northernmost tract extending thence to the furthest limits of Morocco. The language of Bornū, and its resemblance to Mongolian dialects, we have noticed on a former occasion; and we have also remarked upon the linguistic as well as physical resemblances observable between Mongolian tribes and the Hottentots. (See page 219.)

Baron Bunsen, remarking upon the African languages, and holding them all to be ultimately referrible to an Asiatic origin, says, "There evidently has been a southern as well as a northern immigration." But for the supposition of a southern immigration, as a way of accounting for the prevalence of Non-Semitic languages in Africa, we can see no valid reason. He then adds, "The northern was certainly Semitic. The primitive state of Chamism, exhibiting the germ both of Semiticism [or Semitism] and of

Iranism, is left behind in both the northern and southern African formations. This development of theirs, however, does not run in the Semitic line. In the historical Semitic formations, the copula is constantly expressed by the pronominal form (*he*), whereas the Iranian possess the more abstract, and therefore more advanced verbal form (*to be*). In this decisive characteristic most African tongues agree with the Iranian [which (for reasons hereafter to be stated) we derive from Turanian dialects that received many elements found in Iranian from Africa]; as they do in the whole system of conjugation in opposition to the Semitic conjugation, as explained above. As the American, and, in a certain manner, all Turanian languages, are distinguished by their system of incorporation, and particularly by the agglutination of words, together with that of post-position ; so these African idioms bear the type of prefixes, and indicate the congruence, or grammatical position, of the parts of speech by changes in the initials of the words." (Vol. ii. pp. 116-118.)

In the foregoing extract the difference of most African languages from the Semitic is somewhat exaggerated ; though it is, in truth, very great. It cannot be said with propriety that, " in the historical Semitic formations, the copula is constantly expressed by the pronominal form (*he*)." In those formations, the copula is generally *understood*, not expressed : except in the technical phraseology of logic, the pronominal form is an *emphatic* mode of expressing it ;

or, to speak more correctly, the pronoun is in this case a substitute for the preceding noun, and the copula is still understood. But sometimes they express it in the same manner as the Iranian: in the Arabic, for instance, it is not unfrequently expressed by the abstract verb *kāna*, divested of all signification of time, as well as by *kāïnun*, the participial form of that verb. We should therefore say that, with respect to the copula, most of the African languages differ from the general usage of the Semitic, and agree with the Iranian. But though they thus exhibit one of the characteristics of the most advanced languages, their general backwardness has been established beyond doubt by the researches of Koelle, and is well exemplified by one of them, namely the Vei, which (as he has stated in his grammar of that language, page 19,) " is distinguished by an almost entire absence of inflexion." We must observe, also, that the remark which we have quoted respecting " the whole system of conjugation " in " most African tongues " appears to us to be one requiring modification or explanation.

The nations and tribes composing the great *Mongolian* family are distinguished by languages in which we trace various gradations, from the Chinese, now slightly advanced beyond monosyllabic simplicity, to the Turkish and Finnish, the most developed of the Turanian stock, but not passing beyond the agglutinate stage.

The *Malaïc* has been shown to belong to the Turanian class, and to be one of the Turanian languages nearest in the general character to the Chinese; and the languages prevailing throughout the whole Malayan region seem generally to belong to the same stock. On this point, Bunsen says, "I think that Wilhelm von Humboldt established the connexion between the Polynesian languages and the Malay, or the language of Malacca, Java, and Sumatra, and that this Malay language itself bears the character of the Turanian languages of Central Asia. Whether the Papua languages, spoken in Australia and New Guinea, and by the aborigines of Borneo, of the peninsula of Malacca, and some small Polynesian islands, be a primitive type of the same stock as the Malay, which afterwards in many parts superseded it, is a point which must be left undecided till we obtain from the missionaries a Papua grammar. Thus much, however, we know, that it is an earlier and very primitive formation, and one which will probably prove to have only degenerated." (Vol. ii. p. 114). This last observation, as applying to the very remote origin of certain languages, among which that of the "so-called Original People" of the Malayan Peninsula before mentioned seems to be included, confirms the opinion which we have expressed respecting the origin of the Papuans and Australians and similar races. And that opinion is further confirmed by an obvious linguistic connexion found to subsist between the Malayo-Polynesians, from Madagascar eastward, and several tribes of Inter-tropical and Southern Africa; unless those African tribes, or at least their languages, originated either wholly or partly in the region termed that of the Malays.

With respect to the *American* race, which we regard as a branch of the Mongolian variety, we borrow the following important observations from the work of Baron Bunsen. "It is not yet proved in detail, but it appears highly probable, in conformity with our general principles, that the native languages of the northern continent of America, comprising tribes and nations of very different degrees of civilization, from the Esquimaux of the polar regions to the Aztecs of Mexico, are of one origin, and a scion of the Turanian tribe. The similarity in the conformation of the skull renders this affinity highly probable. The wonderful analogy in the grammatical structure of these languages, with each other and with the Turanian tongues of Asia, is universally admitted; and we think that the curious and, at first sight, startling problem, of the apparent entire diversity of the lexicographical portion of those American languages, by the side of that grammatical affinity, will be satisfactorily accounted for upon a fuller acquaintance with the roots, and by the application of our principle of secondary formations sometimes overlaying the ancient stock of roots." He had written thus far in July, 1847; since which, the great national work published by order of the government of the United States of America, on the Indian tribes of the territory of that Republic, has afforded to him ample confirmations of the opinions above expressed.

Referring to that work, he says, "The linguistic data before us, combined with the traditions and customs, and, particularly, with the system of pictorial or mnemonic writing (first revealed in this work), enable me to say, that the Asiatic origin of all these tribes is as fully proved as the unity of family among themselves. According to our system, the [American] Indian languages can only be a deposit of a north Turanian idiom. Indeed, in addition to the evidence already collected by Prichard, the passage of tribes from Siberia (where we also find traces of the same pictorial writing), over the northern islands, is placed beyond all doubt by the work in question. The Mongolian peculiarity of the skull, the type of the hunter, the Shamanic excitement which leads, by means of fasting and dreams, into a visionary or clairvoyant state, and the fundamental religious views and symbols (among which the tortoise is not to be forgotten, ii. p. 390), bring us back to primitive Turanism. As to the languages themselves, there is no one peculiarity in them which may not easily be explained by our theory of the secondary formation and of the consequences of isolation. The unity of the grammatical type was long ago acknowleged, but we have now (as I think) the evidence of the material, historical, physical unity. The Indian mind has not only worked in one type, but with one material, and that a Turanian one." (Vol. ii. pp. 111-113.)
—The analogy between the predominant superstitions of the American Indians and the Shamanism

of certain Mongolian tribes, here noticed, is similar to that which is traced, through the Malayan district, between Shamanism and the Fetishism of the Negroes.

Thus the Nigritian and Mongolian and Malayan varieties of man appear to be allied both in their languages and their religions, and exhibit the strongest evidence of their having existed many ages before the origination of the *Semitic* stock of languages and that which we term the *Japhetic,* or *Iranian,* or, as Professor Max Müller terms it, *Arian.*

The origins of these two stocks of language next claim our attention, and demand a careful investigation, which we will endeavour to pursue with the aid of Professor Müller's valuable contributions to Baron Bunsen's work. But first we must observe, that these two learned authors appear to have struggled with enormous difficulties in the attempt to reconcile some of their opinions, expressed in the following extracts, with their belief that Adam was the first of mankind; difficulties of so weighty a kind as to have obliged the latter of them, as we have before mentioned, to require an interval of some ten thousand years between the creation of Adam and the Noachian period.

Professor Müller says, "We cannot derive Hebrew from Sanskrit, or Sanskrit from Hebrew, but we can well understand how both may have proceeded from one common source. They are both channels supplied from one river, and they carry, though not always on their surface, floating materials of language which challenge comparison, and have already yielded satisfactory results to careful analyzers. It is true, if there were any strong arguments against the common origin of these two channels of speech, the coincidences between them, hitherto pointed out, would perhaps not suffice to silence them. [To this admission we beg to call particular attention.] But, unshackled as we are by any contrary evidence, and encouraged as we must feel by the success of physical research, there is even now sufficient evidence with regard to a radical community between Arian and Semitic dialects, to enable us to say that their common origin is not only possible, but, as far as linguistic evidence goes, probable; while to derive the Semitic from the Arian, or the Arian from the Semitic type, may henceforth be declared a grammatical impossibility. . . . The Turanian dialects share one thing in common,—they all represent a state of language before its individualization by the Arian and Semitic types. But these Turanian languages cannot be considered as standing to each other in the same relation as Hebrew and Arabic, Sanskrit and Greek. In smaller spheres, similar families, like the Arian or Semitic, can be established within the Turanian kingdom. The Tamulic dialects, for instance, are held together by the same close ties of relationship as Greek and Latin, Hebrew and Arabic. They necessitate the admission of a common parent, of a long continued grammatical concentration preceding their gradual dispersion. The same applies to the different branches, which have been called Taïc, Bhotîya,

Malaïc, Mongolic, Tungusic, Tataric, and Finnic. The languages belonging to each of these branches point to so many parent-languages, whence they proceeded, and which they represent under different aspects. But these branches themselves must be viewed as separate in their beginnings, neither of them being subordinate to any other, neither of them being parent or offspring, but all springing side by side from the same soil, though with different powers of growth, and under circumstances more or less favourable to their grammatical organization. Nor can these Turanian stems be considered as standing to one another in the same relation as Semitic to Arian. The separation of these two dialects and their independent growth is the result of an individual act, unaccountable in its nature and origin, like everything individual, while the separation and divergence of the Turanian languages can be explained as the result of a gradual, natural, and simple process, which, out of many things that were possible in the mechanical combinations of roots, fixed a certain number of real forms which, under geographical and political influences, became consolidated into national idioms. [This is another observation to which we desire to call particular attention.] . . . Where the differences between the Turanian languages cease, the first stamina of the Arian and Semitic languages also would be found to converge towards the same centre of life. Radicals, applied to certain definite but material meanings in common by all Turanian dialects, belong to this primitive era, and some of them can even now be proved the common property of the Turanian, the Semitic, and Arian branches."

The learned professor afterwards affirms, that "as to the formal elements, or the grammatical growth of language, no difficulty exists in considering the grammatical system of Sanskrit, the most perfect of the Arian dialects, as the natural development of Chinese—an admission made even by those who are most opposed to the generalizations in the science of languages."

He then adds, "These two points, therefore, Comparative Philology has gained :—I. Nothing necessitates the admission of different independent beginnings for the material elements of the Turanian, Semitic, and Arian branches of speech,—nay, it is possible even now to point out radicals which, under various changes and disguises, have been current in these three branches ever since their first separation. —II. Nothing necessitates the admission of different beginnings for the formal elements of the Turanian, Semitic, and Arian branches of speech,—and though it is impossible to derive the Arian system of grammar from the Semitic, or the Semitic from the Turanian, we can perfectly understand how, either through individual influences, or by the wear and tear of grammar in its own continuous working, the different systems of grammar of Asia and Europe may have been produced." (Vol. i. pp. 476-480.)

Now, with respect to the languages which he terms "Arian" (that is, the Japhetic, called by Bunsen "Iranian," which we shall have to consider more particularly hereafter), we readily concede it to be most probable that, commencing with the Celtic, the language of Gomer (or the Kymri and other tribes), once widely spread through Europe, they were produced by gradual transformations of a highly-advanced class of Turanian dialects, somewhat after the manner in which the Italian and Spanish and French languages were formed from the Latin, though by far greater changes.

For the *Semitic* languages, however, we must claim a perfectly independent origin; admitting only that, in the course of their development, they received many Turanian roots, and probably some Turanian idioms. The most extended chronology that can fairly be regarded as reconcileable with the Bible we hold to be very far from what would suffice to allow of our entertaining any other opinion with respect to these languages: for if they did not originate independently, they must have originated from some other highly-advanced form of speech, requiring for its growth and development, according to the most moderate estimate that we can persuade ourselves to adopt, a period very much longer than that chronology allows. The state of isolation in which Adam and his wife were placed clearly indicates their having originated a language, *or* having received one by revelation; and it seems to us most unreasonable to suppose that this was such as the primeval language appears to have been according to the investigations of Bunsen and Max Müller. Independently of the obstacle to our holding the language of Adam to have been of this kind presented by the few antediluvian generations in the Bible, or the few generations prior to the time when Semitic, properly so called, is *known* to have already originated, even though we make the utmost reasonable allowance for the probable omissions of females, a strong reason, we think, for our not holding it to have been such is the fact of our finding that, among all the names occurring in the Biblical history of the times before the Flood, there is none that does not obviously bear a Semitic stamp. Among them, "Tubal-cain" ("*Scoriarum faber*") may be distinguished as presenting a *partial* exception: this, however, being compounded, after a Non-Semitic manner, apparently of a Non-Semitic and a Semitic noun, can only be urged as implying that *a Semitic and a Non-Semitic language* (with the latter of which the wandering Cainites may be supposed to have become acquainted) *existed before the Flood*: certainly not that the language of the early descendants of Adam was of a kind different from the Semitic. But as it may be objected that these names are perhaps translated from more ancient equivalents (though we see little ground for this supposition), we are content to rest our opinion respecting the language of Adam upon the chronological argument, which we regard as conclusive. We believe that his language, and that of his descendants to the time of the Dispersion, must have embodied the common elements of the several Semitic dialects, in a state of confusedness. The near mutual resemblances of all those dialects appear to us most imperatively to require this inference, while the differences of the three main branches, the Hebrew and Aramaic and Arabic, are such as absolutely forbid our deriving any one of them from either of the others. Of this, at least, we are convinced, by facts which we shall have to mention when we come to treat of the ancient Egyptian language, that if the rudiments of the Semitic languages did not originate with Adam, no reasonable way of accounting for their origin has yet been discovered.

Our next stage brings us to the period of the Dispersion, and "the Confusion of Languages;" and it ˳appears to us that the confusion was the *consequence*, not in any manner the *cause*, of the dispersion (agreeably with a rendering of Gen. xi. 9, proposed in our second chapter, page 94); designed to prevent the descendants of Noah from reuniting.

The race of Shem spread themselves through countries not far from the scene of the dispersion; and their languages, in consequence, became comparatively little varied. Each branch of this race, finding it necessary, as is always the case, to reduce its language to something like uniformity, may be most rationally supposed to have adopted particular idioms in preference to others, and to have had its dialect made to differ further from others of the same stock by natural development and by foreign influences. Thus we believe the several Semitic dialects to have originated; and among these must be included the dialects of the descendants of Canaan, though they were not Shemites; while, on the other hand, the language of the Elamites, the easternmost of the Shemite settlements, must be excluded. It is held by some that the descendants of Canaan (like the Philistines) came out of Egypt, on the sole ground of their being numbered among the descendants of Ham: but after a careful consideration of all the circumstances of the case, we are firmly convinced that, speaking the same language as the sons of Shem, most of them settled soon after the dispersion in the land called by their name, and there gradually individualized the dialects of which the Hebrew is one, in a great measure by mixing with various tribes mentioned in the Bible by the names of "Nephīlīm," "Rephāīm," "Anākīm," "Ēmīm," "Zamzummīm," "Zūzīm," etc., *whose genealogies are unrecorded.* That some of the descendants of Canaan afterwards settled for a time in Egypt, we think highly probable: and it can hardly be doubted that the Phœnicians dwelt in the region of the Erythræan Sea, in Southern Arabia and on the Persian Gulf, at a very early period, before they finally established themselves in Canaan. The latter people we believe to have been a Cushite branch that had become ingrafted upon the Joktanite stock.

The existence of the Hebrew and Chaldee dialects in the time of Jacob is shown in Genesis xxxi. 47: and from what is there said, we think it perfectly clear that the original language of Abraham was Chaldee, that is, Aramaic; and that he adopted, when he settled in Canaan, the dialect that is termed the Hebrew. Reckoning about seven centuries to have elapsed between the dispersion from Babel and the arrival of Abraham in Canaan, we have what we regard as a sufficient length of time for the gradual individualization of the Hebrew and the Aramaic, partly by means of natural development and partly by foreign influences; and in like manner, and in about the same period, we may suppose the principal dialects of Arabia to have assumed their distinct individualities. We know the Hebrew language in very early stages: the Arabic, commonly so called, only in its last two stages: we have no valid reason, therefore, to regard either of these languages as of earlier origin than the other. From the fact that the Arabic bears a much greater resemblance in its modern structure to the Biblical Hebrew and the Aramaic than it does in its earliest known stage, we might infer it to be the oldest of the three: but according to our view of the case, it was less exposed to foreign influences than either of the others until it became thus assimilated to them. It has, moreover, several characteristics of later development; the most remarkable of which is its predominant kind of plural, termed "the broken plural," of which we find no trace in any other Semitic dialect except the Ethiopic, though it remains predominant in modern Arabic; and it should be observed that the Ethiopic is allowed by all of the best Semitic scholars to be a dialect of the Southern Arabic, and not of a very ancient origin. The Biblical Hebrew evidently originated from a language more rich in respect of grammatical forms: and the names of "Methū-shelah" and "Methūshā-ēl," exhibiting instances of what was originally a nominative case-ending, indicate that the language of the *antediluvian* descendants of Adam bore somewhat of the same relation to the Hebrew of Moses and of later ages that the classical Arabic does to the simplified and decayed Arabic of modern times, *the contrary of what Bunsen supposes*. In the history of the transition from the classical to the modern Arabic, occasioned by the spreading of the Arabs among other races, we see exactly what we infer to have been the history of the transition from the prototype of the Semitic to the Biblical Hebrew and the known phases of the Aramaic.

A large portion of the race of Ham, and apparently the greater portion of the race of Japheth, spread themselves further than the Shemites and the Canaanites; the former, into Africa; the latter, throughout a great part of Asia and of Europe; so that each became disunited from the other and from the Shemites: and the differences of their languages from the known Semitic type confirm our opinion that they became intermixed, in greater degrees, in their adopted countries, with tribes and nations more ancient in origin than themselves. The vast extension of the race of Japheth, the early separation of the race of Ham, the consequent retention of the true religion by descendants of Shem alone, and the subjugation of Canaan by these last, fulfilled the prediction of Noah (in Gen. ix. 27), which we thus render : " God shall enlarge Japheth; but shall dwell in the tents of Shem; and Canaan shall be a servant to them."

Our inference respecting the mixture of the Shemites and Japhethites with other races agrees with an opinion of Professor Müller, founded solely upon his studies of comparative philology. Speaking of the "Arian [or Iranian or Japhetic] and Semitic races," and plainly showing that he includes with the latter the race of Ham, whose language was originally the same as that of Shem, and afterwards partially so, he says, "Wherever these two races arrive, they find the land occupied by barbarians, [but who were these *barbarians* that must have multiplied so largely before the time of Shem, if not descendants of Pre-Adamites ?] represented as giants [such as the Nephīlīm are supposed to have been] or evil spirits, and speaking languages unintelligible to the new arrivers." And it was by mixing their original form of speech with some of these barbarian dialects, and gradually remodelling several of the latter, that we hold most of the Hamitic and the Japhetic languages to have been formed. Again he says, shortly after, "They appear at once upon the stage of history, fully clad in their own armour, the enemies of the barbarians, the worshippers of brighter gods, and with a language which has left for ever the tumult of a Turanian arena." (Vol. i. pp. 483 and 484 of Bunsen's "Outlines.")

We could hardly express our own opinion on this subject more plainly than it is expressed in these extracts from a work with which we were entirely unacquainted when we formed that opinion. But we must differ from their author when he ascribes a Turanian origin to these races and to their languages, while he proceeds, immediately, to add, "They are Arians, or Shemites, inasmuch as they are no longer Turanians; and though their antecedent growth must have passed through a Turanian phase, this is overcome when they appear as the heralds of a new era in the history of man. It is only after having conquered in themselves Turanianism, in every sense of the word, that they advance through Asia and Europe as the conquerors of the descendants of Tur. This battle is not yet ended; and the largest share of the earth still belongs to its earlier occupants. The Arian and Semitic languages occupy but four peninsulas of the primeval continent, —India, Arabia, Asia Minor, and Europe; all the rest belongs to the family of Tur. But the countries reclaimed by Shem and Japhet mark the high road of civilization, and comprehend the stage on which the drama of ancient and modern history has been acted. Shem [with whom our author here, again, includes Ham, for to Ham most of the following remarks peculiarly apply,] was in advance of Japhet; and his first colonies represent a stage of language not yet decidedly Semitic, not yet freed from all Turanian influences, and, hence, less distant also from the stream of Arian speech. These were the colonists of Africa, who have fallen back into nomadic habits, but whose language is still the language of the people in Morocco, Algiers, Tunis, Tripoli, and Fez, wherever it has not been supplanted by the tongue of the conquering Arabs. A second colony, not yet decidedly Semitic, but, owing to political influences, more settled in its grammatical system, took its abode in Egypt. A third made its idiom the language of Babylonia and Assyria. These three early colonies exhibit the Semitic in its struggle towards grammatical form and consistency; and the individuality of Shem has not yet in them obscured those traces of a common past which enable us to connect the radical elements of the Semitic with the Turanian, and through it with the Arian family." (Vol. i. pp. 484 and 485.) The same distinguished scholar, recapitulating the results of his Turanian researches, says, "In the grammatical structure of the Semitic languages we can clearly perceive traces of one powerful mind who once grasped the floating elements of speech, and impressed on them his own stamp, never to be obliterated in the course of centuries. The same applies to those grammatical features which constitute the characteristic expression of the Arian dialects. As mighty empires founded by the genius of one man perpetuate for ages to come the will of one as the law of all, the Semitic and Arian families have preserved, at all times and in all countries, so strict a continuity as to connect the language of Moses with that of Mohammed, the poetry of Homer with that of Shakspeare. The principal branches of these two families never stand to one another in a more distant degree of relationship than French and Italian, German and English." (Vol. ii. p. 17).

In questioning the correctness of one of the opinions thus expressed, that of the possible origination of the Semitic, materially and formally, from the Turanian, we must observe that it is one to which both Bunsen and Max Müller have naturally been led by their belief in the descent of all mankind from Adam. Its adoption, however, demands concessions enormously at variance with the Scripture-history of the times anterior to the Dispersion, unless we admit the evidences in favour of the existence of Pre-Adamites presented by the Bible itself, and by physical and historical, as well as linguistic, facts; and if we admit these, needless: first, that a period very far too great to be reconcileable with the Scripture-history (according to Bunsen about ten thousand years, as we have before mentioned,) must be supposed to have intervened between the creation of Adam and the age of Noah: secondly, that a long period must be supposed to have elapsed during the transition from the Egyptian to the true Semitic type. This latter concession involves difficulties which Bunsen endeavours to meet by asserting that "the emigration from Asia into Egypt is Ante-Noachian. [It therefore took place, according to his chronology, about ten thousand years, or more, before the Christian era.] This [he says] explains also the fact of the Egyptians' having no traditions respecting the Deluge; that is to say, the great catastrophe which changed the climate of that primitive abode of mankind, the land between the Caucasus and Ararat in the west, the Altai in the east, and the Paropamisus in the south." (Vol. i. p. 190.) He then proceeds to affirm that "the beginning of Egyptian life" must be referred to a period above 5000 years B.C.; that it "had existed about 2000 years before Menes;" and (to account for the development of the Egyptian race as a distinct nation) that "this period, again, implies a long period during which the localization, and, as it were, the Africanizing, of that race took place." And he shortly after adds, "Khamitic is the first indistinct stage of Asiatic Semitism. This fact is symbolically represented by Kham, as Shem's elder brother, Japhet being the youngest of the three. Scripture calls Shem the elder brother of Japhet, but not of Kham. The expression that Canaan is the son of Kham must, therefore, be interpreted geographically. The departure of Canaan out of Lower Egypt, as part of the people of the Shepherd

Kings, after a thousand years' sojourn in that country, which took place in historical times, and his return to the land named after him, may have frequently occurred before the reign of the Hyksos. Geographically then, and historically, it is true that Canaan was the son of Egypt: for the Canaanite tribes which inhabited historical Canaan came from Egypt." (Vol. i. pp. 190 and 191.)

We will now consider the particular phenomena of the *Egyptian* language, and briefly state, in Bunsen's words, the principal linguistic facts upon which his opinion respecting it is founded; and it will be seen that all the difficulties which it involves are completely obviated by our own belief (a belief which we most confidently hold, and which is perfectly consistent with all the facts of the case), that a portion of the descendants of Ham, settling in Egypt, contended for the mastery of that country with an aboriginal Negro population, overcame them, intermarried with them, and, during the struggle and after it, intermixed their language with that of the more ancient people. Thus we are of opinion that these Noachian settlers formed a new language, of which, as they themselves became predominant, the predominant grammatical character is that of their own original tongue. (As to the inference that Canaan came out of Egypt, we have already expressed our opinion that it rests on a weak foundation; though we readily concede the probability that *some* of the descendants of Canaan settled for a time in that country.)

CHAPTER VI.

"The ancient Egyptian was, as we shall see, a form of speech only just emerging from the monosyllabic state and the absolute isolation of words." (Vol. ii. p. 62.) This remark is exemplified by the Lord's Prayer "in the Sacred language of the most ancient Monuments; composed by Lepsius: in the Demotic of the time of the Psammetics, 6th century B.C.; composed by Dr. Brugsch: and in the Coptic of the Translation of the Gospel [of St. Matthew], 2d century A.D."—"The language of ancient Egypt (Kham, the black land,) has an equally organic structure, but much less developed than the Iranian and Semitic, and is connected in its roots with both, and in its grammatical forms with the Semitic more particularly. This phenomenon cannot be explained, except by the supposition that those two great families were originally connected with each other." (Vol. ii. pp. 10 and 11.)—We explain it by deriving the Egyptian partly from the prototype of the Semitic and partly from an African language to which are traceable many of the roots found in Iranian.— "The Egyptian language," he says, "is a formation of primitive Western Asiatic life deposited in the valley of the Nile, prior, however, to the development of historical Semitism. The facts which prove this are mainly as follows: 1. The roots of the Egyptian language are, in the majority of cases, monosyllabic, and, on the whole, identical with the corresponding roots in Sanskrit and Hebrew. This *is* said advisedly. The proofs will be given in the proper place. . . . 2. The grammatical forms have throughout analogous formations in both : the pronominal system is, however, preponderantly Semitic. . . . 3. The Egyptian language, in forming a sentence, expresses the copula (the junction between the subject and predicate), either, as the Semites [occasionally] do, by placing the personal pronoun of the third person between both, or, as in the Iranian language, by a particle denoting the verb substantive." (Vol. i. pp. 185-187.)

Thus we find that the ancient Egyptian language, as known to us by its monuments, consists of Semitic and Non-Semitic elements; that with respect to the latter, it is similar to Iranian, but "much less developed;" and that it is connected in its grammatical character more particularly, but not exclusively, with the Semitic. To account for these peculiarities, we must observe, that a region of Asia in which only Semitic dialects are known to have been spoken from the earliest period of history lies on one side of that in which was spoken the Egyptian; and on another side lies a region of Central Africa in which only Non-Semitic dialects are known to obtain in the present day. We may therefore infer, either that the Non-Semitic elements of the second region (that is Egypt) once existed in the first (South-western Asia), intermixed with Semitic, that both these elements thence passed into the second (as Bunsen supposes), and that the Non-Semitic elements, nearly, if not entirely, separated from the Semitic, then passed on into the third region (that of Central Africa); or that the Non-Semitic elements of the second were derived from the third; which latter opinion, if we consider only the facts of the case, unbiassed by the assumption of the non-existence of a Pre-Adamite people, is evidently by far the more probable.

If we adopt either of these two inferences, we are necessarily brought to the conclusion, that the Non-Semitic elements of the third region must have been once the same, or nearly so, as those of the second: and even in the present day, notwithstanding the changes which must be supposed to have taken place during more than four thousand years, we find that the languages of most of the countries adjacent to the Nile (such as the Bishārī, the Galla, the Berber, or Barbar, and several others, to which may be added the language of Bornū,) are either mainly or wholly *Non-Semitic, and characterized by striking resemblances to the ancient Egyptian.* Such resemblances are clearly traceable in African languages beyond the range of Semitic influences: and Bunsen's remarks on those languages, which we have already cited, show that most of them agree with the Non-Semitic of the Egyptian in one "decisive characteristic," the manner of expressing the copula, which the Iranian languages have probably adopted from the more ancient Turanian stock, through the medium of some one or more of its dialects of South-western Asia, of a kind similar to the Turkish. To this last-mentioned language, or one of the same family, Sir Henry

Rawlinson finds the original (Non-Semitic) dialect of Babylonia to be analogous; so that it appears to exhibit a state of development to which some of the agglutinate languages had attained in the earliest historical ages; and we have before noticed, on more than one occasion, resemblances which have been observed between agglutinate languages in Asia and idioms of Central Africa. He has also confirmed an opinion which we expressed in the first edition of this work; that there are reasons of no small weight for deriving the Non-Semitic Babylonian, at least in a great measure, from a dialect of Ethiopia; reasons which, combined with facts already mentioned, indicate the high probability of there having been two streams of emigration from Africa into Asia in the ages before Ethiopia had become partly Semiticized in its languages; one, by which Asia and other parts were gradually peopled, flowing mainly through the southern countries of that continent, into China, and through the region which is now that of the Malayans; and the other, at a later period, of a more powerful and civilized race, from Ethiopia properly so called, through Arabia, Babylonia, and other countries, to Western India. To this latter supposed emigration, we shall have to revert: and we shall also have to mention several strong reasons for regarding Africa as the quarter in which originated many of the roots of Iranian found in the language of the kingdom of Nimrod as well as in that of ancient Egypt.

That the Non-Semitic languages of Africa existed in that continent before those having Semitic elements, appears to us to be almost demonstrated by our finding that *the latter, as far as we know, are confined to those parts which are most easily accessible from South-western Asia, the proper region of the Semitic; and that they extend no further than the tracts in which the physical type of South-western Asia is blended with that of the Negro.* Those Non-Semitic languages, however, since the entry of the sons of Ham into Africa, have probably been subjected to as great changes as most other national tongues in an equal lapse of time; while the language of ancient Egypt, consecrated by the religion and the religious monuments of the people who spoke it, remained essentially unchanged until it became that of the Coptic church; and thus it has been preserved, not greatly altered, to the present day, though now restricted to religious services.

As the opinion of Bunsen and Max Müller respecting the origin of the Egyptian language is attended by so great difficulties, we submit with confidence our own opinion upon the same subject, for the reasons already stated, and for many others, here following.—First, as affording a more probable explanation of all the linguistic facts of the case. (Some observations confirmatory of this assertion we have yet to adduce.) Secondly, as being reconcileable with Biblical chronology. Thirdly, as being agreeable with the most obvious indications of passages and words in Scripture which we regard as evidences of the existence of Pre-Adamites. Fourthly, as being confirmed by our finding that the people who spoke the Egyptian language were in their physical characteristics a compound of that variety to which the unmixed Noachians assuredly belonged and of the Nigritian. Fifthly, on the ground of our finding that the Egyptian religion combined revealed truths with the earliest known form of Babylonian idolatry (which perhaps originated in Africa) and with Nigritian fetishism. And sixthly, because, to our mind, it satisfactorily explains whence arose the exploded notion (justly ridiculed by Bunsen, in his "Outlines," vol. i. p. 191,) of an original connection between India and Egypt: for a connection of both these countries with *Nigritia* is indicated by the identity of most remarkable superstitions prevailing throughout the three.

Such, and so many, are the principal grounds upon which we rest our opinion of the origin of the Egyptian language; and several other languages, of the Eastern and Northern regions of Africa, we hold to have originated in a similar manner.

We have termed the Egyptian language "Hamitic," rather than "Khamitic," because we see no reason to doubt its having originated, in the manner explained above, partly from the race of Ham, the son of Noah, and because both of these terms may be used with propriety to indicate its country. If future investigations should show the true date of the

Deluge to be as low as Ussher has placed it (which we think most unlikely), then we should conclude that the first Asiatic settlers in Egypt must have been antediluvian Adamites, as we have observed in an early portion of our fifth chapter. In this case, however, none of the arguments which we have here advanced would be in any degree invalidated.

The foregoing remarks respecting the Egyptian language, with the exception of a few insertions and substitutions agreeable with their original tenour, were written before we were acquainted with the work of M. Renan from which we have added an extract in the introductory portion of this chapter. After stating that several eminent scholars agree with Bunsen, and that others disagree with him, as to the origin of that language, and mentioning (in Book I. chap. ii.) the striking facts of the identity of pronouns, both isolated and affixed, in the Coptic (the latest and best-known phasis of the Egyptian) and the Hebrew, and of the manner of treating them in the two languages, the analogies of the nouns of number, the agglutination of the accessory words, the assimilation of consonants, the secondary part played by the vowel, its instability which causes it to be often omitted in writing, analogies in the conjugation of verbs, resemblances in the theory of the particles, and other characteristics almost identical in the two languages, establishing between them incontestable affinities, he pronounces against the theory advocated by Bunsen. The same subject is resumed by him in the concluding chapter of his volume; and he there (in pp. 430 and 431) makes the following observations, nearly agreeing with our own opinion on this very important point.

" Je n'ai jamais pu me faire une idée claire de ce que serait, en philologie comparée, une famille de langues qui, par sa nature et indépendamment de tout emprunt, fût intermédiaire entre deux autres, tenant à l'une par sa grammaire, à l'autre par son dictionnaire. Le pehlvi, le persan moderne, l'hindoustani nous offrent, il est vrai, un vocabulaire en grande partie sémitique et une grammaire indo-européenne; le turc, un vocabulaire indo-européen et sémitique accouplé à une grammaire tartare: mais ce sont là des phénomènes de mélange relativement modernes et dont la raison historique se laisse apercevoir. Au contraire, quand il s'agit de langues simples et primitives, on ne saurait expliquer que la grammaire d'une famille se retrouvât dans une autre famille, séparée du lexique. Pour maintenir cette opinion, il faudrait soutenir que les Chamites vécurent en société avec les Sémites, longtemps après que ceux-ci se furent séparés des Ariens, puisque la grammaire, qu'on suppose s'être développée à une époque plus moderne, est analogue entre les Chamites et les Sémites, différente entre les Sémites et les Ariens. Mais alors, à plus forte raison, le dictionnaire, qu'on suppose antérieur à l'apparition de la grammaire, devrait être analogue chez les Sémites et les Chamites: or le dictionnaire sémitique et le dictionnaire copte n'ont rien de commun. Au milieu de ces profondes obscurités, l'hypothèse d'un emprunt très-ancien au moyen duquel les langues africaines, par elles-mêmes très-imparfaites, se seraient complétées en s'appropriant le système sémitique de la conjugaison, des pronoms et des noms de nombres, est encore peut-être la plus acceptable. Le copte, le berber, le galla et les diverses langues de l'Afrique orientale nous apparaissent à l'égard des langues sémitiques dans une même position de vassalité."

To the last two sentences in this extract we desire to draw particular attention, as showing that M. Renan has been led by linguistic facts alone to prefer that opinion respecting the origin of the Egyptian language to which we have ourselves been conducted by the same and *other* facts. He adds, in a note, another remark which is worth transcribing: "M. de Slane croit avoir retrouvé en berber la trilitérité des racines, les formes du verbe, et les particularités des verbes faibles et défectifs."

We may here also quote the following remarks of the learned Cardinal Wiseman, in the second of his "Lectures on the Connexion between Science and Revealed Religion," as applicable to the illustration of the origin of the Egyptian language.—
"I will take the liberty of saying, that some instances seem to warrant us in maintaining that, under the pressure of peculiar influences, a language may undergo such alterations as that its words

shall belong to one class, and its grammar to another. It is true that in that case, a new language will be formed, different from either of its parents, but still it will depart from the one which preceded it by the adoption of new grammatical forms. Thus, Schlegel himself allows that Anglo-Saxon lost its grammar by the Norman conquest. [This remark, however, should at least be modified; for the grammar of our language still remains Teutonic.] And may we not say that Italian has sprung out of the Latin, more by the adoption of a new grammatical system, than by any change in words? For if you will compare any works in the two languages, you will hardly perceive any difference in the verbs and nouns: but you find articles borrowed from the pronouns, a total loss of case, and consequently of all declension; and the verbs conjugated almost entirely by auxiliaries in the active voice, and totally deprived of a passive, properly so called. These, in fact, are the alterations which entitle it to be considered a new language. It is true, that in this case, the language has not gone out of its own family for the types of its variations; for these peculiarities are all to be found in other languages of the Indo-European class, as German and Persian; but it is no less true, that the change is very great, and allies the new language to another subdivision, which forms one extreme, while the Latin is almost the other, of the family."—After mentioning some other instances of a similar kind, the same distinguished scholar adds:—"Finally, another example may be drawn from the Amharic; and I will state it in the words of an able writer in a new periodical, deserving of every encouragement (the 'West of England Journal,'—No. 3, July 1835, p. 94):—'So much has been stated merely to show that the question needs to be considered thoroughly, whether languages may not borrow each other's pronouns and inflexions, while the whole material remains incongruous. . . Indeed, the Amharic language, which at first was supposed [to be] a dialect of the Gheez (Abyssinian), and then to be Shemitic, is now alleged by the most recent inquirers to be of African pedigree, and only to have imitated Shemitic inflexions.'"

It should be especially observed, that the mixture of Western Asiatic with existing African characteristics in the physical type and the language of the ancient Egyptians is traced, by means of their monuments, up to a period not more than about three centuries later than the date of the dispersion from Babel, according to the most extended chronology consistent with belief in the historical truth of the book of Genesis; and also that their religion was a compound of Asiatic and Nigritian elements, predominantly similar to that of the modern Negroes. *This we regard as the most important ethnological result to which the study of historical monuments and books, and of comparative philology, has led us.* That the Negroes were precisely what they now are, in their physical characteristics, more than three thousand years ago, we know from the earliest Egyptian monuments, on the walls of which we find them portrayed. But that they inherited from the ancient Egyptians the latter's partially-Negro physical traits, to be afterwards more developed, and the Non-Semitic elements of their language, and the lowest principles of their religion, and have retained all these to the present day, without any trace of the Caucasian characteristics of type, or of the Semitic elements of the language, or of the higher principles of the religion, or of the science or civilization, of the latter people, no impartial judge, endowed with common sense, can, we think, hold to be credible. And scarcely less unreasonable would be the supposition that the first Asiatic immigrants into Egypt had a language purely Non-Semitic, and a religion consisting only in the low nature-worship of the Negroes, and that they ingrafted upon their language its Semitic elements, and upon their religion its higher principles, after a portion of them had passed on into Central Africa, there to remain without any similar improvement, and to lose every trace of the Western Asiatic physical type. Yet, if we insist on the origination of all mankind from Adam, we can see no alternative but that of adopting one of these two suppositions, or a vastly-extended chronology of the Post-Adamic period, coupled with the concession that some of the descendants of Adam quitted the region of the Deluge many ages before its occurrence, so that their posterity escaped it. With this concession, Bunsen's period of about ten thousand years between Adam and Noah would give scope for supposing a migration from Asia into Northern and Central Africa, followed by another migration several thousands of years later into Egypt, after the origination of the Semitic languages; and thus, if we could derive these languages from any other form of speech, for framing a theory that might explain the philological difficulties of the case under our immediate consideration. But even this enormous extension of the Biblical chronology, though it might perhaps lessen, would be very far from removing, the difficulties of the case in relation to physiology or religion; and in our opinion it would leave the origin of the Semitic languages involved in utter obscurity; for we are convinced, as we have before affirmed, that if these languages did not originate with Adam, no reasonable way of accounting for their origin has yet been discovered.

The *Himyeritic* and *Ethiopic*, but more especially the former, and the *Assyro-Babylonian*, deserve particular notice among the languages of which we hold the origins to have been somewhat similar to that of the ancient Egyptian, though predominantly Semitic: for they exhibit too many and too great disagreements with all the well-known Semitic dialects to admit of our believing them to have arisen in any other way than from a mixture of peoples of distinct and very different languages. With respect to the Assyro-Babylonian (which apparently deviates more widely than the Himyeritic, and much more than the Ethiopic, from the general Semitic type), Sir Henry Rawlinson has clearly proved a most important fact, fully sufficient to account for its having arisen from such a mixture; that this language was preceded, in the region south of Assyria, by one of a kind analogous to the *Turanian*, which continued to obtain in Babylonia until near about the time of Nebuchadnezzar, when it was superseded by the language previously confined to Assyria. Thus he has discovered what was doubtless *the Original Language of the Kingdom of Babylonia:* and as Nimrod may be said to have been begotten by Cush without being one of his immediate offspring, we may, with a high degree of probability, trace a colony of the Cushites, through their settlements in Arabia, from Ethiopia, after adopting an African language, into Babylonia, as we have before hinted; in like manner as we may trace some of their brethren from an African settlement, and from the coasts of the Erythræan Sea (where they had probably intermixed with Joktanites), into Phœnicia, and thus account for Homer's coupling Ethiopians with Sidonians, in the Odyssey, iv. 84. That a migration of Cushites from Ethiopia to Babylonia took place, or one in the reverse direction, seems to be indicated not only by Nimrod's being said to have been begotten by Cush, but also by the two applications of the name

"Cush," in the Bible, to regions of Africa and Asia; by the corresponding application of the term "Ethiopians" by several of the ancients, as Homer (Odyss. i. 22), Herodotus (vii. 70), and Strabo (i. p. 60); and by the resemblances obtaining between the Turanian languages (to which the earliest Babylonian has been found to be analogous) and idioms of Central Africa. And that Babylonia was colonized from Ethiopia, rather than that the reverse was the case, may be argued from the apparent fact that the sons of Cush are mentioned in the Bible, probably without a single exception, in the order of their settlements, commencing from Ethiopia, commonly so called, and ending with Babylonia; and from an opinion of Sir Henry Rawlinson, that the cuneiform character originated from hieroglyphs, compared with the old tradition (mentioned in our fifth chapter) that the Egyptian hieroglyphics were derived from Ethiopia. Hence we inferred (and our opinion has been confirmed by discoveries of Sir Henry Rawlinson that have come to our knowledge since the foregoing remarks on this subject were published) that the earliest Babylonian language was at least in a great measure, if not mainly, Cushitic, that is, Ethiopian: not, however, doubting it to have been gradually mixed with a Scythic or some other Asiatic dialect; for it seems to us almost as certain that the Cushites of Asia intermixed with earlier Asiatics as it is that those who remained in Africa blended their race with that of the Negroes.

Agreeably with this view of the case, Herodotus (in Book VII. chapter 70) says that the Eastern Ethiopians were lank-haired, and those of Libya [or Africa] crisp-haired; and that, in his time, they differed in language. The intercourse of the Shemites of Southern Arabia with their Cushite neighbours in Africa, and with Cushites in Arabia also, affords a reasonable explanation of the origin of the Himyeritic and of the language which we term the Ethiopic, as together forming one of the remote branches of the Semitic stock. (See Note 10.)

The *Japhethites*, in the ages immediately following the Dispersion, do not appear, from any historical records, to have founded powerful kingdoms, as descendants of Shem and of Ham did; and accordingly we do not find that they either preserved their original language little altered, like the generality of the race of Shem, or blended it grammatically with the languages of the nations among whom they spread, as did some of the descendants of Ham: but it seems to be most probable that they gradually transformed a highly-advanced class of these languages, as we have before observed, and introduced into them an abundance of Semitic roots, which still remain in European tongues and in the Iranian languages of Asia. Some of them, however, appear to have made very little alteration in the languages of the regions in which they settled; as, for instance, the ancestors of the Basques (a supposed remnant of the Iberians), and of the tribes of the

Caucasus. The Celts (or Kymri and other tribes descended from Gomer) are the nearest in speech of all the other branches of the Japhetic stock to the Turanians: and the appellations of *black* and *fair* by which "the Picti and Scoti are usually distinguished in the Welsh records," as Dr. Charles Meyer has remarked (in Bunsen's "Outlines," Vol. i. p. 151), "seems to refer to a difference of blood, and to imply that the *black* Picti exhibited in their physical appearance a less pure Caucasian origin than the *fair* Scoti."

In the first edition of this work, we intimated the probability of there having once existed a class of Turanian dialects, now lost, from which the earlier Iranian languages were transformed, in like manner as the later (such as the Pehlevi, the modern Greek, the Italian, the Spanish, the French, and the English,) have been transformed from, and made to supersede, other languages of their own stock, by foreign intruding races. We also mentioned the existence of radical elements of Iranian in the language of ancient Egypt: and we have since learned that many roots of Iranian are likewise recognised in the primitive language of Babylonia; and that we may, with a degree of confidence almost amounting to certainty, pronounce this language to be properly Cushitic, and trace its roots of Iranian to an African origin, as we have shown in Note 10. Such being the case, seeing that at least one dialect which appears to

PHILOLOGICAL OBSERVATIONS. 273

have been brought from Ethiopia into Asia, namely, that of the Cushites of Babylonia (as described in the note to which we have just referred), was of a kind analogous to the Turanian, and contained many roots of Iranian, and that the ancient Egyptian language, in like manner, consists partly of elements found in Iranian,—seeing, also, that a colony of Ethiopians is said to have settled in or near India, where Iranian dialects prevail, and that the Turanian is held to be the only kind of language from which the Iranian can have mainly originated,— we think that we have satisfactory reasons for regarding the Iranian languages as transformations of Turanian dialects that had received many radical elements of Iranian from Africa.

It is very remarkable that Iranian elements are first found in the language of *Egypt*, and next in a language almost proved to have been brought from *Ethiopia*. Now, according to the theory of gradual development for which Bunsen and Max Müller contend, we have the following series:— Before the time of Noah, *Turanian*: then, Semitic and Iranian elements combined to form the *Hamitic* language of Egypt: and at a later period, pure *Semitic*. But we find that *one language* which (like the second of these) was *spoken by descendants of Ham* was of a kind analogous to the *Turanian*, with many Iranian nouns, and only some traces of Semitic; namely, the primitive language of Babylonia: and this fact, we think, most convincingly shows that the descendants of Ham found in Africa a language similar to the Turanian kind, with roots of Iranian, which the descendants of Cush adopted with scarcely any change, while their brethren in Egypt so largely intermixed the same or a similar African dialect with Semitic as to form a language of a new general character. When we consider, moreover, that the ancient Egyptians, as we have already shown, are proved by their monuments to have been characterized both physically and in their religion by a mixture of African with Western Asiatic traits, the conclusion which we have just expressed appears to us to rest upon evidence more than sufficient to satisfy every impartial judge. And thus we obtain a most important confirmation of our opinion, that the Deluge (while it destroyed all the Adamites, in the most proper sense of the appellation, except the family of Noah,) did not destroy the whole human species.

Communication between Africa and several of the countries of Asia and of Europe was most probably frequent in very ancient, as it has been in later, times; and may have occasioned great changes in the western branches of the Turanian stock of languages, which, as well as some eastern branches of the same stock, we suppose to have been transformed into Iranian. Thus we may account for the fact, pointed out by Dr. Charles Meyer (in Bunsen's "Outlines," Vol. i. p. 168), that the *Celtic* "in all its non-Sanskritic features most strikingly corresponds with the *Old Egyptian*," the language, we may add, of a people generally believed to have procured the tin for their bronze either from Britain or from Spain, perhaps following in the steps of earlier African traders, for they had that metal many ages before Phœnician ships are related to have voyaged for it.

Amalgamation, in the formation of words, we believe to have originated with the prototype of the Semitic dialects: with this characteristic, Iranian languages possess another, consistent with the opinion that Iranian is a Japhetic improvement of Turanian; namely, an abundance of compound words, beside those formed by inflections. Of such words the Semitic languages present extremely rare instances; little more than a few contractions of two or more particles or other words into one.

The only Iranian language of which we possess any remains of very high antiquity is the Sanskrit: the hymns of the Rig Veda being asserted by Professor Wilson to be "at least fifteen centuries prior to the Christian era;" so that they may be even anterior to the writings of Moses, and yet by eight or ten centuries less ancient than the oldest portion or portions of the Egyptian "Book of the Dead."

Further than this, we need not pursue our philological inquiry. We have continued it down to the times of the first great kingdoms of the Eastern World, and the age of their earliest monumental records, applying our last test of the correctness of our opinion respecting the originations of the principal varieties of our species, founded upon the closest possible renderings of words and passages in the Scriptures; and philological evidences have led us to the same conclusion as the evidences of every other kind which we have examined.

Can the numerous facts which we have adduced as confirmations of this opinion be regarded with any degree of probability as mere fortuitous coincidences?

We hope that this question will be dispassionately and carefully considered by competent judges; not by such as are merely theologians, but such as combine general scientific and literary attainments with Biblical learning: for we have seen that the understanding of the Bible has hitherto increased, with, and by, the increase of human knowledge; and we confidently believe that it will continue to do so to the end of time.

NOTES.

1.

(Page 14.)

The words in verses 8 and 9, "And they heard the voice of the Lord God, walking [or "going to and fro"] in the garden, in the wind (rūăh) of the day, ... and the Lord God called unto the Adam," may receive some light from the passages here following.—"The voice of the Lord [is] upon the waters: the God of glory thundereth: the Lord [is] upon great waters: the voice of the Lord [is] with power: . . . . with majesty: . . . breaketh the cedars: . . . . cutteth out flames of fire: . . . . shaketh the wilderness: . . . maketh the hinds to bring forth, and discovereth the forests" (Ps. xxix. 3-9). "He walketh in the circuit of heaven" (Job xxii. 14). "Who walketh upon the wings of the wind" (Ps. civ. 3). "Thine arrows went to and fro" (Ps. lxxvii. 18; in the authorized version, 17: "arrows" meaning lightnings; and the verb here being that which is generally rendered "walked:" see also a similar use of the same verb in Ezek. i. 13). "Then the Lord answered Job out of the storm" (Job xxxviii. 1: see also Ex. xix. 16-18, etc.).

2.

(Page 43.)

In illustration of the creations pertaining to what Miller terms " the three geologic days," we quote the following passages from his third lecture in the same work.

" In the first or Palæozoic division we find corals, crustaceans, molluscs, fishes, and, in its later formations, a few reptiles. But none of these classes of organisms give its leading character to the Palæozoic; they do not constitute its prominent feature, or render it more remarkable as a scene of life than any of the divisions which followed. That which chiefly distinguished the Palæozoic from the Secondary and Tertiary periods was its gorgeous flora. It was emphatically the period of plants,—' of herbs yielding seed after their kind.' In no other age did the world ever witness such a flora: the youth of the earth was peculiarly a green and umbrageous youth,—a youth of dusk and tangled forests, of huge pines and stately araucarians, of the reed-like calamite, the tall tree-fern, the sculptured sigillaria, and the hirsute lepidodendron. Wherever dry land, or shallow lake, or running stream appeared, from where Melville Island now spreads out its ice wastes under the star of the pole, to where the arid plains of Australia lie solitary beneath the bright cross of the south, a rank and luxuriant herbage cumbered every foot-breadth of the dank and steaming soil; and even to distant planets our earth must have shone through the enveloping cloud with a green [?] and delicate ray."

" The middle great period of the geologist—that of the Secondary division—possessed, like the earlier one, its herbs and plants, but they were of a greatly less luxuriant and conspicuous character than their predecessors, and no longer formed the prominent trait or feature of the creation to which they belonged. The period had also its corals, its crustaceans, its molluscs, its fishes, and in some one or two exceptional instances its dwarf mammals. But the grand existences of the age,—the existences in which it excelled every other creation, earlier or later,—were its huge creeping things,—its enormous monsters of the deep,—and, as shown by the impressions of their footprints stamped upon the rocks, its gigantic birds. It was peculiarly the age of egg-bearing animals, winged and wingless. Its wonderful *whales*, not, however, as now, of the mammalian, but of the reptilian class,—ichthyosaurs, plesiosaurs, and cetiosaurs,—must have tempested the deep; its creeping lizards and crocodiles, such as the teliosaurus, megalosaurus, and iguanodon,—creatures some of which more than rivalled the existing elephant in height, and greatly more than rivalled him in bulk,—must have crowded the plains or haunted by myriads the rivers of the period; and we know that the footprints of at least one of its many birds are of fully twice the size of those made by the horse or camel."

"The Tertiary period had also its prominent class of existences. Its flora seems to have been no more conspicuous than that of the present time; its reptiles occupy a very subordinate place; but its beasts of the field were by far the most wonderfully developed, both in size and numbers, that ever appeared upon earth. Its mammoths and its mastodons, its rhinoceri and its hippopotami, its enormous dinotherium and colossal megatherium, greatly more than equalled in bulk the hugest mammals of the present time, and vastly exceeded them in number. The remains of one of its elephants (*Elephas primigenius*) are still so abundant amid the frozen wastes of Siberia, that what have been not inappropriately termed 'ivory quarries' have been wrought among their bones for more than a hundred years. Even in our own country, of which, as I have already shown, this elephant was for long ages a native, so abundant are the skeletons and tusks, that there is scarcely a local museum in the kingdom that has not its specimens, dug out of the Pleistocene deposits of the neighbourhood. And with this ancient elephant there were meetly associated in Britain, as on the northern continents generally all around the globe, many other mammals of corresponding magnitude. . . . 'Tigers as large again as the biggest Asiatic species lurked in the ancient thickets;' . . . . [and] the massive cave-bear and large cave-hyæna belonged to the same formidable group, with at least two species of great oxen (*Bos longifrons* and *Bos primigenius*), with a horse of smaller size, and an elk (*Megaceros Hibernicus*) that stood ten feet four inches in height." ("The Testimony of the Rocks," pp. 135-138.)

To these extracts we add a paragraph from the "Edinburgh Review" (No. 219) on Miller's view of the narrative of creation.

"It has been objected to this view that the facts do not exactly correspond with the picture—that an extraordinary development of vegetation characterised only a part of the Palæozoic strata—that creation embraced during those times, as well as during the succeeding Secondary ages, many forms of animal, and especially of Icthyic life—that in like manner beasts of the earth had appeared before the Tertiary ages had begun—and that, consequently, no such divisions of time can be accurately applied to corresponding divisions in organic nature. It is no part of our object here to enter into the controversy which may be raised on this and other similar points. But in justice to Miller's view, we must observe that it is founded on principles of interpretation which are not much affected by this class of objection. No one knew better than Miller that the divisions indicated in geology are not sharp or definite, either in respect to their duration or in respect to their productions. His own research had been specially devoted, not to the plants, but to the fish of the Palæozoic rocks, and he had described, as no one else had ever described, the abundant fertility of primeval seas. But he did not consider these facts inconsistent with his view: because he holds the representation given in Genesis to be an ideal representation—but ideal only in the same sense in which the great classifications of the naturalist or the geologist are themselves ideal. It was not to be regarded as teaching the details of physical science, but only as shadowing forth certain great leading acts in the drama of creation, and selecting a few prominent epochs as typical of the whole. The fundamental idea is that the epochs thus selected were representative of corresponding stages in the history of the earth,—stages through which it passed from one physical condition to another, each more advanced than the preceding, with reference to its final purpose. Some of these earlier epochs or days, such as that assigned to the 'Division of the Firmament,' have left, of course, no record in Palæontology: and Miller's picture of this part of the Mosaic Vision may appear to be purely fanciful. Yet it is remarkable that conclusions derived from other branches of the science afford no small probability to his rendering. We observe in the Cambridge Essays for 1857 a very able paper on Geology, by Professor W. Hopkins, in which, with all the care of exact reasoning, and from arguments purely physical and cosmical, he shows the high probability of conditions in the early history of the Earth very similar to those which are assumed by Miller. Nor is it less worthy of observation that, looking at the subject from this very different point of view, he fixes on the vegetation of the coal as by far the most striking indication of what those conditions may probably have been during part of the Palæozoic ages. Doubtless all these conclusions are scientifically more or less uncertain. They must continue to be tested by the progress of discovery. Meanwhile it may perhaps be enough to say that the Theologian will recognise the principle of interpretation assumed by Miller with reference to this supposed vision of the past as at least not wanting in analogy with that which has been long admitted with reference to visions of the future: whilst the geologist must admit that it accords at least so far with the 'Testimony of the Rocks' as to embody a very large amount of physical truth."

3.

(Page 76.)

The remark which we have made respecting the appellation "ādām," with the article prefixed to it, perhaps requires further explanation. We hold that, in the cases which we have specified, when it does not denote the man to whom it was applied in the manner of a proper name, nor relate to his time, it is *properly* a generic epithet, but used as a collective noun, and signifying "the

Adamites," including none *beside* them, and excluding none *of* them (though some are occasionally excluded by the context), whether rendered in the authorized version by a plural or by a singular. It is like "the 'anāk," or "the 'anōk," in Josh. xv. 13 and xxi. 11; where Arba is called, as Rosenmüller says, "*pater Anaki* s. *Anakæorum*, quod non de generis origine, sed de imperio intelligendum videtur." (See Barrett's "Synopsis of Criticisms," vol. ii. p. 92.) In saying this, we do not deny that "hā-ādām" may sometimes be rightly and preferably rendered "the Adamite;" as in the latter clause of Ex. xxxiii. 20, " the Adamite shall not see my face and live;" "the Adamite" here applying to *every* Adamite supposed to see the face of God; and if the existence of Non-Adamites be a fact, meaning, *à fortiori*, "man," as in some other cases. In this instance, and, we believe, in every similar case in which it may be preferably rendered by a singular, "hā-ādām" is a *vague* and an *equivocal* singular, which is *virtually* a plural. We have not met with any exception, unless it be one presented in Josh. xiv. 15 : but here, the reading followed in the Septuagint-version seems to have been not "hā-ādām," etc., but "hā-adāmāh," followed by a feminine epithet and a feminine pronoun; as observed by Rosenmüller (*vide* Barrett, "Synopsis," *ubi supra*); and we regard this as the *right* reading; meaning (not that *Arba* was "the *great Adamite* among the 'Anākīm," but) that " *Kirjath-Arba* was the *metropolis* of the 'Anākīm," as rendered by the LXX.

The word "ādām" bears a near resemblance to "hamōr;" which is originally a generic epithet, applied to "an ass," because, like "ādām," denoting a reddish colour, the colour of that animal in its natural wild state; once feminine (in 2 Sam. xix. 27), like as "ādām" is once expressly applied to the female as well as the male (in Gen. v. 2); and also used as a collective noun (in Gen. xxxii. 6, in the English version 5, where three other nouns, originally singulars, are also used collectively). So, too, it does in its being used as a proper name; being the proper name of a certain man of the Hivites, mentioned in Gen. xxxiii. 19, etc.

4.

(Page 83.)

The writer to whom we have here alluded has argued (in the "Journal of Sacred Literature," January, 1856,) that if "ādām" properly signify "Adamite" or "Adamites," the passage in Josh. xiv. 15 shows that there was a great Adamite among the Anākīm; and hence, "the probability is that they were all Adamites, which [he says] is what we maintain." He then adds, "Now in Num. xiii. 33 the 'Nephilim' are called [or rather some of them are called, in the Hebrew,] the 'sons of Anak of the Nephilim;' the previous passage, therefore, by which we prove the Anakim to have descended from Adam [*probability* being now regarded as *proof*], by implication proves the same of the 'Nephilim.' We go further, and remark that the Emim, equally with the Anakim, are referred to the Rephaim in Deut. ii. 11, and are thus disposed of in the same way. So of the rest."

In reply, we first observe that, if we be right as to the *proper* signification of "ādām," Arba is called in Josh. xiv. 15, in the existing Hebrew copies, "the great

Adamite among the Anākim." Hence it is argued, "the probability is that they were all Adamites." The probability, however, is not a proof: for Arba may have been thus called in the same sense in which the greatest of the monarchs of France might be called "the great Corsican among the French;" and it was for a reason of this kind according to the opinion of Rosenmüller (as we have mentioned in Note 3) that Arba is called in Josh. xv. 13 and xxi. 11 "the Father of the 'Anāk," or "the 'Anŏk," that is, of the 'Anākīm. But, secondly, in Note 3, we have given two reasons, both of which we regard as being of great weight, for preferring the reading of the Septuagint, according to which it is said, not that *Arba* was "the *great Adamite* among the 'Anākīm," but that "*Kirjath-Arba* was the *metropolis* of the Anākīm."

5.

(Page 101.)

In the "Journal of Sacred Literature" (New Series, No. XIV.,) is the following postscript to a notice of the pamphlet which we have mentioned in our preface; written before the remarks to which the present note relates, and proposing for consideration an opinion respecting the Deluge remarkably consistent with the Scripture-narrative of that event, except with regard to the locality.

"Since writing this, I have received a copy of a pamphlet on 'the Deluge,' suggested by that noticed above, and likewise printed for private distribution. The author holds the opinion that the Adamites were a distinct race, and not the progenitors of the whole human species, and points out a curious analogy between the Deluge and a very destructive overflow of the Nile, both as to the time of the year at which the Deluge happened, supposing that the year commenced about the vernal equinox, and also as to the manner in which the waters rose, and the height to which they attained. These views are supported with much learning and ingenuity, and deserve a careful examination. Great difficulties seem to me, however, to stand in their way. The bases of the argument are affected by the impossibility of determining what year was in use in those times, and by the consideration that regular or accidental floods of other rivers might fulfil nearly the same conditions as those of the Nile, while the result is opposed to the fact that the Ark rested on the mountains of Ararat, and to the silence of the Egyptian records with respect to the Noachian flood."

It should be added, that the author of the opinion to which the above remarks relate believes "the usual interpretation of Ararat" to have "no authority whatever." We admit that the Bible does not anywhere distinctly indicate the position of that country; and hence many learned men have differed very widely respecting it: while one, whose opinion has occasioned this notice, holds it to have been somewhere on the eastern border of Lower Egypt, others have fixed upon various localities in regions extending from Asia Minor to Northern India; and, according to the Samaritan Pentateuch, it was in Ceylon! Certainly, then, the opinion which points to the eastern frontier of Lower Egypt is not the *most* improbable. But, for ourselves, we can hardly doubt that the name "Ararat" applies to a part (or perhaps the whole) of Armenia, which is said to be still so called by its inhabitants in their own language.

6.

(Page 102).

"Natural history has produced various changes in current interpretations of the Bible, and is destined in all probability to affect exegesis in a still more salutary way hereafter. Thus it has taught us to see that all animals in every part of the globe could not have been shut up in the ark. The number of distinct species to which mammalia, reptiles, insects, and animalcules can be reduced by the greatest possible contraction, renders it utterly impossible. The ark was not spacious enough to contain pairs and septuples of all the animals now existing on the face of the earth. Besides, animals have their appropriated regions to which they are adapted by nature, and cannot live in others. When, therefore, it is considered that above a thousand species of existing mammalia are known, more than five thousand of birds, more than two thousand of reptiles; of insects an immense number, more, certainly, than one hundred thousand; of animalcules countless millions; and that all have congenial climates; the impossibility of the ark holding them is obvious. Hence the language of the narrative must be restricted. The newly-created animals of *that region* which was the cradle of the human race [or rather (we would say) of that region which was to be overspread by the Flood] were alone brought into the ark and preserved." ("The Text of the Old Testament considered;" etc.: by Samuel Davidson, D.D., p. 358.)

The great authority of Cuvier has often been adduced as favouring the opinion of the universality of the Deluge. "'I agree with MM. Deluc and Dolomieu in thinking,' we find him saying, in his widely-famed Theory of the Earth, 'that if anything in geology be established, it is, that the surface of our globe has undergone a great and sudden revolution, the date of which cannot be referred to a much earlier period than five or six thousand years ago.' But from the same celebrated work we learn that Cuvier held that this sudden catastrophe—occasioned, as he supposed, by an elevation of the sea-bottom and a submergence of the previously existing land,—had *not* been universal. . . . . In referring to the marked peculiarities of the Mongolian race, so very distinct from the Caucasian, he merely intimates, that he was 'tempted to believe their ancestors and ours had escaped the great catastrophe on different sides;' but in dwelling on the still more marked peculiarities of the Negroes, we find him explicitly stating, that 'all their characters clearly show, that they had escaped from the overwhelming deluge at another point than the Caucasian and Altaïc races; from which they had been separated,' he adds, 'for a long time previous to the occurrence of that event.'" (Hugh Miller's "Testimony of the Rocks," pp. 310 and 311: a work presenting evidence and arguments far more than sufficient to satisfy every impartial mind that the Noachian Deluge was not universal with respect to the *earth*, though its author held it to have been universal with respect to *mankind*, except those that were saved in the ark.)

7.

(Page 110.)

The identity of the appellations "Beni-l-Kenz" (or "the Sons of the Kenz") and "Kunūz" has been remarked upon by De Sacy (in his "Chrestomathie Arabe," vol. ii. p. 28, 2nd ed.); "Kunūz," as he has observed, being plural of "Kenz;" and the identity is confirmed by the fact that the principal seat of the Kunūz in the present day (the district of Aswān) was the principal seat of the Beni-l-Kenz in former times. He also cites an Arabian historian as asserting that the Beni-l-Kenz derived their origin from Rabī'ah, which was an Arab tribe: but the truth is, that Arabs of the tribe of Rabī'ah intermarried with families of the Bejā, or Bujā, and thus produced the race called "Beni-l-Kenz." For the fact of the intermarrying here mentioned, we have historical authority (see Burckhardt's "Travels in Nubia," pp. 509 and 510); and the physical characteristics of the modern Kunūz plainly show that they very largely partake of aboriginal African blood. It would seem to be not improbable that the appellation "Beni-l-Kenz" might have been derived from "Kens," which is found upon ancient Egyptian monuments as a name of Nubia or the Nubians; but according to Arabian historians, it is from "Kenz-ed-Dauleh" ("the Treasure of the State"), a common honorary surname of several of the early chiefs of the people to whom it is applied.

8.

(Page 136.)

We have not overlooked the explorations recently prosecuted, during several years, by direction of Mr.

Leonard Horner, to discover the general depth of the alluvium of Egypt, and, by calculations founded upon its secular rate of increase, supposed to be approximatively known, to connect geological and historical time.

In a boring of the soil near the colossal statue at Memphis, from the depth of *thirty-nine feet below the surface*, wholly through true Nile-sediment, the instrument brought up *a piece of pottery*: whence it has been inferred that man existed in Egypt 11,517 years before the Christian era; and not merely existed, but had so far advanced towards civilization as to know and practise the art of forming vessels of clay and hardening them by fire.

It was our intention to have shown that this inference has been drawn from data extremely uncertain; but our doing so has been rendered needless by some remarks in the "Quarterly Review," No. 210, pp. 418-421. It is almost enough to notice one source of error in Mr. Horner's calculations. He says,

"In every situation where the experiment is made, we must have *a fixed point in time* to start from, viz., the known age of a monument whose foundation rests upon Nile-sediment, and upon whose sides it has accumulated by subsequent inundations. If there have been no local causes to disturb the probability that the sediment above and below the foundation has accumulated at the same rate, we divide the amount above the foundation by the number of centuries known to have elapsed from the erection of the monument to the present time, and then apply the same chronometric scale to the greatest ascertained depth of sediment below the foundation."

This rule involves the supposition that the ancient

Egyptians were so absurdly inconsiderate as to found the monument on a spot above which the annual inundation must have risen several feet. Undoubtedly experience taught them to place it upon an elevation, which, in the midst of an alluvial plain, was probably formed of the adjacent compact soil. After the lapse of several centuries, they may have found it necessary to surround it by walls or embankments to preserve it from the inundation; or the continual raising of the site of the surrounding dwellings may have served for this purpose. See what Herodotus says (in Book II. chapter 138) respecting the temple and town of Bubastis; his description of which is confirmed by existing remains.

Other circumstances affecting the inference drawn from the "piece of pottery," such as changes in the course of the Nile, fissures of very great and unascertained depth in the parched soil, the former existence of innumerable wells or pits (few of them, we may observe, less than twenty-five feet in depth, and many of them much more,) from which water was raised by means of *earthen pots*, and the discovery of fragments of *burnt brick* (a material not known to have been used in Egypt before the Roman domination) between the fortieth and fiftieth foot from the surface,—Mr. Horner even mentions pieces found at the depths of fifty-nine and seventy-two feet,—have been pointed out in the remarks in the "Quarterly Review" to which we have referred. Mr. Horner's researches have established nothing more than the fact that the depth of the alluvium is sufficiently great to show that Egypt must have been *habitable* by man some thousands of years before the date commonly assigned to the creation of Adam.

9.
(Page 225.)

The opinion that man was originally in that condition which is generally termed a state of nature is now commonly asserted to be unphilosophical and exploded. But it cannot be justly pronounced unphilosophical, since it has been held by many of the greatest minds of ancient and of modern times: nor can it with truth be said to be exploded, when we find such a man as the author of "Cosmos" unable to satisfy himself that it is false. "We will not," says this profound investigator of nature, "attempt to decide the question whether the races which we at present term savage are all in a condition of original wildness, or whether, as the structure of their languages often allows of our conjecturing, many among them may not be tribes that have degenerated into a wild state, remaining as the scattered fragments saved from the wreck of a civilization that was early lost. A more intimate acquaintance with these so-called children of nature reveals no traces of that superiority of knowledge regarding terrestrial forces, which a love of the marvellous has led men to ascribe to these rude nations." (Otté's Translation, vol. ii. p. 477.) We believe that the higher kinds of nature-worship that obtained in Ancient Egypt, India, Greece, and other countries, mainly originated from attempts to found philosophical systems upon the fetishism of the aboriginal inhabitants of those countries.

10.
(Page 271.)

In a lecture delivered by Sir Henry Rawlinson, on the 8th of August, 1856, before the British Association for the Advancement of Science, on recent discoveries in Assyria and Babylonia, and on the results of Cuneiform research, some opinions expressed in the first edition of this work have been very remarkably confirmed, as will be shown by the following extracts from a report of that lecture in the Athenæum, No. 1503.

"It was found that Cuneiform writing, closely allied to hieroglyphic expression, had been first introduced into Chaldæa by a Hamite race cognate with the Egyptians; that the primitive Cuneiform characters were, in fact, like the hieroglyphs, mere pictures of natural objects, which, when used alphabetically, possessed a value corresponding with the name of the object represented. As the primitive race was composed of many tribes, each possessing its own vocabulary, each natural object had many names, and each character had many values. This confusion, embarrassing enough from the outset, was increased in after times, when the Semitic Assyrians adopted the old Hamite system of writing; for the characters then not only retained their former values, derived from the polyglott vocabulary of the primitive race, but new values were also assigned to them, corresponding with synonyms in the Assyrian language. The discovery that there thus existed a copious admixture, in the Assyrian system of writing, of the old Hamite element, which the Lecturer had announced at Oxford last December, had been of the most essential value, not only in resolving difficulties both of alphabetical expression and of etymology in the inscriptions of Nineveh, but also in pointing the way to an investigation of those far more ancient and more interesting records belonging to the primitive race which were written in the old Hamite tongue."

Some further observations (one of which was the statement that "the science of Assyria even to the latest times appeared to have been recorded in the old Hamite language, which the Lecturer, for the sake of convenience, denominated the Chaldee,") were followed by a notice of "the most important historical discoveries that had resulted from the study of the Inscriptions. These discoveries were classed under three chronological heads: the Chaldæan period, the Assyrian period, and the Babylonian period. The Chaldæan period extended from the earliest dawn of history to the institution of a Semitic Empire on the Tigris in the thirteenth century B.C. There were many traces in the Inscriptions of a tradition that the first colonists had come from Æthiopia under the leading of a hero, who answered to the Nimrod of Scripture, and who was deified in the country as *Nergal*,—an explanation being thus afforded of the Biblical ethnic scheme which described Nimrod as the son of Cush, who again was the brother of Mizraim. This *Nergal* was the God of 'the Chase' and the God of 'War,' and was further regarded as a real historic personage, being invoked by the kings as their 'ancestor,' 'the founder of their race.' He was depicted as a lion; *Nergal*, indeed, signifying in primitive Chaldee 'the great animal,' and being applied to 'a lion' among beasts, as to 'a hero' among men,—and his other names, *Nimrud* and *Aria*, had the same, or nearly the same, signification. *Aria* was perhaps connected with the Greek Ἄρης, as *Nerig*, the Sabæan name for the planet Mars, was undoubtedly a contraction of *Nergal*,—and as *Mirikh*, [or rather, *Mirrikh*,] the old Arabic title for the same planet, preserved the name of the country

(*Mirukh*, Gr. *Μεροη*, for Æthiopia,) from whence *Nergal* came. It was further curious to observe that in all the geographical lists *Mirukh* and *Makkan* (*Μεροη* and *Μακωη*) were placed in juxtaposition with *Hur* and *Akkad*, in evident allusion to the line of the original immigration from Æthiopia along the southern shores of Arabia to the mouth of the Euphrates. *Nergal* was especially worshipped at *Cutha* (a few miles N.E. of Babylon), this city being called by the Talmudists and the Arabs the city of *Nimrud*. Its ancient Chaldee name was *Tiggaba*, answering to the *Digba* of Pliny and the *Δυγουα* of Ptolemy. . . . .

"A nominal list was exhibited of fifteen kings belonging to the primitive Chaldæan race, and there were perhaps an equal number of royal names, as yet doubtfully or imperfectly read. This line of kings began to reign probably in the 23rd century B.C., and continued in power to the 13th century, when it gave way to the Semites, who established their seat of empire at Nineveh. A king *Kudur* of this line, who reigned about 1950 B.C., was pointed out as the probable representative of the Chedorlaomer of Scripture, his distinctive epithet being 'the Ravager of the West,' in apparent allusion to the famous Syrian campaign, in which, according to Genesis, he was defeated by Abraham. . . . .

"The language in which all the early legends were written was of the Hamite family, having been brought apparently from Æthiopia, through Arabia, by the primitive colonists. Many of the terms belonging to it were to be recognized in the *Galla*, the most ancient, perhaps, of the African dialects now available for comparison; and there was also an evident similarity between the vocabulary of this tongue and that of the Arabic, where the latter differed from its sister languages of the Semitic family. There were, however, a considerable number of verbal roots common to the Assyrian and primitive Chaldee,—an additional argument being thus furnished in favour of the theory advanced by Bunsen, Max Müller, and others, that Semitism was a mere development of an anterior Hamitism. The Lecturer, indeed, thought that through the primitive language of Chaldæa, we should be able to trace a connexion between the Semitic languages on the one side, and the Arian and Turanian languages on the other. Viewed according to philological rule, the Lecturer would certainly call the primitive Chaldee, Turanian or Scythic; yet a Semitic germ was to be detected in most of the verbal roots, while a great number of the nouns were Arian."

The exact agreement of several of the statements here made with opinions of our own, previously expressed, requires no comment: but we must offer some remarks upon Sir Henry Rawlinson's inference respecting the proper place of the language called by him the "primitive Chaldee," in relation to other languages with which it is connected.

He thinks that the primitive Chaldee (or the Cushitic language of Babylonia) furnishes "an additional argument" "in favour of the theory advanced by Bunsen, Max Müller, and others, that Semitism was a mere development of an anterior Hamitism;" and that it may enable us "to trace a connexion between the Semitic languages on the one side, and the Arian and Turanian languages on the other." Baron Bunsen, however, to maintain his theory, finds it necessary to assert, that "the emigration from Asia into Egypt is Ante-Noachian" ("Outlines," vol. i. p. 190), and to "demand for the Noachian period about ten millennia before our era, and for the beginning of our race another ten thousand years, or very little more" (vol. ii. p. 12). Is Sir Henry Rawlinson prepared to concede these conditions of Bunsen's theory? If so, he must subscribe to the opinion that the portion of the Bible relating to the times anterior to Abraham is *not historically true*. Our own theory requires no such concession: for we hold that the descendants of Cush adopted an Ante-Semitic dialect of Africa; afterwards, in Asia, mixing it with a Scythic, or some other Asiatic, dialect; and that Mizraim formed a new language, a mixture of the same or a similar African dialect with their own original Semitic tongue. That the language of the former should contain Semitic elements intermixed with African is what our theory would lead us to expect; considering their relationship to Shem, and the close proximity of their African settlement to that of their brethren Mizraim.

THE END.

www.ingramcontent.com/pod-product-compliance
Lightning Source LLC
Chambersburg PA
CBHW020324170426
43200CB00006B/262